SHADOWS
OF THE
BUFFALO

Also by Beverly Hungry Wolf

THE WAYS OF MY GRANDMOTHERS

Also by Adolf Hungry Wolf

THE BLOOD PEOPLE: A Division of
the Blackfoot Confederacy,
an Illustrated Interpretation
of the Old Ways

THE GOOD MEDICINE BOOKS

SHADOWS

OF THE

BUFFALO

A Family Odyssey
Among the Indians

ADOLF and BEVERLY
HUNGRY WOLF

WILLIAM MORROW AND COMPANY, INC.
New York   1983

Library of Congress Catalog Card Number: 83-61365

ISBN: 0-688-01680-4

Printed in the United States of America

First Edition

1 2 3 4 5 6 7 8 9 10

BOOK DESIGN BY BERNARD SCHLEIFER

SHADOWS
OF THE
BUFFALO

INTRODUCTION

"PEOPLE ASK ME if we will ever get along," Blackfoot elder Ben Calf Robe once told us. He said that fellow tribe members often wondered, "When will Indians and whites have respect for each other?" In answer, he seemed to speak for people everywhere, by saying: "I think the time is coming. It will be here when we all have the same color of skin, and we are slowly coming to be that way."

In this age we are witnessing a tremendous blending of cultures and races. Often this is the cause of great turmoil around the world. Some take advantage of this process by destroying people and traditions in order to force their own domination. Wise people generally counsel love and respect as the best hope to save the human race from impending self-destruction.

The following story is about some wise people—tribal elders like Ben Calf Robe—who have inspired us in our homeland, along the Canadian Rockies. We consider these people wise, not because they mastered intellectual dissertations or presented themselves as guides to better ways, but because they have lived simply, and in harmony with Nature.

We want to share the following experiences with you, hoping to show that ours is but one of a multitude of ancestral paths that can still be traveled and learned from, even though we belong to a contemporary society.

But before we begin to talk about experiences that we have had

7

together, we would like to tell you who we were at the time that Beverly and I met each other . . .

As a girl my name was Beverly Little Bear. I lived on the Blood Indian Reserve, in western Canada. Our people are one of four divisions making up the Blackfoot Confederacy of the Northern Plains. In my youth the last of our tribe's buffalo hunters were very old men. Buffalo had been gone from our lands for more than seventy-five years. Among our tribe's old women were still a few who had tanned buffalo hides, and whose first husbands were killed on Indian war trails.

By this time the buffalo hunting and war-raiding days were over and done with. My people were struggling to fit into the "white man's" way of life. It was my childhood dream to succeed at learning this "new" life. I went so far as to marry a "white man," but he ended up leading me back to the customs and traditions of my ancestors.

I often felt ashamed being an Indian child. We were usually treated like lower-class people by the society around us. Full-blooded Indians, like my father, were generally stereotyped as being the humble and naive descendants of "noble savages." In public this made me feel uncomfortable. But at home these same people gave me pride when they told captivating stories about brave family ancestors, or when they sang old tribal songs.

Our household was considered progressive, because it functioned more like a ranch home than an "Indian dwelling." In part this was because my mother's parents were "half-breeds." Both their full-blooded Indian mothers had married white men. One of these was a German immigrant named Joseph Trollinger, who fathered several children that grew to old age on our reserve. My grandmother AnadaAki (or Pretty Woman) was the youngest of them. Still, my mother spent a lot of her youth with an old grandmother who grew up in the buffalo days, and whose later husband was a leading medicine man.

My first close contacts with non-Indians included the nuns who became my school teachers in 1956, when I was six years old. I had to live at the Indian boarding school, which was then strictly run by the Catholic Church. The nuns made us feel that we were "little heathen children" in need of being saved. They got us to believe them.

"The mean nuns," is what we thought of our teachers and disciplinarians. I came from a close-knit family and found it hard to accept these substitute mothers who had no children or husbands of their own. Often I felt they resented us—and our isolated school, to which they had been assigned.

"Just don't do anything wrong," my older brothers advised me about the nuns when I started school. "Listen to them and do as they say, and they won't bother you," I was told. Looking back at that period of my life, I think I followed the advice pretty well. Not that I stayed out of trouble completely—even the smallest mistakes were noticed and punished. But I feel that I gained by my schooling. I learned to accept discipline and to benefit from it. Of course, I had no idea that someday I would put it to use practicing the ways of my Indian ancestors, who also followed many disciplines.

Some of the rules at our boarding school seemed extreme, however. For instance, we were allowed to use the toilets only at certain times each day. We had to line up for our turn and finish quickly. Each of us was given three sheets of toilet paper! I once saw a Sister go into the restroom and drag out a girl who took too long. The girl happened to be one of our class's habitual troublemakers. On this occasion a scuffle broke out, during which the girl grabbed the nun's head, and accidentally pulled off her headpiece. I was startled to see that nuns shave their heads bald.

This same recalcitrant girl received a merciless beating from the priest when she was caught, along with two friends, sneaking out of school to meet some boys. We were all made to watch the punishment so that we would learn a lesson. It was a traumatic experience for us to see our friends whipped with leather straps. We were from Indian households in which traditions generally forbid the physical punishment of children.

Our fear of the nuns was strangely balanced with a deep respect for the sacredness of their lifestyle. Most of the girls had parents like mine, who were devout Catholics, even while the rest of society still thought we were "pagan Indians." My parents respected the tribal traditions and still had some faith in them, but they believed that going to church was a necessary part of learning "the white man's way."

Indian people seem to inherit deep spiritual feelings about life. I have not known a single Indian person who denied all faith in the existence of a supernatural power. I doubt that there is an American Indian who would claim to be an atheist! In the so-called "old days" this strong faith among Indian people was expressed in every part of their life. There was no separate place for religion—my ancestors didn't even have such a word. Religion was in everything. Prayers and other expressions of devotion came frequently, and from their hearts.

Early European missionaries were often welcomed and well treated by Indians because of native respect for all kinds of spiritual beliefs and "religious" activities. Priests who wandered through wild lands, unarmed, performing strange ceremonies, were considered to possess two of the highest virtues among my ancestors: bravery and spiritual power. When the Catholic nuns came, their dedication to celibacy was compared by my forefathers to the strict virtues required by those women of our tribe who perform the very sacred medicine lodge ceremonies, or the tribal "Sun Dance." The Sisters were venerated as "holy women," who were expected to set standards of goodness for the rest of the people. Even we children of the 1950's knew this comparison meant nuns were always to be approached respectfully.

This sacred, almost mysterious, character of the nuns, at school, helped early to inspire my faith in prayers, although the Catholic litanies were much more regimented than prayers I have since learned from my own people. But through my long-ago grandmothers I feel I have an inherited urge to speak with someone mightier whenever I seek inspiration and strength.

Of course, in those days I did not realize that the ways of my grandmothers were as valid as those of the nuns, because at school we were told the opposite. The Sisters convinced us that our forebears were wild people, whose primitive ways had caused them to be sent to hell. I thought God had cursed me by making me an Indian.

For summer vacations we were allowed to go back home. After my father and brothers cut the hay on our own land, we usually took our family tent and moved out on the open prairie, where they cut wild hay. This was on Indian reserve land that none of our tribe's members had claimed for themselves. Usually we were joined by a few relatives and friends, who brought their own tents. These haying camps could be seen all over the reserve in the summertime.

High winds often blow across the prairie, and I recall how they caused a very funny incident in our camp. We used to tie our tents to our vehicles to keep them from blowing away. One morning, after an all-night windstorm, my cousin got into his truck to drive to town. But he forgot that his tent was still tied to the bumpers. Before he realized it, the tent cover was fluttering along the wagon road behind him, leaving exposed an angry family, some of whom were still asleep in their beds.

For me, a real vacation during those summers meant a trip to the mountains, or down to the U.S.A. Our tribe has some land at the foot of the Canadian Rockies, bordering the wild Waterton National Park. Sometimes we saw moose and elk when we went there, and we knew that grizzlies were around. The men in the family always started mountain camping with a hunt. Meat made up most of our food while we were there. That was when we came closest to living like our ancestors, and it helped keep ancestral feelings alive deep within me.

We went to the mountains mostly so that the men could cut logs, which were used to build houses, fences, barns, and corrals. Families who lived near the Belly River were able to float their logs home. My father always hauled his home with horses and wagons. He and his uncle Willie Eagle Plume built the family cabin from these mountain logs.

The men also cut logs and hay to sell, mostly to non-Indian ranchers. There was not much opportunity for money-earning on the reserve at that time. My parents usually went down to pick apples and other fruit in Washington state, when they really needed the work. We had friends and relatives on the Yakima Indian Reservation down there, so we spent a lot of our time visiting and enjoying ourselves. Another uncle of my father's was married to a woman there, and he liked to have us come and stay with him.

At the orchards we worked with Mexicans and other migrant farm laborers from "minority" groups. We were all treated about the same by the growers. Mexicans were usually not very friendly to Indians. Often they just stared at us, and we seldom mingled with them. There were generally several Indian families working and traveling together, for company.

We liked going to the United States because the white people there seemed more respectful than Canadian whites toward Indians. In many places this is still truc today, especially in smaller towns. Storekeepers were friendlier, and seemed genuinely pleased to help us. Compared to the U.S., Canadian society seems more old-fashioned, with pioneerlike attitudes still common near the country's vast areas of unsettled land. Perhaps Indians are seen as the allies of this vast Nature, which has never been fully conquered. There is an air of mystery in this relationship, and many people fear mysteries.

In the States we sometimes made friends with black people. If we worked with them at a fruit orchard, they were usually friendly, and willing to talk to us. Of course, we children had our misconceptions about black people, as well. In the Blackfoot language they are called "black-white-men." One time my brothers told our adopted sister that black people smell burnt. They were trying to fool her. She became so curious that she worked her way close to a young black man, in a market, just to take a whiff of him. He must have misunderstood her intentions, because he began to chase after her. She ran from him and hid behind my father. After that she was nervous around non-Indians for a long time.

When I was old enough to start taking an interest in boys, life changed rapidly around me. Among other things, our school system became liberalized so that it was possible to have boyfriends. That was something new in our tribal history, where traditions had always required a fairly strict separation of boys and girls until marriage. My father was quite conservative about this. He frequently lectured me and my adopted sister, who was of the same age, and warned us of possible consequences. Like typical teenagers, we resented his concern and advice, and learned to get around it.

When I confided in my mother about boys that I liked, she usually informed me that they were relatives, and explained how we were related. Marriage even among fairly distant cousins is frowned upon by tribal custom, and it seemed as if every boy was my cousin. I finally concluded that I would never marry anyone from our own tribe.

We girls learned to keep our boyfriends secret. We would meet with them at dances and other public events, but never so that our relationships were obvious. If we were lucky, we could sneak away to a car for a few kisses, but there was great danger in being seen. I have learned that things were pretty much like this in the camps of the old days, as well. Only then girls who became too loose were sometimes killed by their irate fathers and brothers!

One time I left a dance with a girlfriend of mine, just to get something from her sister's car. One of my aunts happened to see me. She gave me a stern lecture about being out alone after dark, and made me go in and sit by her for the rest of the dance. I finally fell asleep in my chair. Another time one of my brothers saw me with a boy and told my father. But my brother changed the story, and said I was with a different boy—one whom I didn't even like. I got into a lot of trouble, felt heartbroken, and decided to end my life. Fortunately, I lacked conviction to make a good job of it, so I ended up with little more than another stern lecture. My behavior back then seems silly to me now, and I'm thankful that my parents kept me in line most of the time.

For a long time I wanted to become a nurse. When my father realized I was serious about nursing, he talked me out of it. He said it was a dirty job and, being an Indian, I would be given the worst tasks. Like other tribal elders and relatives, he encouraged his children to get educated for occupations that we could succeed at. Thus, one of my brothers studied to be an agricultural researcher, one learned to be a welder, mechanic, and airplane pilot, and another has become the tribe's first lawyer. But I dreaded leaving the reserve for a non-Indian world of higher education.

I finally attended a community college in a small city near the reserve, but from the beginning I felt uncomfortable there. The majority of my fellow students were non-Indians who knew little about my people, and seemed to care less. Possibly they didn't even realize that the college campus was but a little spot in the vast domain that my forefathers had controlled less than one hundred years earlier.

I boarded with a white family, which was my first experience of that kind. They treated me decently, but they charged me far above normal for the privilege. When my inferiority feelings became too strong I stayed away from school and went to the movies, or for drives. My parents found out that I was losing courage, so they told me: "Those who are making you feel unworthy are not the ones who will be supporting your later life—you had better pull yourself together and take advantage of your chance for schooling."

After that I worked harder and found it easier to succeed. I also started having non-Indian friends, which caused changes in me. One of these white friends was a fellow student, a blond-haired girl of my age whose mother invited me to board at their house for a small fee. Their unbiased friendship opened a new door to my way of seeing the world. I realized not all whites thought my people were inferior. These new friends were interested in knowing about my tribal culture, which made me sense that it had some value, after all. Sadly, I also came to realize that I knew very little about it.

While I made some valuable social discoveries, my actual college learning didn't seem to be leading me anywhere in particular. With my newfound self-confidence I wanted to know what else modern society had to offer. I left school and, in the following seasons, traveled, worked in offices as an assistant, and ended up marrying a part-Indian fellow from another tribe. That relationship failed just when I was getting ready to have my first child.

I reached adulthood with a lot of confusion about what I should do in life. It seemed that many of my old beliefs were proving wrong. I realized that most of these beliefs had developed in my mind because of demands made by others, and I wanted to replace them with beliefs of my own. At about that time the mood of rebelling against existing social standards and authority was sweeping non-Indian youths all across the continent, and I found myself getting caught up by it, as well.

One summer weekend I went down to our Blackfeet relatives, in Montana, to attend their big yearly powwow celebration, which was called the North American Indian Days. I was with a girlfriend, and one of my brothers brought us there. She was my first non-Indian friend who came to powwows, and to our family house, where she slept in one of our beds. My parents were impressed by that, since white people often acted as if Indians were too dirty to sleep by.

At that powwow I met Adolf, whom I first noticed as a young white man dressed like an old-time Indian, with braids and moccasins. He seemed to be friendly with several of the elderly Indians in camp. I thought he was very unusual. At that time young Indians didn't often seek friendship and advice from elders, who were usually considered relics from the past, with little knowledge about the modern age in which we were living.

My girlfriend and I were so curious abut this stranger—Adolf— that I agreed to find out what he was about. I soon found myself involved in a very lengthy conversation with him, sitting at the edge of the big tribal encampment. He captured my interest with his knowledge about the traditional ways of my people. I realized he knew a great deal more about them than I. He had ideas for reviving our dying tribal culture, and I was inspired by the challenge, as well as by his determination to succeed with it. I had been searching around for something worthwhile to do with my life, not realizing I would find it right in my own tribal homeland.

The young stranger told me that he was married and had a family, which sounded ideal for our friendship. Several disappointments with men made me want to avoid serious relationships at that point. I was glad when he invited me to visit his family at their mountain homestead, and they made me feel welcome when I arrived. His wife and I adopted each other as sisters, which is a common Indian way of expressing special friendships. When my parents met her, soon afterward, they accepted her as an adopted daughter.

I was especially interested in the simple country lifestyle my new friends were practicing. I thought I might like to live that way myself. I wondered if I could encourage other young people, back home on the reserve, to consider such a lifestyle as an alternative to the frustrations of being Indians trying to catch up with modern society.

In some ways the homestead life of my friends was similar to the way my family lived when I was small. But the spiritual and cultural purpose of their efforts was new and especially appealing to me. For instance, my adopted sister introduced me to the simple Indian ritual of sweat bathing, which I never expected to experience. She and her husband learned it from some people of the Flathead tribe, where men and women both practice it. Later, when I spoke enthusiastically about sweat bathing to a friend on the reserve, I learned that nowadays in our tribe only men take part in this ritual. In the past our women used sweating as their winter baths.

When I got back home from this visit to the mountains, I had many new things to think about. I built my own sweat lodge, behind our old family barn. Few people knew about it, but I persuaded a couple of close female relatives to try it with me. They really liked the experience, as did my father, who used the lodge once or twice on his own. Later the ritual became very popular among Indian youths striving to regain some of their ancestral culture.

When my first son was born my parents helped look after him so that I could work to earn money to support us. I became one of the first Indians from our tribe to obtain a teaching position in the previously strict boarding schools. By this time the federal government was showing its growing uninterest in Indian schools by cutting their funding. Government support was originally promised us in a treaty by which we surrendered most of our lands. With less money, qualified teachers became harder to hire, especially in such an isolated place. Those with only partial training, like myself, got the work for partial pay.

The following summer I took my baby boy to the mountains and made a longer visit with my adopted sister and her family. We got along so well that we talked about making my stay permanent. We even discussed how to base our relationship on the traditional customs of my forefathers, most of whom had more than one wife in their households. The cultural rewards seemed exciting, but our inability to get past emotional restraints learned from modern society doomed our efforts and finally broke down our friendship. I went back home, disillusioned.

I was not home long before Adolf showed up for a visit. He said his family had moved from the mountain farm to a small tourist town nearby, where his wife sought more company. He was planning to winter, alone, on the farm, after a visit to the Montana Blackfeet, where he was going for cultural work. We were glad to still be friends. He intended to continue learning about Indian culture, and I tried to encourage his efforts.

When Adolf stopped by again, on his way back from Montana, I was amazed to hear that he had pledged to become keeper of a medicine bundle. That was something very important that I knew little about, except that it could not be taken lightly. I had never met anyone so young and devoted to traditional Indian customs. I had not realized the depth of Adolf's commitment while I stayed at his family's home, because he spent much time alone. I also had never met a white man who enjoyed being so much like an old-time Indian. I couldn't help wondering if he was really sincere.

The next thing I heard from Adolf was even more startling. He had gone to his wife and asked her to join in taking care of the medicine bundle, with all its obligations and ceremonies, but she wanted nothing to do with it. She thought he was getting too serious about Indian life. He decided to keep his pledge, nevertheless, and asked me if I would take the place of his wife . . .

As a boy my name was Adolf Gutöhrlein, and I lived in southern Germany. At that time the Second World War had just finished. The country seemed ruined, and the people were unhappy. My dream was to go from that land of machines and destruction to live in the forests and mountains of mystical North America. The people of my childhood dreams were the American Indians.

I felt as though my family was rootless, and I was a boy without a people. We had few relatives in the land of my birth. My father had moved there from Switzerland, and my mother from Hungary. My maternal grandparents were Austrian and Prussian. I never had a chance to meet any of my grandparents.

Before the countries had names, my ancestors lived in wild tribes, just like the Indians. I always felt a deep and mysterious longing for that era. But I learned nothing of the ancient and natural ways of these forefathers. History seemed to have left them quietly in the past.

Like many boys my age, I thought American Indians were traditional people who still lived wild, in Nature. I don't know exactly where I got this idea, but I had it as far back as I can remember. I longed to know those wild people, and to live with them in that wilderness land. I did not know that modern-day Indian life is very different from the one that fills the romantic imaginations of young boys. It would not have mattered, anyway, had I known the truth. As a boy in postwar Germany it seemed unlikely that I would ever get a chance to fulfill these daydreams.

The happiest memories from my German childhood are of times spent outdoors. We had no car, so most of our traveling was done by walking. If we had to go far, we went by train. I don't think that happened more than half a dozen times during my ten years there. My father had a bicycle that he rode to the factory where he worked, but as a boy, I didn't have one.

The favorite place of my early world was a grassy knoll behind the street where we rented a flat. It happened to be an old cemetery hill, with flower-covered graves and a little chapel dating back to the 1700's. At the edge of that knoll I forgot about most everything except my pleasant fantasies. The hill faced west, so I was able to watch the sunsets. Often they bathed our town, which lay below me, in fantastic shades of orange and red. When I lay down far enough in the tall grass I could see only the sky and the sunset. Often I imagined tipi camps in place of the town.

An aunt sent us tempting letters from America, where she had gone after marrying a U.S. soldier, at the end of the war. She told my mother it was the land of opportunity. She and her husband finally offered to sponsor us as immigrants. My parents agreed to borrow money for the long journey. In January of 1954 we sailed into the stormy Atlantic aboard the huge liner S.S. *America,* along with hundreds of other Europeans who hoped for a better life. For me, the whole experience seemed almost unreal, but I knew that we were headed for the land of my dreams.

Being an immigrant kid from Germany did not make me particularly popular in the southern California neighborhood where my aunt and uncle lived. Most of the boys in my age group had fathers who were GIs. I was the only foreigner in our school. When the kids played war games, the bad guys were called Nazis and Krauts. What a setting for a German-speaking boy named Adolf!

My parents thought work in America was very well rewarded, and they frequently pointed this out to me. Within a short time they managed to buy a good used car and an older house, although we had arrived in the U.S. with nothing. I caught the working fever from them, and soon had a job delivering newspapers after school. From a nearby sporting goods dealer I learned how to tie fishing flies, which he then bought from me.

One of my newspaper customers was an old widow who treated me kindly. When she learned of my longing for the outdoors, she offered to sell me a small vacation-cabin site in the nearby mountains, for $250. I made monthly payments of twenty-five dollars from my newspaper earnings, and by the time I was fourteen, I had title to my own piece of land. In Germany, a few years earlier, such a thing would have been beyond imagination, even for my parents, much less for a boy.

As a member of the Boy Scouts I got my first experiences in outdoor life. All through my school years I looked forward to the annual summer camps, up in the mountains, where I learned hiking, tenting, and Indian lore. Many weekends were spent at a Boy Scout park, in an undeveloped part of Long Beach, the city where we lived. There, I sometimes sat alone for hours and daydreamed about living all the time in Nature, just as I had while sitting on the hillside back in Germany.

The park was in charge of an old fellow everyone called "the Ranger." Sometimes he invited me into his rustic, ranch-style home, where he added fuel to my daydreams by showing me Indian relics, stuffed birds and animals, and books of outdoor adventures. I was introduced to the writings of James Willard Schultz, who wrote over thirty novels based on his life with the Blackfoot tribe back in the final buffalo-hunting years. As a young man he had left an eastern city, and its schools, for the western outdoors. He married a Blackfoot girl and learned the customs of her people. His stories made me realize that I was not the first to have such dreams. In my subconscious mind they must have begun to outline my future.

School in America seemed boring compared to the strict classes I had experienced in Germany. The pace of studies was vague and slow. The values of education were often proclaimed, but I could never see clearly what they would lead me to. One report card described my feelings well when it said: "Adolf would do much better if he did not spend so much time daydreaming." I sometimes felt as if I were going to school just to take up time from one vacation to the next.

I had no trouble keeping my grades up well enough to stay in schools for seventeen years. I readily learned the facts and figures that modern society considered important enough to give me degrees for, even though they are now only pieces of paper filed away somewhere. Mathematical solutions and technological theories have turned out to be of no use to the way I am now living. Their greatest impact on my mind has been to confuse me, while my heart has tried to accept the simple beliefs of Nature-loving ancestors.

I cannot say that my schooling was a complete waste of time and effort. However, I wish there had been more emphasis placed on doing things—visiting and talking with those who know how to do things, and getting directly involved in the daily world—instead of just sitting at desks in classrooms.

After years of planning to become a lawyer, I finally decided that my strong interest in western American history would be better expressed if I were to become a history teacher. My special interest was research on the life of America's Indian people, which led me to read everything I could find on the subject. In my spare time I improved the Indian lore skills I first learned as a Boy Scout. I found much satisfaction making traditional Indian clothing and other articles. My field of study slowly turned into living history, although I still had no idea how to put these pleasures to practical use.

An old Coahuilla Indian man named Smiling Bear changed my way of thinking about life. We were neighbors in an older residential area of Long Beach, where I rented a small apartment after moving out of my parents' home. Smiling Bear was a handsome, brown-skinned little man, with a big, happy smile for everyone. He had let his wispy, silver-colored hair grow long, although he wore it discreetly rolled into a small bun at the back of his head. He had spent most of his life working as a servant, farmhand, and common laborer, but in his heart he carried a dream similar to mine. He said he wanted to move into Nature and live simply, wearing breechcloths and moccasins like his forefathers. He didn't care that I had no Indian ancestry when he encouraged me to join him. He said we would move to a ''sacred forest'' somewhere in the land of the Cherokees where we could form our own tribe . . .

Smiling Bear lived with an old woman who called herself Morning Star. The widow of a wealthy lawyer, she was planning to come to the forest with us. After her husband's death, grief and loneliness had caused her to seek refuge in the mystical world of Smiling Bear's Indians. Neighbors sometimes laughed at Morning Star and her ''Indian chief.'' Her grown sons were outraged. They had her judged incompetent and got power of attorney over her estate. After that they ignored her.

My friendship with this elderly couple came just when our modern social system was making a major turn in history. Alternate lifestyles were being considered, and daring social experiments were made. Suddenly my childhood dreams no longer seemed so strange, or unreachable. Many youths were looking to the American Indian people for inspiration and wisdom about living in harmony with Nature.

Smiling Bear had a special "magic" for making his new-age tribal life seem like a wonderful ideal. He liked to smoke the herb marijuana to brighten his visions. He said that his grandmother was a tribal medicine woman when he was a young boy. Missionary priests forced her to practice the craft in secret, but she gathered marijuana and other herbs regularly in wild canyons nearby. From her he learned to think of it as a "sacred smoke." He said it was a spiritual helper. His was a different attitude toward a subject that was just then becoming very popular.

But our plans ended when Morning Star died one night of a stroke. Smiling Bear became sad, then weak and feeble, until it became evident that he would never make it to the tribal camp of his dreams. One time when we talked together about this, he cried. He said I should learn from his experience not to wait all my life to fulfill my dreams . . .

Smiling Bear died not long after Morning Star. He left me with the will to move into Nature as a modern-day pioneer. Like many other young people, my goal became to live self-sufficiently and to "get back to the land." Although I had no experience with gardening or farming, I looked forward to learning these practical things. I began by studying books, and by spending spare money on tools and supplies. A small part of my apartment turned into a misplaced farm shed.

It still amazes me whenever I think how quickly a large part of our modern society readjusted its philosophy back in the sixties. It seemed exciting and enlightening to question things that had been accepted without much thought for so many generations. No longer was the stereotyped "White Anglo-Saxon Protestant" considered to be God's own chosen hero. Those of us with light skin became aware of terrible mistakes made by earlier members of our race against Africans, Orientals, and American Indians. We became conscious of a new dimension in the old idea that "all men are created equal."

Yet, deep within, it was hard for most of us to accept that the world contains no "chosen people." Some turned to mystics and gurus from distant lands, hoping to find a replacement for the long-cherished goal of a Christian heaven. Some thought such a goal could be reached here on earth, and that the ways of America's native people would help. They seemed to be the only ones who had a history of living in harmony with the Nature of this continent.

An old Hopi wise man named David Monongye spoke kindly to young romantics of that period, including myself. He said his ancestors left prophecies that foretold the coming of "white brothers" who would wear long hair and want to live like Indians. He thought this was good—that we could work together to save the land from further destruction by modern technology. He thought there was deep meaning to the similarity between the names Hopi and Hippie. To the many who were inspired by him, he became known as "Grandfather David."

This wise elder said the ancient prophecies of his tribe indicated that the world was getting ready for a "purification," which he likened to the "Judgment Day" of Christians. He said only those in tune with the "Spirits of Nature" would survive. His talks encouraged many to leave the cities and try a new form of country life.

Toward the end of my formal education I applied to live among Indian people as a VISTA volunteer. A representative from that government agency came to our college campus looking for recruits, telling of such things as food co-ops, housing projects, and other important social changes that I wanted to help with, and learn from. My application was accepted, but I was told that my interest in traditional Indian culture would conflict with the program's direction. Instead, I was assigned to a city ghetto, so I withdrew. I had already decided that my future was definitely outside of city limits.

Next a campus recruiter from the Bureau of Indian Affairs helped me to get hired as a boarding-school teacher. I was to work on a Sioux reservation in South Dakota. This time my interest in native culture was thought to be an asset, since the BIA was trying to change its image from that of a ruthless enforcer of non-native ways to that of a government ally.

Marriage to my girlfriend, Carol, changed my plans for a teaching career on a reservation. Before I received the necessary degree, we learned that we were to have a child. We decided to begin parenthood in the city, near our own parents and friends, rather than in some unknown place. Then a semester of teaching local high schoolers showed me that this was not the way to satisfy my longings for living history and culture.

For the next two years Carol and I talked about making our permanent family home in the country, while I unloaded ships in Los Angeles Harbor, sorted mail at the post office, and made leather clothing and craftwork to earn money. We operated a small store that was based on an old-time trading post, where we sold our handiwork and met many friends. The closest of these shared with us a longing for rural group life.

Carol and I made several trips from the city to search for land. We traveled through the Pacific Northwest and saw many places that we liked. Along the way we met a few others who were doing the same thing. I realized I had inherited my father's longing to be close to mountains, although his yearning had been for the Alps and mine was for the Rockies. Near the head of the Columbia River, at the foot of the Canadian part of the Rockies, we finally bought 140 acres of partial wilderness for $5,000. The previous owner was so eager to sell the isolated place that she let us have it for a small down payment and $25 a month. Similar places nearby were bought by other young families. Local residents thought we were all crazy to be paying such "high" prices for the land, though the same parcels now bring ten and twenty times as much.

During one of the trips in search of land we ended up at a large tribal celebration in northwest Montana. It was on the Blackfeet Indian Reservation, not far from Glacier National Park. That was my first visit to a real tipi camp, and thus an opportunity to bring alive a favorite childhood dream. I met some of the tribal elders, who made me feel welcome, like a friend. I put on the traditional costume that I had made, and joined in their dancing. I had no idea that the visit would turn out to have a major impact on my life.

Within that camp was a very aged man of special significance. He was Jim White Calf, or "Last Gun," the last old Indian who had hunted buffalo and taken an enemy's scalp on the war trail. He was over one hundred years old, and still very active and faithful to his ancestral ways. I now realize that he was the last living person able to help me make some kind of direct contact with the wild Indian life of my fantasies. That I met him at all was very good luck, combined with a lot of strange mystery.

My relationship with this aged-man-from-another-era was very brief, compared to the length of his life. Yet within my heart he was able to light up a faintly glowing ember of natural faith inherited from primitive ancestors. He showed me enough of his own way of practicing that kind of faith that I made a vow to dedicate my life to learning and following it. I told him this, and I asked if my race and modern upbringing would prevent me from learning his mysteries and powers. He said: "Anyone can live in harmony with Nature, if they try." He gave me a small symbolic initiation, and said it would help me to live according to my dreams. He made it seem so very simple . . .

On another reservation an old Salish Indian woman named Mary Ann became our "grandma." Near ninety, this woman lived all alone in a little log house. It sat alongside a gurgling creek, at the edge of a beautiful grassy meadow near the foot of the snow-topped Rockies. She inspired us with her simple and quiet ways, and she seemed honored when we told her that we would like to learn that kind of lifestyle.

This "grandma" set up a small tipi by her house and invited us to stay with her for a time. She told us many stories from her past, and painted romantic visions. When she was a girl her people still lived in their ancestral mountain wilderness, away from the reservation. She was one of the last to learn the old, traditional life. To us, she represented evidence that such a life could still be followed.

Every day she went out to haul water in buckets, chop wood for cooking, and bathe in her little stream. Her feet were always covered with soft moccasins made from deerskins she had tanned. I was convinced that we, as mere youths, could succeed with a lifestyle that someone so old and alone was still following happily.

During our stay with this grandma I sometimes went to visit her neighbor, Louie Ninepipe. He also lived alone, in a log house. Like her, he wore his hair long, and in two braids. His hair was still coal black, while hers had turned to a beautiful creamy white. It was very thick, and hung below her waist. Often she wore it doubled up, with the tips tied behind her neck.

Louie Ninepipe was a widower, and the last of a large and well-known family. With brothers Adolf and Andrew he was the leader of a popular Indian singing group that traveled all over the plains. They were among the first Indians to record a commercial album, which is still available from Folkways Records. In his final years Louie met one of his many foreign fans—a young lass from England—who came to keep him company in the log cabin. Their marriage made newspaper headlines as a "fairy-tale wedding."

When I met Louie the wedding was still in the unknown future, and he was often lonely. He enjoyed telling me about the past. He taught me Indian dancing, and how to make a rawhide drum. He showed me his "love flute," and let me record his favorite songs. He played some ancient love songs, and jokingly said he would use them to find one more sweetheart in life . . .

The homestead land that we bought in Canada was just a few hours' drive north of where "Grandma" and Louie Ninepipe lived. It lay in a valley similar to the wild one they had grown up in. Thinking there would be other young people inspired to try such a life, I wrote a little booklet with stories of these Indian elders, and with some related thoughts and information. Using one thousand dollars of our saved-up money, I had four thousand copies of this booklet printed. These, our tools, and some other belongings made our grubstake for life in the Canadian wilderness.

In the 1960's it was still fairly easy to get legally settled in

Canada. A college degree, a bank account, a down payment on land, and a load of booklets seemed enough to show immigration authorities that we had a future planned in their country. Many youths were then thinking that Canada might be the new "promised land." It still had vast areas of unsettled wilderness where one could go and live as one pleased. It also had a prime minister with shoulder-length hair. No other place in the Western Hemisphere seemed so close to contemporary ideals.

Of course, it was very easy to sit in a crowded city and make ambitious plans for living quietly in the country. It was a different thing to cut those city ties and face reality on the land. Where we moved to there was no electricity or telephone. The nearest doctor and supermarket were an hour's drive away. There wasn't a neighbor to be seen or heard from our place, which didn't even have a house on it. We put up a small, handsewn tipi, and cooked in a lean-to shack.

I loved the simple life from the start, and wished it were even wilder. Having Nature for a neighbor was better than I had been imagining all those years. When our car broke down I decided to do without it, so I gave it to a friend in trade for our first winter's firewood. Eagerly we cultivated and planted our first garden, and though it did poorly we were proud of the meager crop. We got chickens and rabbits, and when stray dogs killed them we learned to house them better so that it wouldn't happen again. For the children we got goats, whose milk tasted strange until we learned not to tie them near certain wild plants. I even got horses to ride and work with, though their feed drained our budget, and I spent a lot of time chasing them through the woods whenever they managed to get away.

Learning this new life kept us busy for the first year, and we had little time to get dissatisfied. But slowly we came to long for different futures. Carol wanted more neighbors, I wanted fewer. In the cities we had friends who wanted to join us, but we couldn't agree with them about land ownership, work opportunities, and basic needs. Even among our fellow settlers the expected group relationship was torn by jealousies and differing opinions. None of us seemed mature enough to create the new-age utopia of our city dreams.

During the first summer on that homestead I left the family for a week and hitchhiked to the other side of the Rockies for a visit with Indian friends. It was time, again, for the annual powwow, which seemed to draw me like a magnet. An elderly Blackfoot couple wrote and invited me to stay in their tipi, which was a chance I did not want to miss.

The old couple was surprised when I showed up alone, and on foot, but they made me feel welcome. Their little tipi was already set up in the camp circle by the time I arrived. For several days I stayed with them. In the evenings I danced, wearing my costume and watching the older men to learn the footsteps and subtle body movements. It was a form of pleasure dancing, much different from the ceremonial dancing done away from spectators. It was a modern version of the dances that used to celebrate war-trail victories.

During that encampment I searched for young people with whom I could share my thoughts, but I found only one—a young woman from the nearby Blood Tribe. She was related to the old couple I had already become friendly with, and she wondered what brought me to camp with them. I told her something about my childhood dreams, and about my family back on the homestead, across the mountains. We talked far into the night, realizing that we were at the start of a strong relationship, although neither of us imagined that we would end up as husband and wife.

The following stories tell of our coming together, and of some experiences that we encountered while learning to blend two races and cultures into one family. I was older and further along the traditional path than Beverly (which often felt strange to me, as a non-Indian), so our relationship began with me as the dominant partner. This was in keeping with customs then still followed by the elders who became our closest friends, as well as our advisors. Their philosophy was: ''Behind every strong man is a strong woman.'' Only later, as those elders slowly passed away, did we learn how to follow their paths walking side by side, according to more modern thinking.

In reading this book you will find that I (Adolf) am the story-teller. The story is as much Beverly's as mine, and through frequent discussions and readings of our notes, we drew on both our memories to produce this book. But having me do the final writing was much easier than confusing ourselves, and readers, by taking turns at the typewriter.

1

My life was in the midst of an emotional crisis when I found myself going to an old Indian man and wife to seek advice and guidance. It was a beautiful autumn day in 1971—an ideal day, in my memory, for making important life changes. The air was crisp and cool in Browning, Montana. The morning sun shone brightly across the wide-open plains. Thin gray smoke spiraled softly upward from the chimney on top of their roof.

I was back in Blackfoot Indian country to visit my favorite "old folks," Louis and Maggie Bear Child. They were born around the end of the "buffalo days," and were among the last representatives of the ancient Indian life. Being around them seemed like being in the shadows of the buffalo . . .

Not far north of that land is the reserve of the Blood Tribe, fellow members of the large and powerful Blackfoot Confederacy. On that morning Beverly was there, teaching young girls how to cook and sew at the Indian boarding school. She had no idea that the old folks and I would soon be making plans that would change her life as drastically as they would mine.

I made this visit because I wanted to talk with Louis and Maggie about the failure of my first marriage, and the breakup of my family. I also told them about the death of my father, which happened at the same time. I told them that I was lonesome for relatives, and lonely for a people. I mentioned my childhood dreams of living like an Indian, and wondered if they thought I could try that.

31

The old folks lived in a tar-paper shack at the edge of Browning's official junkyard. From their front door they had a splendid view of auto wrecks and old, broken farm equipment. The place turned into an impassable swamp whenever it rained heavily, or when snows melted. I never asked the old folks why they picked this awful spot on the desolate prairie to make their final stand. I just know that they lived there as gaily and happily as two chickadees in a cozy tree.

Before moving to their junkyard estate they had lived together in a little log house along Cutbank Creek, on a secluded part of the reservation. There they often camped during the summers, picking wild plants and berries. Frequently they got together with relatives and neighbors for powwow dances and sacred ceremonies. But one spring day a flood came raging down from the nearby mountains, taking many of the log cabins and the lives of some neighbors. After that the old folks moved into town.

They were kind and understanding people, with many friends, near and far. They had only been together for fifteen or twenty years. Most of their lives they had spent married to earlier partners, with whom each had raised a family of children who were now elderly men and women themselves.

The old folks didn't have much in the way of windows on their shack, which reminded me of being in a tipi. They must have heard me drive up, though, since one of them called out for me to enter as soon as I knocked. I turned a loose, worn doorknob and pulled open a creaky wooden door. Warm air, mingled with mysterious odors, came rushing past me to reach the cool outdoors.

I stepped into a dark, enclosed porch that was dominated by a collection of heavy coats, sweaters, and hats, all hanging from nails and hooks around the walls. The floor was covered by an assortment of shoes, cowboy boots, and rubber galoshes, to which I added those that I normally wore over my buckskin moccasins.

The tiny porch led into a small, narrow kitchen that contained only the most basic necessities. There was a wooden cupboard that had been painted numerous times during its life with uneven brushstrokes and various colors. The latest layer was pale blue. A few well-worn metal dishes sat on shelves once hidden by cupboard doors no longer there. Next to this was a sink with no faucets. A plastic pail full of water sat near the sink. It was filled by buckets brought from a nearby well. Another plastic pail sat underneath the sink, to catch the used water.

In one corner of the kitchen was a small table and three painted chairs. A beat-up cast-iron cookstove constituted the rest of the kitchen furnishings. Against the wall, by the stove, were stacked freshly chopped pieces of firewood that looked like scraps from building sites. The few food articles that I could see were bread, a package of margarine, some boxes of noodles, coffee, sugar, and some tins of canned meat. All of it was stamped "U.S. Government," so I knew it was ration food handed out weekly at the Blackfeet Indian Agency for those in need. The old folks certainly lived about as simply as they could.

An open doorway led from the kitchen into the main room of the shack—the only other room. Just inside, on the edge of an old metal cot, sat a dark-skinned little man with silver-gray, close-cropped hair. His face beamed with a big, white-toothed grin that seemed to go from ear to ear. This was Makes Summer, or Joseph Young-Eagle-Child, a good friend and a fellow powwow dancer. He was always glad to see me, and always he disarmed me with that big smile.

Makes Summer was a longtime bachelor known for living as sort of a handyman with various married couples—always way older than he—who looked after his room and board. At this time he happened to be staying with Louis and Maggie, bringing in buckets of fresh water from the well and lumber from the scrap piles. He was also the one who brought hot, glowing coals from the stove in the midst of the room that they all shared, so that the old folks could make incense upon them whenever they wished to pray, which was often.

Makes Summer called out to the old folks: *"Hai-Yah!* Here is my boy, Hungry Wolf." He was in his seventies, and he called me his "boy" because somehow he understood my fascination with old Indians like himself, and he wanted to please me. Besides, he seemed to have no boy of his own, although I later learned that he did have children from a long-ago and short-lived marriage.

He got up to shake my hand, and we ended up giving each other a hug. He evoked feelings of warmth and friendliness that came from his many years among old-time Indians, and in the outdoors. One writer who tried to meet him mentioned later that he was an elusive man who said little and soon disappeared into the woods. However, that writer was a big, loud fellow from Texas, while Makes Summer was a quiet little man from the North.

The old folks made sounds of approval when they heard my name. The old man repeated it, in the Blackfoot language, saying several times: "Makwi Unotche, Makwi Unotche," while Maggie covered her mouth with one hand, which is a traditional way for women to show modesty in times of surprise or pleasure.

I stepped across the room to shake hands with them. They were sitting on their metal-framed double bed. As I took Louis's outstretched hand, he said, with a jolly grin and a twinkle in his small, dark eyes: "Gee, you must have some magic! You always show up right after we talk about you. We just been talkin' about you this morning, ain't it?" He turned and looked at Maggie, having used a local expression for "isn't it so?"

I might have taken his suggestion—that I have magic—seriously, thinking the old Indian was crediting me with supernatural powers. But he had made similar statements to me on earlier visits, so I figured he just wanted to make me feel welcome. Besides, maybe *he* had the magic, since he always seemed to talk about me just before my arrivals!

When I took Maggie's hand, she pulled me toward her for a hug. She was dressed in an old-fashioned calico gown of the style worn by Blackfoot women since light cloth was first brought by traders in the late 1800's. The bottom of the dress came nearly to the ground. Only the tips of her moccasins stuck out from underneath. They were made of hand-tanned buckskin, on which she had embroidered pretty, colorful flowers with tiny glass beads.

The dress was soft pink, and also covered with flower patterns in various colors. It came snug around her neck, and had long, open sleeves. On her wrists she wore bracelets of old-time beads, and around her neck she had a long buckskin thong that appeared to have something hanging from its end, way down beneath her dress, where it could not be seen. Probably it was some kind of sacred medicine amulet.

Around her waist Maggie wore a narrow belt of oiled harness leather, covered with tiny beads sewn on in geometric designs. It was a traditional style of belt. Combined with the dress, moccasins and bracelets, it was evidence that Maggie was one of the few "authentic" old-time Blackfoot Indian women still living on the reservation. When going to town or to public gatherings she always wore a fringed, woolen shawl over her clothing. At other times she usually wore a heavy coat or jacket.

Louis said that his father was a "white man," although records list him as a mixed-blood from some eastern tribe. He apparently came out West in the 1800's with two brothers, each of whom married into a different tribe. Among the Blackfeet Louis became known as Bear Child, and on paper he got the first name of Jack. Louis carried his father's last name, but was more commonly known as Louis Plenty Treaty. His father gave him that name because of his experiences as a guide and scout for emigrant parties. Along their routes he often had to make treaties with different tribes so that the wagon trains could pass through their lands. Louis was very proud of the history behind his name.

While the old folks and I were involved in our warm greetings, Makes Summer went over to a large closet that took up a good part of the small room. He rummaged through several things until he pulled out a plain brown shopping bag. When he got a chance to interrupt, he said, temptingly, "I've been saving this for you," while he cast a downward glance at the bag. He went back over and sat down on the edge of his bed, then he continued: "I'm going to give it to you right now, because I'm sure glad to see you." He began to pull something out of the bag, then he suddenly seemed to have second thoughts, and he laid the bag back down. "I'd better make some incense first," he said, more to himself than to us. Then I knew that the bag's contents were sacred.

Makes Summer went out into the kitchen and came back with a large metal spoon. By the wall across from his bed stood a round, wood-burning heater. Warmth was radiating from a quiet fire within it. He went to the heater, raised its metal lid, and used the big spoon to bring out a red-hot, glowing coal. From under his bed he pulled out an old auto hubcap, into which he placed the burning ember. Then he reached into a small canvas sack that hung from a nail above the head of his bed. Out of it he took a small green braid of sweetgrass, which is a popular native incense. One end of the braid was tied with a strip of colored cloth, while the other end was loose and showed signs of having been torn. From this he broke off a small piece, which he sprinkled on the hot coal. Instantly sweet-smelling smoke curled up into the air and filled the room with a pungent odor. Makes Summer began to pray.

Blackfoot traditions require that every important event be preceded by prayers. Each prayer is usually accompanied by incense. Generally a coal is taken from a fire with a special set of wooden tongs, made from the forked branch of a berry bush. The coals are deposited into a special altar kept by the head of the bed—nowadays usually a small wooden box filled with fine dirt. In this case, Makes Summer was performing the ancient ritual in very modern and functional style, using his spoon and a hubcap.

Makes Summer's prayer was in the Blackfoot language. I only understood a few words of what he said. At the same time he pulled a small bundle from the paper bag. It was of red cloth, wrapped with a buckskin thong. He held the bundle over the sweetgrass smoke, as a symbolic cleansing and blessing. Four times he held it into the smoke and took it back. The last time he untied it and showed me what was inside. It was an old-time Indian hat, made from a strip of brown fur.

"It's my fur hat," he said, using a hushed voice that might also have mentioned a long-gone relative. He spoke with a dialect common to elders of his generation. It caused him to pronounce fur like "farr."

"I got this from Sun," he explained. "They gave it to me in a dream while I worked for them—the old men, Weasel Head and Chewing Black Bones. They're the ones who showed me the Way.'' He was referring to his tribal duty as Weather Dancer during the very sacred Sun Dance, which to the Blackfeet is known as the medicine lodge ceremony. The two old men he spoke of were Weather Dancers in years past—he was initiated for it by them. They had taught him something of their magic, and so he inherited their position from them. He was saying that they had appeared in one of his dreams and instructed him to make this hat a symbol of the power of Sun, and other elements. In similarly mystical ways are explained the origins of most Blackfoot sacred articles, and the ceremonies that go with them.

"We're supposed to stay in that medicine lodge for four days and nights," Makes Summer explained. "During that time we're not supposed to drink water, eat food, or go out. We just stay in the lodge to pray and dance and try for the weather to be good and the people to stay safe." I understood what he meant, because I had been studying about these rituals and ceremonies in old ethnological books and papers. Until then, however, I had experienced little of this firsthand.

Makes Summer explained the symbolism of the hat and the various small objects that were attached to it. About a certain round, carved seashell he said: "This is Sun—he's the one that helps me to make good weather . . . This one [a small, crescent-shaped item] is Moon, the night-light—she's the one for making storms . . . These here [pointing to eagle plumes] are for good winds . . . These other [ermine skins] are for good winters . . . The fur that this hat is made out of is for all the animals, and also for Earth . . ."

He was speaking slowly, and in a way as if no one were there to hear his words. But then he turned and handed the hat to me, saying: "I'm going to prove its power to you, today! By tonight you're going to know it, because the weather's going to make a big change, just for taking this hat out and praying with it!" After he said this, he looked at me carefully, as if to watch my reaction. I didn't know what to say, or think, so I kept quiet.

"At the time of the medicine lodge ceremonies I only take this hat out of its wrappings when the weather is getting bad," he continued. "Then the weather changes and gets better. But today it is already good, so it will turn just the opposite." I still didn't say anything, although my school-educated mind was probably dubious about such magical expectations. In conclusion Makes Summer added: "You can just keep this hat at home. But if we ever have another Sun Dance—if they ever give the medicine lodge ceremonies again—then you can bring this hat and come in with me, and I'll teach you to be the Weather Dancer, just like I was taught by Weasel Head and Chewing Black Bones."

At that point I felt so thrilled that I took off my silver-and-turquoise ring and gave it to him. He seemed to like it, and he quickly found a finger that it fit on.

After this Maggie brought out a small clay-bowled pipe that she kept in a little handsewn leather pouch, inside of her everyday purse. She had a special smoking mix of her own, but she only smiled when I asked her about the ingredients of it. No doubt she gathered certain prairie plants that had special meaning to her, perhaps because of instructions she got from supernatural Spirits, or from long-gone tribal elders. She had been initiated to many important rituals in her life, and was commonly thought to have mystical powers.

All of us sat and smoked the pipe in silence. Although the clay bowl was only a small one—perhaps the size of a man's bent thumb—it held enough to last for some time. Makes Summer moved from his bed to a rocking chair, at the foot of the old folks' bed, so that it was easier to pass the pipe in a circle. We all continued to sit in silence, even after the pipe was smoked out. Makes Summer leaned back and gently rocked himself, with his eyes closed.

I sat and thought about the sacred hat, and what it represented. I was surprised at Makes Summer's willingness to speak about it and its origins. I had read that Indians were very secretive about their religion, especially about their spiritual dreams and the contents of "medicine bundles" that resulted from such dreaming.

I soon learned that the Blackfeet did not generally practice these secretive ways, except in cases involving very personal matters, or the functions of certain tribal societies. The contents of most Blackfoot medicine bundles are well known, and may be seen by anyone, though only certain persons may handle them. In fact, the dream stories of their origins—and of the sacred powers that they represent—are generally regarded as tribal legacies that take the place of written histories among other people. Thus, instead of secrecy, such things are treated with pride and respect.

Ironically one of the few remaining Blackfoot medicine bundles associated with a lot of mystery and secrecy was right then hanging on a wall by the bed of Louis and Maggie, although I didn't know it. I saw the aged-looking rawhide cylinder that it was kept in. Even at a quick glance I knew it was old and special, coated brown from hanging near countless tipi fires. Underneath the shiny coating were subtle geometric designs, painted back in the buffalo days with soft earth colors, using little stick brushes. The whole thing was worn smooth as a result of handling by keepers from many generations. When Louis saw me glancing at it, he said: "That's my old headdress," and left it at that.

It was not until much later that I learned Louis was the only member from the Montana Blackfeet of the traditionally powerful Horns Society, which is still very active among the Bloods of Canada. The headdress symbolized Louis's position within that respected group. It was the ancient style of Blackfoot headdress, on which the eagle feathers stand straight up on the wearer's head, rather than sloping toward the back in the style that has been more recently adopted. I saw Louis wearing this headdress the next summer, at the Blood Sun Dance encampment, when he performed an annual sacred dance with his fellow society members.

Both Louis and Makes Summer were members of another tribal group, the Crazy Dog Society. In the past, members of the Horns were usually elderly men, proven in battle, and possessing wisdom about sacred things. The Crazy Dogs, on the other hand, were young and active warriors—depended upon by the rest of the tribe for camp defense and policing. They were known and feared by the people of other Plains tribes, most of whom fought with the Black-feet. But by the time of my visit the society seemed on the verge of dying out because of old age among its remaining members.

Louis was one of two special members of this society, known as Bear Braves. Their regalia included moccasins, belts, and armbands made of bear fur, and headdresses with pairs of bear claws worn to look like tiny buffalo horns. It was their duty to go around the camp and confiscate whatever food they found in order to feed the rest of the society members. They carried bows and blunt-tipped arrows, which they were allowed to shoot at anyone who tried to keep them from taking food.

While we were talking about the Crazy Dogs, Maggie got up and said she was going to "fix some little lunches." When I told her that I had left a bag on the kitchen counter with moose meat, of my own hunting, all three of the old people made sounds of gladness. Louis began to sing an old-time song in time to the tapping of a slim stick against the end post of his metal bed. Makes Summer went over and sat on his bed with a newspaper.

Half an hour later Maggie came back in with plates of steaming hot food. Although her supplies were meager, she had been able to give the meal a certain taste and quality that suited our simple visit just fine. Even Makes Summer put away his newspaper and looked hungry. I figured he was one of the few elderly Blackfeet who could read, since he had studied the pages so intently. Most Blackfeet born after the tribe got settled on its reservation were made to attend missionary schools for at least a year or two. Makes Summer told me that he was one of these, though he said he spent more time working in the missionaries' gardens than studying books. I believed this, after I looked at a newspaper with him and found him holding it upside down!

All three of the old folks spoke good English. Among the Canadian Blackfoot divisions there were still several elders who spoke no English at all. English came naturally to Louis, since his father had served as a guide and scout. Besides, during the early 1900's he worked as a guide and interpreter, mainly for a young, wealthy graduate of Yale University named Walter McClintock, who spent several seasons making written and photographic records among the tribe. His book, *The Old North Trail,* is a classic account of Blackfoot culture.

During our meal the conversation slowly drifted to a favorite topic among all Indian people—family and children. Over boiled moose meat, potatoes, bread, and coffee I tried to explain in simple terms why my wife and I had split up. Unlike other people whom I knew, the old folks didn't try to pass any judgment on the matter. Nor did they try to tell me what I should do next. Louis did say: "Well, you're home here, and you're always welcome." That was just the kind of encouragement I needed. Among the Blackfoot people this kind of comment is about as formal an adoption as is made. I have heard and read stories about elaborate ceremonies by which non-Indians become "tribe members," or "chiefs." These are honorary gestures, often with political overtones, made by tribal leaders. It is like a mayor giving "the key" for his town to some noted visitor. That doesn't mean every family in town wants the visitor to drop in.

There was a time when tourists coming to nearby Glacier National Park were able to buy "honorary Blackfoot citizenship," complete with dramatic adoption ceremonies. But this was only a New York travel agent's idea for making the vacations of his clients more exciting. Many a "greenhorn" went back home convinced he was a genuine Blackfoot Indian, since he was given a piece of paper that said so. The Blackfeet are much too proud and individualistic to make a common tribal agreement about adopting anyone.

There was just a small group of Indians involved in these Glacier Park affairs, although they went on for many years, starting around 1915. Those who took part were expected to camp in their tipis and dress in their traditional clothing. Since they were also given food and payment, as well as tips from camera-carrying tourists, it was an ideal situation for those who wanted to spend their summers being "real Indians," instead of ordinary reservation dwellers. The adoption "song and dance" was a small compromise to make for so much pleasure.

Louis seemed to be adding to his comment about their home

being mine when he said, "There are lots of good-looking women around the reservation who could use an eligible husband!" But Maggie became indignant and said: "He's up in Canada—he doesn't want a girl from around here." Then she winked at me and added, "The best-looking girls are the Bloods, anyway." She was saying this because her parents were both Bloods, although they had lived among the Montana Blackfeet for most of their lives.

Suddenly Louis broke out with a traditional Blackfoot rivalry song, used by his Piegan division to make fun of the Bloods. The words of the song were: "Bloods all have snotty noses." He sang loudly, and he accompanied the words with sign language by holding his cupped hands downward, in front of his nose, then moving his fingers down over his lips to show something running from the nostrils.

Maggie hardly let him finish the tune before she responded with one of her own, which Blood warriors used to sing at their Piegan relatives and rivals. The words were: "Piegans are lying all piled up." While singing, she placed her hands one on top of the other, several times, to show the piling. This referred to a time when a Piegan war party was wiped out and humiliated in defeat. After their singing, both of the old folks laughed heartily and hugged each other.

Maggie must have decided that the subject of a wife was too important to end so soon. She went on with the following advice: "When you are going to choose another wife, look for the daughter of a good woman—neat and hard-working. Such a girl will probably become like her mother. That is what the old people used to say." She added that her own mother had been a hard worker and a faithful wife. She had even accompanied her husband on the war trail, and helped him in fights with the enemy. Maggie's father, Weasel Tail, was a well-known and fearless warrior. One time he lay down in the trail of an approaching grizzly bear, only to jump up and stab the animal to death when it started pawing him around.

Maggie said if I found a good Indian girl for a wife I would have to give expensive gifts to her parents. She said this very seriously, although the custom is hardly followed nowadays. She said that her own first husband had brought many fine horses and other valuable presents to her parents, in order to convince them that he was sincere in wanting their daughter for a wife, and also to show that he was capable of providing for a family. Her parents later gave back horses and other goods that were nearly equal in value, so that the whole matter turned out to be mostly a token exchange. From this custom many non-Indians have concluded that Indian parents "sold" their daughters to be wives as though they were simply pieces of property.

Our discussion of Indian traditions led me to bring up a serious matter for which I wanted Maggie and Louis's advice. A short time before my visit with them I had made an unusual pledge, during a period of immense panic. It began while my first family was still living together on our homestead. We had gone to visit an elderly couple who were our friends. At that time our daughter was walking and talking, but our one-year-old son, Wolf, was still pretty awkward. During the visit he ran around the house until he tripped, and fell headfirst into the sharp corner of a heavy, marble-topped coffee table. Wolf ended up with a hole through the middle of his forehead that looked large enough to stick my finger into. Dark red blood oozed from the wound, and gave me a tight knot in my stomach. He screamed briefly, then lapsed into a stunned silence. It was the first emergency I had ever faced with a child. The nearest hospital was more than half an hour's drive away. I thought my son might die, or else that he would have permanent damage from the injury. I was very frightened.

I drove to the hospital over a two-lane country highway, going as fast as I dared. I prayed hard, using all the words and thoughts that came to mind. I believe it was the first time in my life that praying was really a serious attempt to communicate with, and seek help from, higher powers. Up until then I always had pretty much what I needed in life, so that my occasional prayers lacked any real serious purpose. Suddenly I found myself in a predicament that seemed beyond any ordinary human solution. I forced myself to have faith in my requests for spiritual assistance, and I meant it when I promised to fulfill some vague traditional duty in the future, to help make my devotion to prayers grow.

When I told the old folks about the traumatic experience with Wolf, they gasped, shook their heads, and waited eagerly to hear the end. They seemed noticeably relieved when I told them that we got to the hospital just as our family doctor was coming out the front door. He took Wolf right back in, cleaned his face, stitched the hole shut, and said he'd be fine the next day. Louis said: "Gee, you're lucky! Your prayers were heard, and the Creator helped you just in time." Since then I believe that the Creator has put within every one of us the spark of devotion. For many it takes a real crisis before that spark flares up enough to make us learn how to rely on spiritual faith.

After the details of the story were discussed a while longer, I asked the old folks what I could do to fulfill my traditional pledge. A few times since the accident I wondered if I should just forget about it, and be glad that everything worked out so well. But the thought of it would not leave me alone, so I was glad to share my situation with these trusted people. There followed a lengthy discussion between themselves, all in Blackfoot, which I did not understand. The tone of the talk was serious, so I gathered that they were debating how an outsider like myself could fulfill such a sacred vow. Even Louis quit making jokes, and his smile was gone for the time being.

Maggie did most of the serious talking, while the two men listened and made occasional comments. Makes Summer stared at the floor, while Louis looked mostly at his wife. Now and then he tugged thoughtfully on the ends of his thin braids, and looked at my own hair, worn the same way. Once he sucked in his lower lip and got a faraway look, then suddenly shook his head from side to side and said, quietly and in a drawn-out manner: *"Saaah."* I knew that meant "no."

Finally I saw all three heads nodding in agreement, as the old folks shifted about and their air once again became relaxed. "We was trying to figure out how you could do this," Louis informed me. "Guess the best way would be to get hold of one of them medicine pipe bundles. That's what they're for, you know—to fulfill a promise you make when you or one of your kids is sick, or in trouble. They'll say: 'If my baby gets well, then I'll get such-and-such a pipe bundle.' But you've got to give a lot of goods and payments for them! It's a serious thing, not easy. That's the way the Spirits will know that your vow was sincere. You pay good for the transfer. After that it's yours, and you'll benefit a lot from it."

Makes Summer added: "First we thought you could take part in the Sun Dance, to make your vow good. I said I'd teach you about weather dancing, already. That would be good enough. But these folks don't think there'll be another Sun Dance, so you might be putting it off for a long time. It's been several years since our tribe had such a ceremony. It's not good to wait with a vow, if your boy has already gotten better. Besides, it's a lot easier to get a medicine pipe than it is to put up a Sun Dance!"

I had been thinking of taking part in a Sun Dance myself. I didn't know how complicated the ceremony was, or how seldom it was performed anymore. But what they were suggesting was much different, and more involved. I certainly didn't imagine that an outsider like myself would have any chance in taking over the care of such an important tribal article as a medicine pipe bundle. I had thought only rich museums got such things.

Medicine pipe bundles were traditionally cared for by chiefs and leaders of the Blackfoot people. At one time there may have been a couple dozen of these bundles among the twenty thousand or thirty thousand members of all four Blackfoot divisions. Within their hide wrappings were contained many sacred articles symbolic of the natural world in old-time Blackfoot life. There were tanned skins of birds and animals, for which special songs and dances had to be learned. There were rattles, whistles, and carved sticks, used during the lengthy rituals. Most important, within each bundle was an elaborately decorated pipestem—longer than a man's arm—which was highly venerated, though rarely smoked. Smoking was a prelude to most social functions, but for those purposes smaller, less-decorated pipes were used.

I knew that there were only a few of these sacred pipe bundles left among the Blackfeet. I also knew that their annual opening ceremonies were still well attended by those who kept alive the faith in Nature that was passed down by their ancestors. I had been invited to attend some of these ceremonies by the bundle keepers. But when I made my vow I had no plans to become so deeply involved in the ways of the Blackfeet, or any other tribe, as this advice of the old folks suggested. I was taken aback by the thought of its possible consequences.

But the old folks didn't seem to take the matter with much concern at all. I had told them of my situation, and my vow, and they had decided on a solution. It was up to me to accept their advice, or to change the subject and forget it. They would not have interfered in my decision, either way.

I asked Louis: "Do you think there is any chance of someone giving *me* his medicine pipe bundle?" I said I thought those bundles belonged only to leaders and special people. Louis shook his head and replied: "Yes, that's the way it used to be when I was young. But nowadays a lot of the customs that go with them have been put aside. Sometimes the bundles are just treated like old souvenirs!"

Maggie told me that I was a "smart young fellow," and that I could try learning the customs and ceremonies to help keep them from being lost. She said the last renowned leader of those rituals had just died a few years earlier, and that his father had been a white man from France. My enthusiasm for living history got me excited over this possibility, although I still wondered how I would ever get started.

"My boy owns one of those pipe bundles," Maggie finally explained, "and he's been saying that he's getting too old to look after it. If I have a talk with him about it, he might let you take it over." I knew this son of Maggie's—a thin man of about Makes Summer's age, and a fabulous dancer. I never realized that he was the keeper of a prestigious bundle, as well.

Before I knew it, the old folks were giving me instructions on how to approach this elderly son in the traditionally proper manner. They said I would have to present him with a filled pipe. If he accepted it, that meant he was willing to transfer the bundle. In that case, I would have to give him a horse, or something equally valuable, to show my sincerity. At the actual transfer of the bundle I would have to be prepared with several horses, and lots of money, blankets, and dry goods. I quickly figured I would use my share of the proceeds from the sale of our homestead, although I had hoped to invest this money in a little piece of land somewhere else.

The old folks said I should think about their suggestion and come back prepared another day, if I wanted to go ahead. They offered to come along when I made my formal request. But suddenly the whole matter reached a climax when a car drove up outside and Makes Summer—who went to look—announced excitedly: "It's him!"

Before I could get the importance of his arrival into focus, the man in question came in through the doorway and said, *"Okeeh!,"* which is the standard Blackfoot greeting. He recognized me instantly and came over to shake my hand, saying with a smile: "Hey, there, you lost?" I told him I was just visiting with the old folks, although my mind was busily thinking what else I might say.

I sat nervously while son and mother engaged in apparent small talk. Louis lit a cigarette, then passed the pack to his stepson, who also took one. Then I noticed that Makes Summer was busy filling a small, stone-bowled pipe that I had given to him on an earlier visit. He was very intent on his work, while I tried to figure out if he was doing this for me, or if he had other plans for pipe smoking.

Meanwhile, the son turned to me and began talking in English. He said he had just taken an hour off work from his construction job. He was employed by the Blackfeet Agency to build an addition to some family's reservation house. He had no idea that we were talking about him just before his arrival, and I decided not to mention it. He talked about his car—it wasn't running well—and about some payments that were overdue to the Blackfeet for lands leased out by them to oil prospectors.

I was hoping that Maggie, or one of the others, would bring up the subject of our discussion, preferably in English so that I could keep up with it. I was anxious to hear how he would respond. Instead, however, Makes Summer motioned for me to come by his bed when he felt a break in our conversation. He handed me the pipe, rather secretively, and whispered: "Kneel down and hand it to him. If he takes it, give him some money and tell him it's in place of a horse."

I turned and hesitated, because the man was again talking to his mother. It seemed strange to think of him as anyone's son, since he looked nearly as old as the others in the room. His short, bushy hair was gray, and most of his teeth were gone. With his dark, wrinkled skin and high cheekbones he looked like an old-time Indian warrior. I felt a tinge of fear when I realized the seriousness of the request I was about to make of him.

He must have sensed that something was up as he turned and looked at me, expectantly. Several times his eyes darted from mine down to the pipe that I held, nervously, in my hands. Quickly I moved over in front of him, knelt down, and extended my arms to hold the pipe close in front of his face. He seemed almost to move backward, as he muttered in surprise: "What's this?" I told him: "Here is a smoke for you; take it!"

For some moments everything in that room stopped. Those seemed like long moments to me. I felt myself trembling upon my knees, and my mouth dried up quickly. Then, without moving, as though I had him pinned down with a weapon, the man demanded: "What do you want from me?" I was confused—the old folks had only told me what to do after the pipe was accepted. He wasn't accepting it—he only asked me what I wanted. I looked around the room pleadingly, hoping someone would speak for me. Then Maggie said: "You better tell him what you want," so I just blurted out: "I'm asking you for your medicine pipe."

There followed another period of silence. The bundle keeper seemed to be taking his time, as though he were testing me. I didn't know what to do, so I did nothing, and waited. Finally he gave me his reply. "All right," he said, carefully measuring his words, "I'll let you have the medicine pipe, if that's what you want. But you're going to have to pay me what I ask for it!" I told him I was willing to do that, though my head was buzzing so strongly from the intensity of the situation that I would probably have agreed to anything he asked, just to get the drama over with.

With slow, firm movements he finally took the pipe from my hands. I felt as though a heavy load had been removed from my shoulders. I let my arms drop and tried to relax. He told me to stay where I was, then he raised the stem of the pipe into the air and began to pray. I learned, later, that he asked for pity and guidance on behalf of both his family and mine. He also spoke to the Spirits of the bundle and asked them to begin helping me with my life. When he finished praying, the old folks added their sounds of agreement, and held their hands over their hearts, according to Blackfoot custom. Then Makes Summer lit a match and held it so that the bundle keeper could smoke the pipe.

Everyone sat quietly while he smoked. When he finished he asked me if I had any idea what a great honor and duty I was asking him to give up. I thought I did, and said so. He probably knew that I did not, but he said nothing. Instead, he began to explain some things to me. He said:

"My wife and I have had this bundle for over twenty years. It's done a lot of good for my family—not just my own, but also my brothers' and even my old mom here. They all helped me with the transfer payments, back when it was first transferred to my wife and me. We gave a lot for it—over twenty head of horses, a cow, blankets, clothing, and cash."

I knew enough about Blackfoot customs to realize that he was preparing me for the amount I would be expected to pay. An old keeper usually lists all his payments at the time that he agrees to pass a bundle on to someone else. It would be an insult for the new keeper to offer less for the bundle than had been given before. If the former keeper felt that there was a lack of proper payments, he could pack up the bundle in the middle of the ceremony and call off the transfer.

Maggie's son said that none of his relatives were willing to assume the many duties and obligations required for keeping the bundle, and that he and his wife were getting too old. He said they had been talking of giving it up for some time already, and that several white men were eager to buy it. He said he would prefer to pass the bundle on to someone like me—that I would at least pray with it and make its daily incense. But I would have to match an offer of four thousand dollars cash that one of the white men had made just recently.

I swallowed hard at the mention of the amount, and felt a cold sweat break out on me all over again. My share of the homestead money would amount to far less than that, and I would have to use some of that to pay several old bills, first. Still, I felt strongly about the obligation I had already made, so I muttered a feeble "yes," when he asked me if I still wanted to go ahead.

He then explained that I would have all winter to prepare for the transfer ceremony, which he wanted to have in the spring. He said: "These medicine pipes were first given to us by the Thunder Spirit, way back in ancient times. Since then the bundles have always been opened every spring, after the people hear the return of Thunder." He said he and his wife would have to hire a wise couple who knew the complete ritual, which he did not. They would transfer rights to me and my wife which would then allow us to learn it. He would also have to get four men to drum and sing the many sacred songs that the ceremony requires. In addition, he would have to provide plenty of food and tobacco for the many guests whom he expected to attend this event.

At least he was going to pay for all these things himself, out of the money I was to give him. Then he added: "I told you that my payments included a lot of good horses, but now I'm too old to go horseback riding. That's why I asked you to pay me with cash, instead. My wife and I will be able to get a few things around our house that we've been needing."

With that final advice he bid farewell to us, went outside, and drove back to his job. The old folks seemed pleased that things had gone so well, and I was somewhat cheered by their happiness. But I felt very dazed at the same time, and I sensed that I had taken on quite a heavy burden.

By the time we drank more coffee and talked about medicine

pipes and related things, most of the day had gone by. For some reason the world outside our dimly lit shack had remained like a distant fog throughout the visit. I never went out, and I don't recall anyone else going, either. At any rate, as I began to think about leaving I realized that it had gotten quite windy. Now and then a gust blew strong enough to butt loudly against the walls of the flimsy shack, and to rattle its tin chimney.

When I looked out the door from the little porch, I could hardly believe my eyes—a genuine snowstorm was howling across the lonely prairie and covering everything in white. Right around the door snow was already piled knee-deep, where the swirling winds had brought it. Within another hour all the grass on the prairie was covered over, and the highways leading in and out of Browning were closed. It was the season's first blizzard, and it blew in with a fury rare even on the northern plains.

Makes Summer had come to the door with me, to say farewell. When he saw my surprise upon finding the storm, he grinned broadly and looked at me as if to say: There you have it! Neither of us needed to mention his mystical weather prediction made earlier that day.

It was not until the middle of the following day that I was able to drive back up to Canada. The short route over a mountain pass was closed from the storm, so I had to take the longer way, past Duck Lake. This is just a gravel road that winds its way over prairie hills, right along the edge of the mountains. In the early reservation days it was a wagon road connecting the Blackfoot divisions, and before that it was a well-known intertribal trail. In some of the low spots along this road snow had drifted into piles as high as my truck's hood, but it was so powdery that I was able to plow right through. For over an hour I drove without seeing another vehicle, unless I count those that have been abandoned along this isolated stretch over the years. During that time the storm cleared up completely and the sky turned a crisp blue that looked almost surreal. The air turned bitterly cold, and I knew that winter had arrived.

I was eager to tell the members of my now-split-up family about the medicine pipe bundle. During my lonely drive I began thinking this might provide enough inspiration to bring us back together for another try. But things turned out quite differently.

Along the way I stopped for an overnight visit with Beverly and her family. Their home on the Blood Reserve was little more than two hours from Browning. Originally the two reservations were supposed to join at the international boundary, so that the closely related tribes could continue to live as neighbors. In fact, the huge reservation of the Montana Blackfeet still runs along the edge of Canada. But the Blood lands, although part of the largest Indian reserve in Canada, has been trimmed down (mostly by hook and crook) so that a wide strip of non-Indian land now separates it from the U.S.A. Modern, educated Bloods have recently been at work sorting out the confusing documents that purport to explain how this land-trimming took place without permission from the Bloods.

Beverly's family followed progressive ways that did not include ancient medicine bundles, or their ceremonies. Nevertheless, when they heard about the medicine pipe they encouraged my plans to obtain it. Both of Beverly's parents had grown up around grandparents who were noted medicine pipe keepers and leaders of the ceremonies. In fact, her dad's grandfather taught the ritual to her mother's grandfather, who was younger. In the traditional Blackfoot lifestyle these duties were considered something like intellectual pursuits, and it may have seemed appropriate that an educated newcomer like myself should get involved in them.

However, Beverly's parents knew nothing, yet, about the breakup of my family. They still assumed their daughter would be a regular visitor to our homestead across the mountains. Her mother even suggested that she be initiated for the bundle with us, so that she could be at ease in its presence. This is a custom often still followed by close family members of bundle keepers.

I knew a fair amount abut medicine pipe bundles from my ethnological reading. However, at this point I felt that advice from a qualified medicine pipe man was in order. I had heard a certain old Blood man's name praised by several people in this regard, so I asked Beverly if she could bring me to meet him. Her mother offered to come along with us and interpret for me the story of my situation.

We found this old man living with one of his grown-up children in a very modern house. He welcomed us, and when he learned that we came for a serious talk he brought us to a bedroom and closed the door. He immediately asked for a smoke, and said that a cigarette would do when I told him that I had brought no pipe. He spoke good English, and it soon became obvious that I could just as well have gone to see him by myself. He said that he was willing to be the instructor for the medicine pipe transfer, and he told us how generously he had paid his own teachers for this knowledge many years before.

The new instructor explained a few basics to us, then he told me that I should go and bring back the rest of my family so that he could perform a certain ritual that should come next in the process. When I said that I would be back with them the following week, he added: "For this that I am going to do, I paid my instructor a good horse." He meant, in other words, that I should expect to pay a good horse as well—or, at least, the equivalent of one. I suddenly began to wonder if I would be able to afford this old man's services.

The next day I left the Blood Reserve and headed north for the city of Calgary, on my way back to the homestead. For a couple of hours I rolled along over the snow-covered prairie highway, feeling both excited and melancholy. I was eager to share the good news with my wife, but I also had some misgivings about her reaction. The huge wheatfields and seemingly endless skies of that country helped make me feel more insignificant. Having grown up in a small town, surrounded by dark forests, I found it hard to get used to such vast, empty spaces. At the same time, the plowed fields and barbed-wire fences of ranch life reminded me that this very land had once been the wild and natural domain of my adopted Blackfoot ancestors.

In Calgary I went to visit an archival library housed in a stately old building in the midst of a park. I wanted to see what information was available about medicine bundles that I had not already studied. My search there was so successful that I made numerous visits to read unpublished papers and look at old photographs in the following seasons. I even found pictures of the bundle keeper as a young man, and of Makes Summer performing as the Weather Dancer during a past Sun Dance. My involvement in living history was expanding.

That day I also bought a whole apple box full of handmade moccasins for one hundred dollars. They were offered to me by an old trader, who said he got them directly from the Indian women who had made them. Every year he went into Canada's huge Northwest Territories and bought furs from the trappers, on which he made lots of money. He said he wasn't interested in moccasins, because they weren't worth so much. He just bought them because they were made by the trappers' wives, and he wanted to keep the good will of their husbands. Ten years later he could have gotten his hundred dollars from just one or two pairs of the pile that he sold to me.

The cab of my truck was filled with a tantalizing aroma when I continued my drive from Calgary. The moccasins had been smoked over slow, outdoor fires. This made them brown, waterproof, and sweet-scented. It was the perfect essence for traveling the snow-lined Trans-Canada Highway into scenic Banff National Park. Adding to this drama was a herd of seven elk who calmly grazed by the roadside, just a few minutes beyond the park gates. While this is not an unusual sight for this region, I am, nevertheless, always drawn to pull over and pause for a while, thrilled by the mere thought of such noble wild animals still roaming their ancient trails in a continent as modern as North America.

The medicine pipe bundle had fairly well captured my feelings and thoughts. Its presence by me was so strong that it seemed I had a passenger riding with me, although I drove through the mountains alone. By the time I got to the little tourist cabin where the rest of my family was staying, I was nearly bursting with enthusiasm for making another attempt at our life.

But when I spilled out the story of my new and deeper commitment to old Indian ways, I was faced with a threatening silence. Mention of the proposed event chilled any prospect of reuniting with Carol, and the conversation that followed made it evident that we were heading in different directions. Suddenly we both seemed to know that we had reached a stage in our relationship where major changes and decisions were necessary. We knew that our actions would affect us and our children from then on. It seemed like an awesome responsibility for two young people who were barely beyond being American teenagers.

Soon I found myself back on the highway, still westbound, heading for the homestead in British Columbia. It had been sold, but the new owners let me keep a tiny cabin and a few acres around it. I wanted to go there and think, and maybe write another book during the winter. The medicine pipe was still strong on my mind, and I was determined to go through with the transfer. I wasn't traveling alone with these thoughts, this time, because I had taken Wolf with me. He was barely two years old, and carefree. He made me laugh through my tears.

When we got to the homestead it looked deserted. House and cabin were empty and locked. Even the birch trees looked gloomy without their leaves. When I shut off the motor the silence of the place became so loud that I thought I heard little children laughing. I felt muscles twitching uncontrollably in my face as tears welled up in my eyes. There was a great heaviness in my heart as I walked down the little grassy path toward the house we had built for ourselves. A sunlit scene of two children playing in the yard flashed across my mind . . . Rabbits and horses nearby . . . Smoke curling up from the chimney . . . Maybe fresh bread and hot chocolate inside . . . I finally fell to my knees and let my emotions drain out on the ground.

Wolf knew nothing of my misery, since he was asleep in the truck. By the time he woke up the only trace of my sorrow was my red eyes, which he didn't notice, and a big smile, which he did. We were standing on the bottom of the valley and from there we could only look up. Together we went to the guest cabin, where I lit a fire in the stove. With a few toys on the bed, and the promise of warm food coming, Wolf played happily by himself while I got things arranged for our stay.

The next morning we lay in bed until long after daylight, talking and amusing each other. I told Wolf of the things I thought we should do, and he acted very agreeable. It didn't matter that he understood hardly any of what I said. The main thing was to see him enjoying my company and attention.

When we got up we found the valley damp and foggy. It seemed too lonely and gloomy for a young father and his son. Even with my newfound cheer I found it hard to look down the field at our house. It gave me an empty feeling deep inside—the kind of feeling one gets in a stadium, after a ball game, or in a theater, when the show is over. I realized Wolf and I would not be content in such an environment.

The two young couples who had bought the homestead from us were glad to hear that I would not be staying after all. They had come up from California to "do their thing," as was common at that time, and I guess they preferred to do it without the presence of someone older, who already had his own "thing" going. They agreed to pay me for the cabin, which I figured would cover nearly half of the bundle transfer. Now, some years later, one would have to pay what we got for the *whole* homestead just to buy that cabin, and the couple of acres with it.

With most of my past ties cut I had no place to call home except with the old folks, and other friends among the Indian people. There I knew we would find friendship and welcome. I thought Wolf should have someone to look after him in a motherly way, which I knew I could not do. I also felt I should have a companion to help learn the ways of the medicine bundle. I decided to ask Beverly if she was willing to join me.

I found her at the home of her parents, taking care of her newborn son and her aged grandmother. I told her that my family was permanently separated, and I asked her if she was willing to live with Wolf and me. She said that she was, and she also reaffirmed a willingness to learn her ancestral traditions with me.

Beverly's parents had gone to work in the boarding-school laundry. She said that our first challenge would be to break the news to them. She warned me that they might not take kindly to the idea.

They had already seen her split up with one husband who was from outside her own tribe. They wished her to get a higher education before making another try at family life. They wanted her to take advantage of the modern schooling that had been denied them. Besides, they already thought of me as a son-in-law because of my marriage to their adopted white daughter—my former wife, Carol. They might find it hard to understand why I would want to give up my white ways so totally and move right in with the Indians. At that time most Indians wanted to move in the opposite direction.

Beverly's unsuspecting parents were glad to see me when they got home from work later that afternoon. All day they had stood on hard cement floors, at the underground laundry room, in the same school they attended as children. They must have been tired, but still they welcomed me with happy smiles and friendly greetings. I found this attitude toward guests quite common among Indians. It seemed noticeably different from the ways of many city people I had known, who wanted advance notice of visits, and preferred to be left alone at mealtimes. In most Indian households guests are offered food even if they show up in the middle of the night.

Beverly's parents thought it was nice of me to be traveling with my little son, rather than alone. They tried to keep me entertained with various topics, not noticing the nervous glances Beverly and I were exchanging. Before either of us could bring up the serious subject of our new plans, her father invited me to go along for a visit to an elderly relative of his. I was glad for the opportunity, since this meant a drive of several miles across the prairie, and a chance to talk privately.

He listened silently, and without comment, when I began to tell him of my desire for religious dedication, and how this was bringing me to seek a home among his people. When I told him that his daughter and I both felt strongly about these matters, I think he began to figure out that I was building up to something. Still, he made no reaction when I finally forced myself to say that Beverly and I intended to take up life together. For the rest of the drive neither of us said a word.

The visit to the relative was unsuccessful—there was no one at his house. When we got back to the family's home, the silence continued for a while, until there was a brief family consultation, to which I was not called. Until that night my usual place to sleep, when visiting, was on the living room couch, near Beverly's father and any other grown boys who happened to be staying in the house. But after this discussion I was told to go and sleep in one of the bedrooms, with my new family, while Beverly's parents took over the couch.

Our relationship was accepted with resignation more than with enthusiasm. Beverly and I were both young adults, and we had each made one big mistake, already, with family life. Her parents kindly decided not to interfere in our second effort. Nevertheless I got little sleep that night, thinking of the whole matter over and over. I remained fully dressed, worried that a change of heart might see me thrown out the front door in the middle of the night.

The night passed without incident, however, and the next day dawned clear and cheerful. Beverly's folks went to work, and she and I were left alone to make plans for our new situation. We wanted to find a place of our own to live, where we could bring elders to visit without interruptions. Beverly said she knew of an abandoned old house down along the nearby Bullhorn River, which we might be able to rent cheaply. We agreed to try living simply, and to learn the old-time Indian ways. I even talked about getting rid of our truck and traveling only by horseback, or with a horse-drawn wagon. Both methods of transportation were then still common on the Blood Reserve. So was simple Indian living.

A twenty-minute drive from Beverly's home brought us down into the wide bottomlands of the Bullhorn River, which was just a small stream. We saw the yellow house from a distance—before we dropped down off the prairie on a dirt road that crossed the active part of the river over a large metal culvert. In the sheltered bottoms grew trees and thick bunches of bushes. That cheered me up, since I had worried about feeling insecure in a house out on the open prairie. This old house had several stately trees growing by it.

The house seemed fairly large compared to most others on the reserve at that time. It had belonged to a big family. Its location seemed like an ideal setting for the tipi camps of my childhood dreams. Within the last century it had actually been the site of such camps. I wished there were people who would join us in making such a camp again.

The walls of the house were covered with stucco, but squared logs could be seen underneath, where the stucco had cracked and fallen off. The four-sided roof of the edifice was covered with wooden shingles that were once painted red. Years of neglect had left them dry and faded. A stone chimney had seen no smoke for many winters. Yet the old building still looked quite solid, although some of the windows were broken. We knew that a few days' work would turn it back into a pleasant home.

Uphill, some distance away, stood another yellow house, this one more modern. It belonged to a son of Dick Soup, the elderly owner of the place. Himself a widower, Dick lived with his son and his son's family, looking out on the land that had once made him among the tribe's most prosperous ranchers.

In his eighties Dick Soup was one of the last Bloods to carry his own Indian name on official records. His father was a Blood warrior and medicine man named Black Plume. His mother was a woman of mixed ancestry, half Indian and half white. She died while he was still an infant, so he was nursed with soup instead of mother's milk. Thus, he got the name Soup, to which was later added the first name of Richard. He had a brother who was then a noted medicine man and ceremonial leader. This man's Indian name was Skunk, but on official records he carried the last name of Black Plume, his father. Dick Soup and Bob Black Plume came from a very traditional household. Their father had two wives, and each of the boys had a different mother.

Dick Soup was very pleased when he learned that we wanted to fix up and rent his old house. For twenty-five dollars a month he said we could treat the place as if it were our own. Soon after we got moved in he came to see us, with his son, and asked if we liked the place well enough to give three hundred dollars for it. For that price he said he would include a couple acres of land, and all the outbuildings except for a corral and a horse stable. His son's family had no vehicle, so they kept a saddlehorse in case an emergency required them to rush to a neighbor.

I got the first taste of my social status as a newcomer living among the Bloods when Beverly brought me a permit, issued by tribal authorities, which said that I could stay for six months "as a guest of Beverly Little Bear." She said at the end of that time I would have to renew the permit or leave the reserve.

Most of those who lived on the reserve with permits were schoolteachers, church people, and government employees. But one man who had married a woman from the tribe used her family's land to build up an enterprising cattle operation. His success was not well received by members of the tribe, especially some of the poorer people. As a result, we heard frequent rumors that this man would be "kicked off the reserve," and all other non-Indians along with him.

We hardly got settled in our new home when word came from a relative of Beverly's who had a good horse for sale. Someone told him that I wanted to live like an old-time Indian, but that I didn't own a single horse. In Blackfoot traditions an individual's wealth and success is measured by the number and quality of his horses. In the Buffalo days an average family of six required at least fifteen or twenty horses to move their tipi, bedding, belongings, and themselves from one campsite to the next.

Today most Blackfeet drive cars, and many are so busy with jobs and other obligations that they scarcely find time even for pleasure riding. Only those involved in ranching or the rodeo circuits still find horses essential. Nevertheless, a number of families own impressive herds. Few tribe members would ignore the sight of a lively horse galloping across the grassy prairie, its tail and mane blowing in the wind like symbols of wild freedom.

I was offered a quarterhorse that was said to be small and well built. It sounded like an Indian pony of the past, and it had some fame as a racer, as well. When one of Beverly's brothers said that the two-hundred-dollar price was a good buy, I took his word, since he was a rodeo cowboy. My own experience with horses—other than those that kept running away from the homestead—was limited to huge draft animals that hauled freight wagons in the German town of my youth. I was always afraid of them, especially after I saw our elderly landlord run over and trampled by a team that had gone out of control on an icy downtown street.

Older people on the reserve spoke of times when ordinary horses brought only fifty cents each. Back then, large herds roamed everywhere, and government agents complained that they destroyed grazing land that could have been used for cattle and other valuable livestock. That helped explain why one medicine bundle transfer included the exchange of one hundred head. Today a good horse is worth a lot of money, and even an untrained range animal brings at least a couple hundred dollars.

The relative who owned the horse rode all morning into the face of that season's second blizzard to keep his end of the bargain and deliver the animal to my door. It was a gelding, and I named him Blood, in honor of the people among whom he lived. He was a sorrel-colored horse, with white socks and a look of friendliness that made me feel relaxed. He did not have the air of aloofness that keeps me from getting intimate with many horses.

While Beverly took the relative back home in our truck, I took the horse out for a trial ride. I thought he would be fairly worn out from his long trip, so I used only a hackamore, instead of a regular bridle, and I rode without a saddle. The quarterhorse was easy to mount and comfortable to ride. Sitting directly on his back helped keep me warm, as the snowstorm had not let up. Time lost all meaning, down along the Bullhorn River. Once we got away from the house we followed trails that could not have been much different in the days of buffalo.

Everything went well until we came to a dark object lying on the ground by the trail ahead. The horse saw it first, and I sensed that he didn't care for it. He began to shy when we got near, and I let him go way around. It was a calf, recently dead, and I didn't like seeing it, either. I let the horse know how I felt by loosening the reins and nudging him lightly with my moccasin-covered feet. I had forgotten that he was trained for racing. He took my suggestion seriously and was off in a flash. We rushed out into the open bottoms, away from the river, at top speed. Snowflakes pelted my eyes so I could hardly see, but the snow-covered ground made the adventure seem less dangerous than it really was. I had never ridden so fast on a horse, or so smoothly.

Later, when I tried to share the excitement of my ride with Beverly's father, I learned the folly of it. He had been around horses all his life, even as a trick rider at public performances. He said I was lucky not to be lying in the riverbottom with a broken neck. I had not thought about the many gopher holes and badger burrows that lay hidden under the snow. Had the horse stepped into one of those, it would have been disaster for both of us. Many buffalo hunters met their tragic deaths that way.

Beverly was especially concerned about the dangers of horse-back riding. As a young girl she had watched, in the company of her parents, while her oldest brother was killed riding a wild bronco during the world-famous Calgary Stampede. He had already completed his trial ride and wanted to get off, but one of his boots got caught in the bucking horse's stirrup.

Beverly's parents tried to cushion the impact of my arrival among their people by giving advice, and by trying to get me involved in the daily social life of the reserve. No doubt they understood much better than I the cultural and racial gap that I was trying to bridge. They were dismayed to learn that I preferred living in relative seclusion, meeting mostly with elders and those people who would reinforce my growing beliefs in the old ways. This helped give my presence on the reserve an air of mystery, which some resented. But I was so overwhelmed by the potential for learning "living history" that I scarcely paid attention to anything else for the next couple of years.

I soon learned the truth of a popular saying, "When an outsider marries an Indian woman, he marries half the tribe." After growing up almost without relatives, I was amazed by the size of my new family. Every time we went to town, or to a dance, there seemed to be aunts, uncles, and other in-law's—especially cousins. What was more, they all seemed to be proud of their relationships to one another, even though they had their share of arguments and disagreements, as well. I could certainly no longer claim to be without a people!

My father-in-law was eager to introduce me to his uncle, Willie Eagle Plume, who had raised him after his own father died. The son of a great Blood warrior and leading medicine man named Eagle Plume, Willie was respected for his knowledge of tribal customs, legends, and ceremonials. As his new son-in-law I was eligible to inherit this information from him, if we should grow close. I'm happy to say that he and I liked each other from the moment we met. I clearly recall a particular night . . .

It was cold and snowing, as another storm was just getting underway. Beverly and I had driven over to visit her parents, as we frequently did. When mother-in-law and daughter got involved in "women's talk," my father-in-law asked me if I'd care to go along to do some visiting. I agreed, put on my coat, hat, and overshoes, and sat on the passenger side of his Ford truck. I was still new to the reserve's unmarked road system, so I soon felt lost in the dark. Adding to my confusion was the loose, powdery snow that a light wind was blowing around outside, so that it was nearly impossible to tell the road from the surrounding fields. At times the snow slithered across our path like a gigantic, powder-white snake, eerily illuminated by our headlights.

We finally pulled up to a small frame house that looked like many built on the reserve during the 1940's and 50's—a generation or two after the time of our own stocky house. We were on a bluff, overlooking the Bullhorn River, so close to our house that on a clear day we would have seen the trees in our yard. I later learned to know the old trail that made a short and direct connection between our houses, but that night we had driven many miles to go around the easy way.

Lights were on inside the house, although there were no vehicles parked out front, save for an old black Mercury that had no wheels, and was otherwise hopelessly wrecked. My father-in-law knocked loudly on the door a couple of times, then turned the knob and entered without waiting for an answer. Indian relatives don't generally make much of a formality about entering each other's homes.

Hot air rushed out toward us when the door was opened. In the background I briefly saw the forms of young children, scurrying through another doorway into an adjoining room. They seemed like little chicks in a farmyard at the approach of an unknown shadow. I later learned that they were some of the old man's grandchildren, of whom a few were most always on hand, while their parents were busy elsewhere.

Inside the brightly lit but barren main room sat an elderly man, alone, on a wooden chair. Next to him was a cast-iron heater that was noisily burning wood and radiating lots of heat. A single light bulb hung from the ceiling, without a shade to soften its harshness. The old man got up to shake my father-in-law's hand, at the same time leaning forward to kiss him. In a gentle voice, which sounded kindly, he called him by his childhood name, "Kheysenohn," which means "brother" in Blackfoot. Most people used his adulthood name, Eagle Tailfeathers, or his official name, Ed Little Bear. His cowboy friends still called him Eddie.

My father-in-law said a few words in Blackfoot, at which the old man turned toward me with a smile, and extended his right hand. I took it and noticed immediately the powerful grip of a man who had worked hard in his life. He gave me the impression of one both humble and proud—a peculiar characteristic of many elderly Indians. We said nothing to each other as my father-in-law pulled over a chair for me to sit on.

For the next hour or so I sat on that chair, listening and watching. The conversation was all in Blackfoot—punctuated by liberal use of hands and sign language—and my father-in-law did most of the talking. The older man listened intently, now and then speaking a few soft words in reply. Their talk was Blood Reserve men's talk, I found out later—things about the weather, the people, and the crops. I came to learn that such talks are always saturated with wishful references to the past. There is a general longing to turn back the times, though it is nearly smothered by an attitude of resignation that the past is gone and the present is here to stay. In this way Indians seem to be no different from conservative and traditional people everywhere.

Now and then the old man turned from the conversation to look at me briefly, returning my silent, contemplative gazes with warm and toothless smiles that suited his pleasant face very well. Many happy wrinkles creased his dark brown skin. His silver-gray hair was just past the point of its apparently regular cutting—it hung a bit over his ears and over the collar of his long-sleeved western shirt. His clothing was plain and well worn, yet he had a dignified bearing about him.

At first I thought that perhaps he lived alone, but an elderly woman soon came from the adjoining room and brought a pot of tea, along with several blue enamel cups. She looked very shy, and said nothing. She was a very small woman, with whitish hair in thin braids, and small hands that were noticeably gnarled from arthritis. She was the old man's second wife, after the first one died. Her Indian name, "Midget," was a reference, in Blackfoot, to her small stature.

As my father-in-law's companion, I was not formally introduced to the old man beyond the handshake, nor did we exchange any words of opinion. Indian society does not generally follow the custom of naming strangers to each other when they meet. It is assumed that important people already know each other's name, and unimportant people will have a chance to learn them with the passing of time. As an outsider, I sometimes felt awkward visiting in a room full of people and not knowing their names, nor they knowing mine. By this time I was no longer using my European last name, Gutöhrlein, which means Good Little Ear. It was a hard name for many people to pronounce. Besides, I preferred the name Hungry Wolf, which was given to me by an earlier Indian friend. It described some of my characteristics, and seemed to fit well with my new lifestyle.

During that first visit I figured Willie Eagle Plume was an elderly, conservative, full-blooded Indian who spoke no English. It appeared that he followed few of his cultural and traditional ways. I didn't imagine that soon the two of us would become the closest of friends, that he spoke fluent English, and that he was full of tribal lore and dedication, which he would share with me.

On the drive back to the house my father-in-law did say that his old uncle seemed to have liked me quite well. When I told him that I felt similarly, he encouraged me to go and visit the old man often. Then he told the story of how he came to be raised in his uncle's household. After his own father died, his widowed mother remarried a proud man who was quite wealthy. This man already had children of his own, whom he treated better than his new stepson. When his uncle learned that little "Kheysenohn" was unhappy, he came with a horse and buggy and brought him back to his own home.

At that time the Eagle Plumes lived in the same area as the house that we went to visit. Old Eagle Plume was then still alive and in charge of things, although there were several other adults in the family. Among them were two of his three wives, including SikskiAki, the mother of Willie. Within a few months of his birth one of the other wives also had a son, so that he grew up with almost a twin brother.

The uncle was born into this interesting household in the spring of 1903, some twenty years after his father's last battle. In that short time Eagle Plume had become a successful rancher, owning herds of livestock as well as fields of grain and a large vegetable garden. However, he left most of the ranch work to other able persons in the family so that he could concentrate on his traditional doctoring and the leading of sacred rituals. Because of his tribal wisdom he was often referred to as "Professor Eagle Plume."

Although the uncle carried his father's last name proudly, he was best known by his own Indian name, Atsitsina, which means Prairie Owl Man. This name came about when a young relative was playing with Old Eagle Plume's two baby boys. She noticed that the younger one had peculiarly dark and shiny eyes, which reminded her of an Atsitsi—a small owl that lives in burrows on the prairie. The parents liked this description well enough to turn it into a name, adding the suffix *na,* from *Ninna,* which is Blackfoot for "man."

Atsitsina turned out to have a major influence upon my life, along with another old man whom I met about the same time. I first saw this other man sitting on the ledge of a big storefront window at the meat market in Cardston, the nearest town. I thought I recognized him as soon as I saw him, because he resembled an old Indian of whom I had dreamed. Even from across the busy street I felt attracted to him in a way unlike anything I had felt before. I had no knowledge of his great reputation for spiritual and mystical powers.

Beverly said this man's name was Willie Scraping White, and that he was a kind old widower. She didn't know much about him except that he was considered one of the last "old-time Indians." Although he was dressed in a heavy coat, slouch cap, and rubber boots, I could see that he wore his hair in braids and that his face was covered with the red earth paint that is sacred to most Indians. We agreed to go visit him at his house, which was not far from ours.

It was a dark night when we drove there to introduce ourselves. Although Beverly had occasionally driven this old man to town, whenever she found him walking along the highway, he didn't seem to recognize her. He lived in a little, one-room house, next door to one of his granddaughters and her children. It was nighttime, and from the highway we could see a light burning through the windows of his place. A dirt road led from there through tall, uncut prairie grass right up to his door. Just before we turned our headlights off I noticed the frames of several sweat lodges, out behind. They remained from purifying rituals he had gone through.

We went up to the door, knocked once, loudly, and right away heard a voice telling us to come in. As we entered, I immediately sensed a strong presence of sacred powers. Doubt and weakness began to overcome my original intentions, and I wondered how to explain our arrival in the silence that was waiting for us. We left our overshoes in a small entryway and stepped into the main room, where three old Indian men sat waiting expectantly.

The room was lit by a bare light bulb, which seemed to be a standard fixture in the simple homes of many old Indians. This one created a strong contrast on everything I saw. While I tried not to look at anything in particular, my eyes were attracted at once to many pleasant scenes. Sacred-looking bags and bundles hung from nails on the rear wall. Several brown-toned photographs were mounted inside old frames. In the middle of the room stood a vintage upright heater, giving off glowing warmth. Its stovepipe went up to the ceiling, where it was bent to follow a course across the room and into a brick chimney at the back. A metal box, filled with coal, stood next to the heater.

Heavy winter coats and an assortment of cowboy hats and slouch caps hung from nails and hooks by the doorway where we stood. A worn old dresser was pressed against a far wall. The clutter of things on its top seemed doubled by their reflection in a large mirror mounted right above. Three iron-frame beds took up most of the floor space in the small, single room. One old man sat on each of the beds, and all three were silently looking at us. I felt as though we had disturbed a fraternal gathering, and that we were now expected to make our purpose known.

The oldest of the three was Willie Scraping White, with his bed at the rear. He squinted his eyes, trying to see past the bright light and learn who was in the doorway. His many wrinkles and powerful features were exceptionally pronounced by the brightness reflecting from the red earth paint on his face. The paint went up into the forelock of his otherwise white, long hair. The forelock was brushed back to casually cover the line where his hair was parted into two thinning braids, which hung down over his ears. Strips of red flannel cloth were tied at the ends of the braids. He wore a long-sleeved flannel shirt, gray trousers, and an old pair of buckskin moccasins, whose toes were decorated with beadwork of tiny flowers and leaves.

When the Old Man learned that we had come to see him, he reached out his hand and we each shook it in greeting. The size and strength of his younger years was still evident in his grip. My lips were dry, and my knees were trembling, as I felt that I was undergoing some kind of an important test. I wanted to be courteous and shake hands with the two other old men in the room, so I went to the one whose bed was across from the Old Man's. Too late, I realized that I should have gone around, instead of straight across, for I had walked between the stove and the sacred bundles. In Blackfoot tradition I had breached proper etiquette by disturbing the sacred path between a household's source of fire and its medicines.

The old men shook my hand, by turns, and quietly pointed out my error. They said it in Blackfoot, but I knew from the tone of their voices what they meant. I felt badly shaken, in addition to being overwhelmed and shy. All this time I thought I knew a lot about Blackfoot customs, from my reading and personal practices. Yet I acted so ignorantly when this rare meeting took place.

I tried to apologize, but the Old Man didn't seem too upset. I stood with my head down while he said a few things to Beverly in a pleasant tone. Near our feet stood a small wooden box that was evidence of the household's traditional faith. It was filled with earth and several strangely shaped stones. Braids of sweetgrass and other ceremonial paraphernalia lay alongside. It was an altar, where the Old Man made his incense when he prayed and sang.

This was the kind of thing Beverly and I wanted to learn, and I wondered if I had spoiled our chance. When I asked the Old Man if we could come back and see him another time, he said he would look forward to our visit. I gave him some fresh braids of sweetgrass that we had brought along.

Outside, in the chilly night, the impact and power of this encounter suddenly caused an uncontrollable shaking in my body, as though I had become possessed. In the darkness I thought I saw the laughing face of old Last Gun, the buffalo hunter who first inspired me to try following traditional Blackfoot ways. He seemed to be telling me that I had much to learn from my mistake. I felt perhaps this was a sign that I should dedicate myself more to practicing traditions, rather than just studying them. It reminded me of an old Indian saying about white men: "Smart, but not wise."

A few days later we went back to see old Scraping White again. It was in the daytime, and he was home alone. He seemed very pleased to see us, and said nothing about the incident of the other night. He asked if I had an Indian name and when Beverly told him what it was, in Blackfoot, he thought for a moment, then responded in captivating English: "Wolf, Hungry!" At the same time he rubbed his stomach, to show hunger, and laughed aloud.

He was familiar with names dealing with wolves. His real father had been named Wolf Old Man, although he died early and his little son grew up with a stepfather, whose name was Scraping White. For more than half of the Old Man's lifetime the tribal head chief was named Crop-Eared Wolf, though he also carried the name Shot-on-Both-Sides. White Wolf was the name of a warrior and medicine man whose particular teachings had been handed down to him. In fact, in his old age he had taken as a final name in life that of his own father, Wolf Old Man. He said we should call him by that name, and he found it worth noting that the little boy in our family had the fitting name of Wolf Child.

In traditional Blackfoot society there are basically two kinds of so-called "medicine men," or "medicine women." One group were those who doctored. They received their main guidance through dreams and visions, which usually resulted in mystical rites combined with the use of certain wild plants and herbs. The others were ceremonial leaders who learned tribal songs and prayers from elderly couples with more experience. Many Blackfoot people gained enough wisdom to practice one or the other of these, but only a few became noted for both. Wolf Old Man turned out to be the last of these.

During our second visit with Wolf Old Man he mentioned an upcoming traditional ceremony that was going to be sponsored by a certain family on the reserve. Beverly thought she understood him to say that he would have a leading part in it. After we left his house I wondered if it would be possible for us to attend. A kindly lady, who was a relative, learned of my desire and offered to ask the sponsors if we could come.

We went along, but found the family hesitant about inviting a stranger to their ceremony, especially a non-Indian from somewhere else. They pointed out that participants in the ceremony must have gone through many ritual initiations in order to be able to sing the required songs. They said that I might have filled one of the lesser duties during the ceremony, such as the lighting of the ceremonial pipes and the serving of food, but these had already been spoken for by other men. Then they added that the sponsorship of such a ceremony is very costly, and they hinted that a contribution might help to get me in.

The lady relative conducted this interview with the sponsors in the Blackfoot language, while we sat nearby. When I learned about the request for money I felt insulted. I wanted to take part in something I considered sacred, not to buy a seat to attend someone's private rites. Had I known more about such matters I would have understood this as a hint, and left. Unfortunately, the whole exchange suffered somewhat from lack of proper interpretation, since the relative knew hardly anything about the ceremonial customs of her own people. The sponsors thought a contribution toward the ceremony's expenses would indicate how strong my desire was to attend, since I obviously had no other business there. When I made no response to the request, the kind relative reached into her own purse and handed over a five-dollar bill on my behalf. The sponsors seemed pleased enough and said that I should be there at the ceremony's start, so that I could have my face painted as a blessing bestowed on friends and relatives of the sponsors by the leader. The other participants could then decide if I should leave after receiving the blessing, or if I might stay through the whole event.

Beverly and Wolf came with me when the night of the ceremony arrived. It was to be an all-night ceremony. In Blackfoot it is referred to as "everyone smoking together." This is due to the many long-stemmed native pipes that are kept filled and rotating among the crowd.

By the time we arrived, several old people were already present. All of them stopped to look at us as we entered. One or two had seen me previously, and they got up to shake my hand. We were given chairs on which to sit near the doorway of the main room. Further into that room participants were sitting on cushions and mattresses next to the floor, in a circle along the walls. Several decorated tipi curtains of canvas were hung so as to cover those walls, and to block out the windows. This made the interior of the room quite like the inside of a Blackfoot tipi. The place of honor, at the very back, was prepared with a soft-tanned buffalo robe, but the occupant had apparently not yet arrived.

An old man who was seated nearby began talking to me in English, trying to explain the purpose of the ceremony. The sponsors had evidently mentioned our request before we came, since he kept referring to the sacredness of the gathering and saying that it was not common for outsiders to attend. The general concern seemed to be that I was coming only to observe these ancient rites—perhaps even to criticize or make fun of them—and that this might distract from the spiritual feelings and efforts of the whole crowd. However, Beverly let me know that no decision would be made until the arrival of the ceremonial leader.

Several people came and went, while I sat quietly and tried to be unobtrusive. Then a car drove up outside, and at mention of its occupants the room took on an air of expectancy. Shortly afterward Wolf Old Man came in, saying nothing but allowing his arrival to be noticeably felt. With him came the two old men who had been at his house during my first visit. One of them, the driver of an old white Ford, was the Old Man's cousin, who always chauffeured him around.

I was pleasantly surprised when the Old Man was led to the seat of honor, though it quickly became obvious to me that he was the logical leader of the ceremony. Someone handed him a large canvas sack, which had been brought in from the car at his command. He untied it and took out a number of well-used leather pouches, four rawhide rattles, and other ritual objects needed for the ceremony. He acted so casually that I felt he was very wise at his task.

After he finished unpacking and got settled back on his comfortable-looking buffalo seat, someone explained to him about my presence, and my request. His eyes seemed quite worn from old age, but he searched around until he found me in the crowd, then he smiled. He told the others that we were already friends, and that he would be glad to have me stay all night. Beverly translated when he said: "We all came here to pray, and it would not be right for us to tell someone that he cannot stay and take part. You are worried about him being sincere, but I say that this will be between him and the Creator. If he should be doing this only for fun, then it will do him no good. But it will not hurt us, either. However, if he believes in what we are doing, then it will benefit him just as well as it benefits us."

Suddenly the whole gathering took on a more relaxed attitude. There was general talking, and occasional joking that caused loud laughter. Several people even spoke to me in their conversations. I felt sorry for myself because I understood hardly anything of what went on. With the Old Man's approval I was given a different seat, on one of the mattresses further into the room, and among some of the old men who were to be participants.

We had mentioned the proposed medicine pipe transfer during our second visit with the Old Man. The elder whom we had first gone to see about the matter was also present. There followed a discussion in which the people seemed to approve of the idea. Of course, they would have nothing to lose by it, since the bundle was coming from another division than theirs. The Bloods still had six medicine pipe bundles of their own. When something was said about my having an Indian wife, it was agreed that the two of us should try to learn the duties required of bundle owners. Had I been planning to take over a bundle from among the Bloods, I imagine there would have been some objection.

After another session of talk, in Blackfoot, one of the elders said to me: "They think that you should change your name before you take over the medicine pipe bundle. In some ways your present name does not sound very good in our language." Beverly later explained that Makwi Unotsche is the proper Blackfoot translation for Hungry Wolf (or, more accurately, Wolf Hungry), but that in common talk it came out as a crude expression meaning a wolf that is hungry for something other than food.

Name-changing is an ancient Blackfoot custom that seems to have caused confusion for everybody, including the Indians. The basic order of it is this: A newborn child is often named for some unusual characteristic, or some event associated with its birth. This might be Crying Child, Brown Woman, or Big Thunder. Occasionally this name, which is given almost at a whim, stays with the person for the rest of his or her life. More often, children are renamed after they reach the age of understanding—say, five to ten years old. Usually a noted spiritual leader is asked to do the naming. In the past noted warriors and chiefs were often given this honor. If the child's father felt proud enough, he could choose the name himself. Otherwise he asked a grandparent, uncle, or other relative to select one. The name-giver prays for the child, then calls out four great accomplishments in his life, or else narrates the background of the chosen name. Names given at such times are often ones noted in past tribal history and carried by many different persons through the ages. Certain names are so old and famous that they describe characters in tribal legends. Often these names were last carried by a close relative of the child, so that they are something of a family totem.

On hearing Blackfoot stories, it is not always clear just which individual of a certain name is being mentioned. This is especially so when several who had that name accomplished noteworthy things. To add to the confusion, names are sometimes exchanged among living relatives, for a variety of reasons. For instance, if I happen to like my brother's name better than mine, I might simply begin using it, perhaps giving him my best horse in return for the honor. This was done particularly by active warriors, who often followed a variation of the naming custom by taking on a new name during any important battle or incident. Some men used a dozen or more names in their lifetimes. To have had four and five names is still not unusual among the elders whom we have met.

After the ceremony, when Atsitsina heard what had been said about my name, he told us that he would gladly give me another name from the history of my new family. He said it would be one to go along with Beverly's, who carries his mother's name, SikskiAki. It means Black-Faced Woman, and was given to her by an older brother of Atsitsina, in memory of their deceased mother. For this reason Beverly had a special place in her old uncle's heart.

Atsitsina carried a variety of names in his own lifetime, although everyone knew him best by the whimsical name of his baby days. By turns he was known as Big Snake, Bull Horn, and Natosina, or Sun Chief, which he was carrying when I met him. That was his father's old-age name, and it was said to have been used by medicine pipe keepers for many generations. Atsitsina had been such a keeper three times, and the name was given to him during the transfer of the first one. He said that from then on I could have the name as my own.

Having given me his name, Atsitsina tried out the name of another ancestor, Bad Moccasins, but it never really caught on among those who knew him well. One time he told us: "Now that you two have the names of my parents, you must give my childhood name to another son, if you should have one." Not long before he passed away, Beverly gave birth to our youngest boy. During his last visit to our mountain home Atsitsina played with the boy and said he felt good to know that his whole childhood family was alive in spirit through our use of his names.

During the night of the smoking ceremony I thought several times about names—not knowing I myself would be given another so soon. Indian names have always interested me, and I have eagerly studied their histories whenever I could. Much of my early speaking and understanding in the Blackfoot language was limited to the pronunciation of people's names. This was of much help in our new social circle, composed mostly of traditional people. When speaking to each other they seldom used anyone's "white man name," even if that name was so seemingly Indian as Edward Little Bear or Willie Eagle Plume. In Blackfoot conversations Indian names of persons are used almost exclusively, and they are commonly heard even when people are otherwise speaking in English.

I learned early how to tell when a person being mentioned in Blackfoot was a woman. The word for woman, *Aki,* is almost always placed at the end of the whole name, such as SikskiAki, or her grandmother, AnadaAki, meaning Pretty Woman. Women don't seem to change their names much in life—often not at all. Even today most of the older Blood women were named, as little children, by noted old warriors. These names are considered especially lucky, so most women prefer to grow old with them.

The warriors often gave gruesome-sounding names to otherwise pretty girls. Killing-in-the-Water-Woman, Smashing-His-Head-Woman, and Shot-in-the-Dark-Woman are some examples. The holy woman of the Blood Sun Dance at that time was an old widow who had been virtuous throughout her life. Yet she had the unlikely name of Stealing-Different-Things-Woman. I doubt that she ever stole anything at all, and her name continues to evoke nothing but respect and dignity in the tribe.

The night of the ceremony passed very slowly. There was much singing, praying, and smoking of pipes. I understood virtually none of what was said, and only very little of what was done. But I enjoyed the feeling of sacredness that pervaded everything. It was like the feeling I had when I first saw Last Gun, the old buffalo hunter and sat at his feet in front of his tipi.

Wolf sat next to me, but he slept most of the night. The room was not divided in half, as in other ceremonies, for men and women. The men sat at the head of the room, on both sides of the leader, and the women sat closer to the door. Men and women prayed, smoked pipes, and sang together. In fact, some men turned to their wives for help in recalling sacred songs that had been transferred to them years before. Most of the songs came from ritual transfers, and the singers explained how they were given the various rights to them. The whole event was a night-long recitation of the tribe's ceremonial history, with brief reenactments of the many normally lengthy rituals.

As I watched these elders during their sacred gathering, I longed more than ever to learn their ways and to feel as one with them, as they seemed to feel with each other. But I wondered if they would live long enough for an outsider like myself to receive all the necessary initiations. There seemed to be no one in the crowd under sixty-five years of age, and several people were quite a bit older. There was a discussion of ages at one point, and the Old Man won by saying he was ninety. At his passing, four years later, we learned from agency records that he was actually three years older than he thought!

The ceremony had several breaks, during which people went outside and relieved themselves, or stayed inside and talked with each other. Tea and coffee were served all night long, which made the occasional breaks all the more necessary. At the beginning and at the end of the ceremony food was served to everyone present. For this the participants had brought their own bowls, cups, and utensils. A standard invitation to a traditional ceremony names the guest, states the place and purpose, and ends with the advice to "bring your own bowl." In the tribal camps such invitations are called out loudly by special announcers who walk around so everyone can hear them.

The food is usually provided by the sponsors of a ceremony. In this case it included cooked meat, bread, fruit, cookies, and other articles bought in stores. For some ceremonies a sizable amount of money is spent to feed the large number of guests. The food is expected to go beyond immediate eating—most guests bring empty pillow cases in which to take home the surplus for their children and grandchildren.

The food served at the end of this night-long ceremony was much more traditional than the store-bought items at the beginning. It included a special soup made by boiling sliced beef tongues (in place of buffalo) and wild berries in a broth of fresh beef blood. This was thickened with flour and sweetened with sugar. It tasted very good, and had a tonic quality, since rituals and prayers were made during its preparation.

Early in the ceremony Wolf, Beverly, and I had our faces painted by the Old Man. Before that he painted the sponsor of the ceremony, the sponsor's elderly father (for whose benefit the ceremony had been pledged), and two or three of the elderly participants. Afterward he painted at least ten or twelve other people who seemed to be members of the household, or their relatives.

This sacred painting is much different from the so-called "war paint" of dramatic stories. It is a way of being blessed with a symbol of the blood and flesh of our Earth Mother. Indian dancers often paint themselves for visual effect, as did warriors of the past on their way to meet enemies. Sacred painting is more subtle, with the meanings of its various designs buried deep in ceremonial mysteries. The special earth paint is gathered in little-known places, and always with the proper ritual.

The Old Man prayed while he painted the faces of those who came up to him. At a certain point he also sang a song used specifically for that purpose. The experience was a truly sacred event that I felt strongly in my heart, even if my mind understood little of its significance. I know many Catholics who have been equally moved while taking part in a mass, even if they understood very little of the Latin that was spoken. I think the Old Man expected this would happen to me when he told the others that I could stay.

It was shortly before daylight when the ceremony finished. There was no rush by anyone to leave. In fact, a few of the people lay down on mattresses and went to sleep. They were waiting for younger relatives to pick them up later in the morning. The Old Man left right away with his cousin, the chauffeur. Before he went, Beverly told him that we'd like to have him come to our house, and he was agreeable. We set a date for the following week, and a time, which he called: "Right after midday."

When the day of the visit arrived, I again got nervous and wondered how I should act as host to a very old and distinguished medicine man. Wolf and I waited at home while Beverly drove the few miles to the Old Man's house and brought him back. Just before they arrived, I began to think it was all too good to be true, and that she would probably come back home alone. But no, she pulled the truck right up to our door, to shorten the walk, and I saw from the window the heavyset face and flat-brimmed hat that resembled no one else but Wolf Old Man. He was the most distinguished visitor I ever had, if that gives you some idea of how excited and shaky I was.

All my life I have lived in homes where shoes were not allowed. For me, this custom began in my mother's European household, where the reason for it was cleanliness and etiquette. Since I've lived out in the country, the practice has been even more useful in that way. In addition, it has become an obligation concerning certain duties of our faith. Moccasins are allowed in the house, but not machine-made shoes.

Since an occasional visitor has grumbled about these footwear restrictions, I wondered how the Old Man would react. But the matter turned out to be of no concern, since he always wore handmade moccasins anyway. When he went outside he wore rubber shoes over them, but he took these off again as soon as he was indoors.

Beverly led the Old Man to an overstuffed chair that we considered the "place of honor" in our living room. Before he sat down he asked for help in taking off his coat—which turned out to be two coats, a long, heavy overcoat of wool, and a regular suit coat of dark material. He also took off a long black scarf that he wore around his neck, knotted at the front.

He approved of the seat by saying something about ceremonial persons not being allowed to sit near the doorway. He explained that this was to keep others from passing back and forth in front of them, which is against their disciplines. Also, near the doorway children would be more likely to play or become distracting, which is to be avoided.

When Beverly asked him if he was hungry, he said he had just finished his midday meal. However, he was glad to accept a cup of hot tea, which is a favorite drink among Indian elders. He also accepted the cigarettes that I gave him, although he already had an open pack in his shirt pocket, and he told me to put mine into his overcoat. Later, when he noticed that I did not smoke, he apologized somewhat for his own habit by saying: "I didn't smoke cigarettes for most of my life, and I don't know why I started in my old age." Smoking was a habit common to nearly all the elders we have known.

When Beverly translated this information I thought perhaps the Old Man had previously smoked a native pipe instead. But he said he had never been much of a pipesmoker either, saving that as a ritual for sacred and ceremonial occasions.

During that first day's visit the Old Man and I established a pattern of communication that was to last throughout our relationship. His English was passable enough to use when we two were alone together. However, as long as Beverly was nearby he spoke mostly in Blackfoot, taking regular pauses while she interpreted his words. At those times he used English mainly for special effects, which he often accompanied with laughter. His pronunciation was so clear, and his voice so loud and strong, that I managed to follow his conversations even when he spoke nothing but Blackfoot. Of course, I often wished that I could understand *all* of what he said.

Not even Beverly understood him clearly all the time. He spoke in the old Blackfoot dialect, which is called "high Blackfoot." It tends to be more complicated and expressive than the modern Blackfoot spoken by Beverly's generation. Those who are younger than she usually speak an even more diluted version of the language, if they know it at all.

The Old Man regularly spoke about things from the past that Beverly has never experienced, thus she never learned the Blackfoot expressions peculiar to them. On the other hand, Wolf Old Man did not know too much about our modern world, and there were things about it that she could not tell him because there were no Blackfoot words to explain them.

This minor communication problem led the Old Man to make a suggestion that surprised us. When he wanted to tell tribal legends and history, he asked us to use a tape recorder, which he called, in Blackfoot, "a thing that will take my voice." That way, he explained, we could listen to the stories again and again, even after he was long gone, and slowly learn them. He was concerned that otherwise they might be lost. In addition, he said we could get someone like Beverly's mother to listen to them and correctly interpret the things we did not understand.

The Old Man said he wished to be brought home after having supper with us. When the time came near he wanted to know the position of the sun. When we told him it was still some distance up in the sky, he relaxed. He said he did not care to go out on the roads after dark, because "there are too many crazy drivers." Later we learned another reason for his concern. During his term as keeper of a medicine pipe bundle he had learned to make incense and prayers every day with the last light of Sun.

When the Old Man sat down at our table, he asked what we were having to eat. Told that the meal would consist of steak, salad, and potatoes, he was glad. He explained that he could not eat rabbits, because of sacred duties with one of the tribal societies, or bear meat, because of his relationship with medicine pipes. He said soon we would have to follow this latter rule ourselves. A mystical event, in the long-ago, caused bears to to become considered sons-in-law to all medicine pipe families. Traditional Blackfeet should not come close to their four-footed son-in-law, or even speak his name. It is an old custom that many Bloods were still following to some degree at that time. When medicine pipe keepers speak about their "son-in-law," the bear, they call him "Sticky Mouth."

The Old Man drank tea with his meal, but he also insisted on having a glass of water on hand. He drank some of this before eating, "to make my stomach start working," he explained. The rest he saved in case someone should get up or move around in the room where he was eating. Such activity was not allowed by the instructions he was given during one of his mystical power-dreams. He was told this might cause him to choke, so he should have water ready. When we brought him to restaurants, on later occasions, he always tried to get a table at the rear, and to sit with his back to the doorway. These disciplines helped him to keep tuned to his spiritual powers.

From different things he told us that day, we realized Wolf Old Man was a very important traditional leader in the tribe—much more so than we had imagined. Not that he ever said he was important, in any way, except to point out that many people were depending upon his prayers and ceremonial services.

Among other things, we were astounded to learn that he regularly led the opening ceremonies for medicine pipe bundles. He was happy to hear our plans for having such a bundle transferred to us. Suddenly I realized that he should be our teacher and guide in this endeavor. In a rush of enthusiasm I told him this, and watched as he nodded his head in agreement, a silent look of pride and satisfaction on his face. Neither of us realized what a lifelong commitment I had made, just then.

At that time there were about a dozen medicine pipe bundles among the twenty thousand or so people of four Blackfoot divisions. At least that many more of these bundles were in various museums. In Blackfoot history and culture they have long been the main symbols of Nature-oriented tribal faith and lore.

The bundles remaining in the tribe were still venerated by a majority of the people, even those who otherwise practiced the

Christian faith. These were sacred tribal heirlooms. Yet only five or six old men were qualified to open the bundles, and no one of younger age had begun the lengthy practice to take over these vital duties. True, ethnologists and scholars had been allowed to film and tape pipe bundle ceremonies, but without the personal spiritual understanding of initiated leaders, the recorded rituals are only dramatic entertainment, or a subject for scientific study.

It turned out that the Old Man had learned most of his medicine pipe knowledge from Beverly's great-grandfather, Heavy Head, who died the year she was born. Moreover, Heavy Head had learned them from old Eagle Plume, the father of Atsitsina. It seemed very natural to the Old Man that we, as their modern relatives and descendants, should carry on these teachings. Sometimes, when we talked to him about this strange chain of events, he would sit quietly, thinking. Slowly he would shake his head from side to side, and muse: "The Creator has very mysterious ways!"

When the Old Man talked to us he never made mention of my ancestry. He certainly never said that there were things I could not learn because I was not born an Indian. It has been publicly said by some Indians that white men can never learn to understand Indians and their ways. If this is so, the Old Man knew nothing about it. In that case, we wonder where the idea comes from. The Old Man summed up the matter by declaring: "When it comes to praying, the Creator accepts all of us equally. It is up to each one how he prays, and how sincere are the words of his prayers."

2

WINTER OUT ON THE PLAINS was every bit as exciting as I had always imagined it to be. There were strong winds, sometimes blowing so hard that it was impossible to walk. There was always the immensity of the sky—so vast and unobstructed that it gave me a whole new perspective of the universe, especially at night. I learned to feel much smaller and less significant.

Sometimes the blue sky was blotted out by endless masses of dark clouds that rolled overhead in advance of fearsome blizzards. When wind and snow combined, the whole prairie disappeared under white, drifting masses that cut off all visibility and made any sort of traveling absolutely impossible. The forces of Nature show their supreme powers at such times!

After one blizzard Beverly's father drove down to our riverbottom home to check on us. The sky was clear and blue, but the air was a vicious 45 degrees below zero, Fahrenheit. When he drove up we happened to have our door standing wide open, to clear out the previous night's air. When Beverly told him this he looked with disbelief at the hot, steaming air that was rushing out into the cold, and muttered: "This is a hell of a time to be airing out your house!"

It was a hell of a time for more than that, especially for horses, dogs, and other living things that roamed in abundance across the reserve. In places the blowing and drifting snow had piled up in layers so hard that horses and cattle found it all but impossible to paw through for even a little feed. Livestock owners had to drive around to their herds and drop off bales of hay just to keep them alive. I felt especially sorry for those horses whose owners were not able to give them such individual attention. Some families still had large horse herds as part of their traditional Blackfoot customs. Their horses were often left to fend for themselves until they were needed.

Joe Young Pine was an elderly neighbor, along the Bullhorn River, who still had his own herd of horses and ponies. I once bought one from him, and he used others for pulling his wagon and sleds. In fact, Joe loved horses so much that it made him a half-breed—he was half Indian and half cowboy!

Actually Joe had no European blood that we know of, but he sure practiced a life of "home on the range." He kept his hair cropped short, and always wore boots and hats. Back in 1939 he was one of several Indian rodeo champions selected to go to Australia and give demonstrations of rodeo skills. He told us it was the trip of his lifetime, but that he got much too homesick to really enjoy it. Blood Indians seldom like living very far from their tribe.

Joe lived with his son, Jerry, on land that had been settled by Joe's father, old Young Pine. This man was a chief of the Many Children Band, within the Blood Tribe, to which our own family belongs. In those days chiefs served for life, as long as they continued to work for their people. Each band had a chief, who met in council with the others. One of them was elected to be the tribe's "head chief." After the Indians made treaties with the government, these chiefs were supplied with uniforms, to symbolize their status. On one of Joe's walls hung a framed photograph showing his father in such a uniform. It had stripes down the sides and an elaborate belt, and looked sharp with Young Pine's long braids. In his earlier years he was a great warrior and horse raider, and in his old age he was keeper of a medicine pipe.

Joe Young Pine was a cousin, as well as neighbor, to our uncle, Willie Eagle Plume. He was often called by the Blackfoot name Dog-with-a-White-Spot, which was inherited from his father. Atsitsina and Joe were lifelong friends along the Bullhorn River, which was named after their uncle, Bullhorn. Sometimes when I was with both of them they would talk secretively to each other, half-whispering and frequently laughing. When I asked Atsitsina what it was about, he would try to act innocent and reply: "Oh, we're just talking about our young days." Others told me that he had been a noted clown and prankster, though only the jovial disposition remained to indicate this in his old age.

Besides being a friendly neighbor and relative, I found Joe Young Pine an interesting man because he was one of the last to travel around with a team of horses and wagon. I talked to him about taking up this simple custom in place of my truck, and he agreed to help me. It didn't matter that the remaining wagon-users on the reserve were all old men in their sixties and seventies. Not many years before, buggies and wagons had still outnumbered automobiles, and even Beverly's parents used them until about the time she was born. Joe summed up his feelings about it like this:

"Very few people on the reserve had an automobile when I first got one. I was still young then. But now that most everybody has at least one car or truck, I'm back to using my team and wagon. I like it real well. I'm never in a hurry, and I always have time to stop and visit with whomever I want to. I don't just go by in a cloud of dust. Of course, I like it because it is cheap, as well. I never have to worry about gas money, oil changes, or stuff like that. When there's any drinking going on around the place, I don't have to worry about somebody taking off in my car and wrecking it. That used to happen to me."

Although the cowboy side of Joe was most obvious, he was still very much of an old-time Indian at heart. He had been keeper of a medicine pipe bundle for several years, with his first wife. He attended the all-night smoking ceremonies whenever he could. He even joined the sacred Horns Society in his old age, which was unusual. It was more common for those of middle age, or even younger. By the time I knew Joe, he was the only one who still came to ceremonies with a wagon and horses, although most of the elders said they traveled that way until just ten or fifteen years earlier. Some of them still rode horseback for occasional pleasure and visiting.

I recall one cold, icy night when Joe arrived at a ceremony with his horses. He was so bundled up that it was hard to recognize him, although his old wagon could not be mistaken. There was steam coming from his swaddled form, and more of it from his hard-working animals. There was the sound of heavy breathing, along with that of harness straps being pulled and metal rings clinking together. Sometimes the wagon groaned when one of the horses tugged on it, or backed into it.

Every time we took a break that night, Joe went to see his horses. He talked softly, while giving them snacks from his sack of extra food. Under the seat of his wagon was a little bag of oats, from which he also gave them a few handfuls. He had the team tied to a wooden power pole, from the top of which a solitary lamp provided the only illumination on that otherwise dark and overcast night.

Sometimes Joe drove his team into the Bullhorn River and parked so that the wagon's wooden wheels could soak up water. This caused them to expand tightly against their iron tires. Of the six or eight wagons still in use on the reserve I think his was the only one with wheel problems. The rest were equipped with air-filled rubber tires, often taken from wrecked motor vehicles. These gave a much smoother and quieter ride on the reserve's rough and rutted roads. Joe's old wagon could sometimes be heard creaking and squeaking a long way off.

Like most people's houses on the reserve at that time, Joe's had no indoor plumbing. But unlike most other homes, his had a hand pump—out front—from which he got fresh spring water by the bucketful. That was because the river flowed just down the bank from his house. When wells are drilled for reserve homes further out on the prairie, the water usually contains so much alkali that it's no good for drinking.

However, when winter winds blew really cold (sometimes with a chill factor of 60 or 80 degrees below zero!), Joe's hand pump froze solid and quit working. Then Joe would hook his team of horses to an old wooden bobsled with iron runners. The sled had a flat top large enough to hold him and a metal barrel. With this he would quietly glide up the frozen riverbottom to a spring that flowed from a bank into the river, just beyond our house. Only the jingling of harness metal gave away his movements. Luckily for Joe, this spring never froze up, even when the river itself became a solid strip of ice.

Getting that big barrel filled with water must have been a tough chore for an old man when the snow was deep and the trail slippery. He wasn't the only one on the reserve getting his water that way. Often his son, Jerry, performed the task of getting water with the horses instead. Other times Joe's wife would ride with him, holding him tightly, and they seemed to enjoy the vigorous run. On the way back they always had a sheet of canvas tied securely over the barrel, to keep from taking a freezing bath with the splashing water.

Joe and his wife had only been together a few years. I was intrigued by the late-in-life marriages of Joe and other elders. What was unique and most fascinating to me about these unions was that the partners had usually known each other since childhood, but had only become intimate long after marrying others and raising families with them. Old Indians usually have very active and fulfilling social lives, unlike senior citizens in many communities, who are often lonely and nearly friendless.

Widowed Indian men frequently marry the widows of their former best friends, or else the widowed sisters and cousins of their own former wives. These customs go back to the early days of hunting and war, when husbands often failed to come back home from their trails. Best friends and fellow members of tribal societies always looked after the families of those who died. Men were expected to take into their homes the widowed sisters of their wives, as well as the sisters' children, even if their homes were already full. This tribal form of social security is still common today.

Multiple marriages and extended families add much confusion when one is trying to trace relationships in Blood history. Kinship terms like ''mother'' and ''grandfather'' apply to a variety of relatives, some not even of the same blood. When showing old photographs to elders it is common to have ''dads,'' ''grandmas,'' and ''brothers'' pointed out even when the individuals being referred to were only best friends of the parents, or the parents of best friends.

Another confusing aspect in identifying persons from the past is that chiefs generally call all tribe members "children," and they, in turn, call their chiefs "fathers." In Blackfoot the word *Ninna* refers to both chief and father, as well as to any other man, though there are slight changes in pronunciation. This seems to indicate that the people of the past did not consider "chief" to be a title in the way that outsiders often think of it. A good chief was one who looked after his people as though they were his children.

This, incidentally, is why American Indians began calling U.S. Presidents "Great White Fathers." When Indian representatives explained government treaties to their tribes, they said, in effect: "The President will take over and use most of your lands, and he will treat you and your descendants as his children, making sure to supply your needs to live." Similar tales were given to Canadian Indians, who made most of their treaties during the reign of Queen Victoria. Among the Blackfeet she is called "Chief Woman," however, not "Great White Mother."

For some reason I became intrigued by the traditional custom of men having more than one wife. For a life in the wilderness this seemed a good way for women to have companionship in households where men are often outdoors, or far away from the household. The chores of simple and rugged living would be only half as much for each of the wives if there were two of them. This could be especially useful during the years when there are many small children in the family. Of course, such an idea was easier to justify before the days of women's liberation. Now, many women would probably demand extra husbands instead, saying two could do twice as much rugged work and thus make life more pleasant for the wife.

Having more than one wife was a common Blackfoot custom, though having more than one husband was not. But we have heard of such a relationship among our neighbors, the Kootenais. One of that tribe's leading elders, until his death around 1960, was the son of a beautiful woman who lived with two husbands in a small cabin. It was never made clear which husband was the elder's biological father, and elderly Kootenais claim he had traits from both.

There were practical reasons why so many Blackfeet men had

multiple wives. Men were always being killed on the warpath and on buffalo hunts, so there were always more women in the tribe. Luckily, one good hunter was able to supply more hides than one or two women could easily prepare into leather, and more meat than they and their children could eat. As the children grew, so came more hunters and tanners into the household.

The last Blood man officially known to have two lifelong wives was Crow-Spreads-His-Wings, who died at the age of ninety in 1953. He was a medicine man noted for herbal doctoring, as were both his women. They outlived him by a few years. He was a half-brother of Wolf Old Man, both having had the same father. Crow-Spreads-His-Wings and his two wives were said to have had a happy and peaceful marriage throughout their many years together.

Of course, had I asked a group of elders to tell *me* who was the last man with more than one wife, they would probably have laughed and pointed at each other! While Blackfoot customs have always put heavy emphasis on the fidelity of women, they have accepted infidelity among men in somewhat the same light as capturing enemy goods on the war trail. It is a game of the lonely and daring. Even so, in the old days, a man faced possible death at the hands of a lover's husband—if he were caught—the same as if he were making a raid in an enemy camp!

Government agents discouraged the practice of having multiple wives. Together with Christian missionaries, they later outlawed the custom altogether. However, there was particular difficulty getting the Bloods to understand such regulations, since their biggest group of non-Indian neighbors are Mormons, who are known in Blackfoot as "Men with Many Wives." Actually the government was mostly concerned with ending the practice among younger Indians, rather than in splitting up old families. What would have become of the many homeless widows who were living as second wives? And how would all their children have been divided?

That the practice lasted well into this century was obvious from the fact that many of the elders we knew grew up in households that had more than one living wife. In the case of Last Gun, the buffalo hunter, his father—White Calf—had at least nine wives up until the time of his death, in 1903. Of course, he was the tribe's head chief, whose household was expected to feed and host many people.

Atsitsina told me that his father slept alone, while his two wives slept together, side by side. The family lived in a one-room log house, which must have been cause for some exasperating moments! No wonder they liked to move outdoors into tents and tipis, as long as the weather allowed it. Old Eagle Plume was said to have had so many powerful dreams and visions that it was necessary for him to sleep alone anyway, so as not to be disturbed during one of them. Even now, elders do not like to be awakened by anyone during their sleep, for fear of having some important dream interrupted and spoiled.

I tried to learn from Atsitsina what arrangements his father made for private visits with one or the other of his wives. He and I usually spoke very openly about such matters. But this time he quickly let me know that he considered his father's private life none of our business. When I suggested that the information might be of direct use to me someday, he laughed rather cynically and said: "Sonny, that don't work good nowadays!"

On another occasion I spoke with Wolf Old Man about the same subject. He had been married several times, though never to multiple wives like his brother, Crow-Spreads-His-Wings. He summarized his feelings about polygamy with a simple bit of wisdom:

"Two ways," he said dramatically, holding two crooked fingers in the shape of a V before his face. "Fellow that has one wife, she dies, and he is left alone with nothing. Another fellow has two wives, one dies, he still has one left!"

I recall another of his favorite sayings. "Two ways," he said, again showing two with his fingers. "Fellow that has bad eyes is no good for anything. Another fellow has crippled legs and is no good for anything. Me, I've got bad eyes *and* crippled legs, so I'm no good at all!" At that he would laugh heartily, knowing that back in the rough war and buffalo-hunting days he would, indeed, be finished. Blind and crippled people were usually abandoned when there seemed no more hope that they could be cared for.

Except for those two ailments, the Old Man was actually quite healthy and strong. Twenty or thirty years earlier he had battled with stomach troubles that nearly caused his death. Doctors and relatives had given up on him. He said a combination of white man's medicines and herbal brews let him survive the dangers that time. But as our own winter waxed stronger—and the snowdrifts grew deeper—we began to worry about him. His little house was heated only by one old metal coalburner, which someone had to fill and tend quite frequently. The trail to his outhouse became an obstacle course for his weak and unsteady legs. He was just then getting used to walking with two wooden canes instead of one. Of greater concern was that sometimes the stretch of road from his house to the highway became impassable, which could have complicated any sudden need for him to get outside help.

Fortunately, Wolf Old Man had a doctor in town whom he considered a friend as well as a reliable physician. The two had mutual respect for each other's curing abilities. They agreed that a bed in the hospital would be safer than one in an isolated house on the open prairie.

This doctor had a modern office in a clinic, and he did most of his serious work in a new, efficient hospital built on the "white" side of the highway that forms the boundary of the reserve. But Wolf Old Man didn't go there. Instead, he moved into a vintage structure of red brick known as the Blood Indian Hospital, on the reserve's side of the road.

All operations and serious ailments were treated in the so-called "white hospital," because the Indian hospital was more of a convalescent residence and rest home. Several other elders were already staying there when Wolf Old Man arrived. He was given a bed across from Guy Wolf Child, who was born in the same year as the Old Man. Since he liked to go into town frequently to see his friends anyway, the hospital stay was a good social exercise during the season of unsure traveling.

We wanted to do something that would help encourage the Old Man during his hospital stay, and at the same time cheer ourselves about his predicament. So we made a pledge to sponsor a smoking ceremony for him. It was to be held upon his release from the hospital, early in the spring. He was quite pleased when he heard about it, and said that he would pray every day for success. By then I was attending these ceremonies quite regularly, with his guidance and with Beverly for company.

In my previous reading I had seen little mention of smoking ceremonies, which seemed surprising after I learned their tribal importance, and the frequency with which they still occurred. There seemed to be at least one smoking ceremony every Friday or Saturday night, and sometimes there were two or three on the same weekend. Those nights were preferred because younger relatives served as helpers and pipe lighters, as well as coming to have their faces painted. Many of them went to school during the weekdays, or else to work. Besides, even the elderly Indians followed the Christian custom of considering weekends special, and Sundays ideal, for religious activities. Most medicine pipe bundle ceremonies are held on Sundays.

It was not long before the elders said I was qualified to participate in smoking ceremonies. Several of them gave Beverly and me eligible initiations, beginning with Last Gun, the buffalo hunter. Each of these allowed me to sing one song during the night. Four songs made up a round, followed by a pause. I was allowed to sing two of the usual four rounds. The upcoming medicine pipe bundle transfer was good for four more songs—another whole round—for which I had to hire a former bundle keeper to do the singing.

There were then still half a dozen men who could lead this ceremony. They usually took turns, so that none got too worn-out from the strain of the night-long ritual. Their job was somewhat like that of a conductor in an orchestra—coordinating all the various songs and movements throughout the night. Some participants were unable to recall all the songs of their own initiations, and others had never learned them at all. In such cases, they were required to "hire" someone else to sing for them, usually the leader, and for this help they paid a couple dollars.

One night the relatives of Atsitsina sponsored a smoking ceremony for the benefit of a sick family member. The event was held in Atsitsina's living room, which had been cleared out for the occasion. The leader of the ceremony was another of Atsitsina's cousins and close friends, John Many Chief, who was also called White Horn. He was skilled at songs and ceremonies, and acted especially proud of this. He had learned much of the knowledge from his uncle, old Eagle Plume, while living in that family's household. He considered this uncle to have been the finest kind of man, and it seemed to annoy him somewhat, at first, that I carried the uncle's final name, Natosina. During the evening he continually referred to me in the Blackfoot language as Hungry Wolf, until Atsitsina reminded him that I was now known as Natosina. He retorted: "That is an important name, you should not be giving it away just to anybody!" To this Atsitsina replied: "He is not just anybody, he is our son-in-law!" That ended the matter, and old White Horn never called me anything but Natosina after that.

He was somewhat upset with me for not spending more time with him. Whenever we met he told me: "Why don't you come around and visit me, instead of always Willie Eagle Plume and old Willie Scraping White? That old man is too far up in age to teach you much. Besides, I speak better English and know more of the ceremonies." Based on the opinion of other elders, he was probably speaking the truth, but I explained to him that I was already busy trying to learn the things these two were teaching me, and I could not sufficiently devote myself to anybody else. Besides, he was actually related to both of them, as well as being an uncle of my father-in-law, so I considered the whole matter to be among relatives, in any case.

At one point during the night of the ceremony at Atsitsina's house, someone asked White Horn to sing an "Iniskim" song. Iniskim are small, peculiar stones that are often shaped like buffalo, which they symbolize. In Blackfoot history the mystical power of these stones was first given to a woman of long, long ago, during a time of great famine. The buffalo herds had left Blackfoot country, and the people were starving. This woman found the first of the Iniskim. In a dream it showed her the ritual for calling the buffalo back, which the people are said to have done successfully. Since then, countless stones of similar shape have served as personal and family "good luck" charms. Their songs and ceremonies formed the basis of many Blackfoot rituals, some of which are still practiced.

It was soon learned by the elders that I was particularly interested in these Iniskim, for which nearly all of them had received initiations, as well. Their proper use was one of Wolf Old Man's specialties, and he was known to be instructing us with his knowledge and songs. Several of my eligible songs at smoking ceremonies were for Iniskim that had been transferred to Beverly and me.

At any rate, when the leader of a ceremony finds himself unable to recall a song, he turns to someone who is noted for that particular song's initiation and asks that person for help. In this case, White Horn suddenly found himself unable to start an Iniskim song. Looking up and seeing me sitting right across from him, he impulsively blurted out: "All right, Natosina, the Iniskim song!" He told his friends later that he didn't really think I could sing one right off the bat like that. But I had already been silently humming my own favorite song while he tried to remember his, so there was hardly a pause between his request and my loud response.

When the song was over one of the elders said: "Well, White Horn, you had better pay Natosina something, since you had to hire him to sing your song!" Others made similar comments, while White Horn sat quietly and took it all in. Not one to be left humbled, he finally said to me: "Aw, you sing like a white man!"

Atsitsina sometimes made a similar observation about my efforts, though he waited until we were alone to remark on it. He and White Horn were noted singers, and often said they couldn't be beat. One of Atsitsina's younger relatives put his remarks more kindly during a later break, when he enthusiastically said: "Gee, we didn't know you could sing so good. You sound just like Elvis Presley in his prime!" Some of the other young people laughed or giggled, and I still haven't figured out if the comment was meant as a compliment or an insult.

In my own defense I will say that sometimes the elders accepted my presence with them so much that they expected me to be just like them, even in my singing. For quite a while I tried hard to fulfill their expectations—and Beverly thinks I came as close as possible—before I finally realized that being exactly like an elderly Indian need not be a priority in my spiritual endeavors.

Sometimes Atsitsina would teach me one of his songs. When he heard my rendition he would mimic me, stretching out his neck and using a high, squeaky voice. Then he would command: "Sing like this!," and repeat the song with his own husky, old-Indian voice. I used to tell him, "How am I going to sound like that when I am not an old Indian myself?" He would just look at me with pity and disgust and keep singing. I doubt that I will ever sound like an old Indian—I will certainly never *be* one—but over the years I have learned to quit stretching my neck, and as I grow older my voice seems to get deeper and stronger.

Atsitsina had other ways of trying to make me into a better "Indian." For instance, he wanted me to pluck my whiskers instead of shaving them daily. Full-blooded Blackfoot Indians have virtually no body hair except on top of their heads (where it often grows long and thick). They never wear beards or goatees, like the members of some other tribes, such as those along the Pacific Coast. Hair grows upon their faces, all right, but generally as individual strands that are plucked out as soon as they are noticed. Atsitsina always carried a pair of homemade metal tweezers in his pockets just for this purpose. He often spent his idle time plucking carelessly around his chin and neck in search of stray hairs. Sometimes he would visit with a couple of his elderly friends and they would all sit and perform this peculiar custom.

In my case, it was not until I had several sores and reddish blotches on my skin that the old man agreed it was too late for me to begin his method of keeping the face free of hair. I was willing to put up with the pain of it, but it took me so long just to clear one small area that all the rest was again covered with hair before I got done.

Through hints from elders, and by my own careful observations, I began making little changes of behavior and appearance that were strictly in keeping with old Blackfoot ways. This had not been my original intention at all. Specific tribal devotion is not exactly vital to living in harmony with Nature. For me, this must have come as the result of deep-down feelings of patriotism, for which my German and Swiss ancestors have been particularly noted.

I learned that wearing long hair parted down the middle of the scalp is the common Blackfoot style for women. Among men it was usually considered the style of enemy tribes, especially of the Sioux. The Blackfoot name for the Sioux is "Parted Hairs." One of the few Bloods who favored this "enemy" hairstyle was old Eagle Plume, who picked it up from a Sioux with whom he became best friends some years after the warpath days ended.

I also found that the elders disliked seeing young people with their hair unbraided. One time I wore mine that way, and somebody asked me for whom I was mourning. It is a Blackfoot custom to leave the hair unbraided after the death of a loved one—or else on certain very sacred occasions during Sun Dance and other sacred ceremonies. In the past old people regularly went around with their hair loose, because they usually had such large families that they were constantly losing one or another of them, and thus were kept in mourning. This is rarely done today, since the majority of people have short hair.

From the Old Man we learned also that we should no longer cut our hair. This is among the many traditional requirements of medicine pipe keepers. I began to follow his custom of braiding my hair the same way each morning. Long hair turned into a symbol of my faith, rather than an object of personal glamor, although the same faith requires one to have pride in all that one does. I wrapped the ends of my braids with thin buckskin thongs, as did many elders, until I adopted a habit common among some, including Wolf Old Man and Last Gun, of using strips of red cloth. Others wore material of different colors, mainly blue, white, or black. For each color there was a special connotation dealing with elements of Nature.

I also got into the habit of using certain common Blackfoot expressions that I constantly heard spoken around me. *Ah!* meant "yes," and *Sah!* meant "no." *Hunya!* meant "Is that so?" To younger people it was like saying, "Oh, yeah?" Sometimes I said *hunya?* frequently, out of courtesy, as others did, when someone was telling me a story in Blackfoot. However, this was a mistake, since it made the storyteller assume I was keeping right up with the talk, even if I was completely lost, or at least thoroughly confused.

Sometimes I got impatient for Beverly to translate what someone was saying, or upset if she wasn't along with me to help. It was very frustrating to be alone with an elder who was telling a good story in Blackfoot. If I didn't tape the story, it was seldom retold. I could usually digest only enough to know that I wanted to fully understand the rest. In that manner I have permanently lost some important knowledge.

With time I learned to *speak* parts of the Blackfoot language, and less well to *understand* it. It is very complicated, lacking the particular system and direction of written languages. There are a number of varying words for each thing, depending on the circumstances that surround its use. Thus, to learn individual words for such common things as shoes, horses, and tipis is of little use for conversation. The same words are often barely recognizable in sentences, where they are cut up and divided by adjectives or adverbs indicating where, when, and how. The more I learn of the language, the more hopeless I feel that I will ever master it.

Since a few of the elders we were close to spoke very little English, I continued trying to learn Blackfoot. Yet I was always afraid to use what I did learn, for fear of making mistakes. This was especially true when there were younger people around. A slight mispronunciation, or even a misplaced accent, can change the meaning of a word or statement completely. And never let it be said that a Blackfoot will allow such a mistake to pass unnoticed! In fact, young and old alike don't hesitate to laugh out loud and make fun of errors, while repeating the mistake over and over. This was at first a very unsettling experience for one who went to schools in which a stick was used to punish mistakes.

My father-in-law took particular interest in my efforts to learn the Blackfoot language, though he was also very critical of errors, even when made by other members of his family. He enjoyed telling the story of a Catholic priest who had practiced hard to deliver a sermon in Blackfoot. He was doing well until he reached his closing remarks, which were supposed to be: "And let us all meet one day in heaven." However, his pronunciation made one word a bit too long, so that he ended up saying: "And let us all meet again, drunk." My father-in-law thought this was very funny every time he told me about it. He said all the Indian people in the church broke out laughing. For me, however, it was only more evidence that my efforts to learn Blackfoot had little chance of real success.

Atsitsina also gave me regular language lessons. Sometimes they went quite well, as when he and I were traveling somewhere alone. At other times he was very impatient, and would get disgusted if I mispronounced the same word more than once or twice. I tried to tell him that my mistakes with Blackfoot words were similar to his mistakes with English (which also sometimes turned out humorous!) but he didn't consider that to be worth debating. He wouldn't even accept my argument that he still made many errors while speaking English, even after hearing the language for nearly all of his seventy years, whereas I had only been hearing Blackfoot for a short time.

What made me feel worse, one summer, was the appearance of a "white" linguist from some university. This man had studied a number of unusual languages, and for the previous year had devoted himself to learning Blackfoot. For that purpose he hired an interested and clear-speaking elder from the Siksika division, with whom he spent a lot of time. However, until his casual visit to the Sun Dance camp this linguist had not been heard of by the Bloods.

It happened that a neighbor woman of ours—the elderly wife of Joe White-Man-Left—was working with her daughter to put up their family tipi. The linguist parked nearby and strolled over to watch them work. The woman asked her daughter in Blackfoot: "Why is this white man just standing there and staring at us?" The linguist replied in the same language: "I am interested to see how it is properly done." Without a moment's hesitation the woman got up and went inside her nearby tent. She later said that she felt so startled and embarrassed that she could do nothing else.

The story quickly made the rounds of the camp, and the linguist was addressed by all manner of people. He came back to visit another day, when my father-in-law happened to be present. Before long, Beverly's father was conversing at great length with the linguist, an experience he seemed to enjoy. In his youth he had known other white men—mainly priests and storekeepers—who could speak the Blackfoot language fairly well. But he eventually came back to us with a gleam of satisfaction, saying: "Well, I gave him a test to see just how well he knows our language, and he failed!" Then he proceeded to give a complicated explanation about similarities between the words for apple and potato, and their plural sounds. Something unusual is done with them, though I missed understanding just what that was. Unfortunately for the linguist's reputation, so did he.

But a couple of elders chided me and said: "Look at that white man, he has hardly been around us and he speaks better Blackfoot than you!" I felt bad at first, until I talked to the man myself and learned that he knew very little about Blackfoot life and customs, apart from the language. When I said this to the elders they agreed that I should just keep going along as I had been.

One day I asked Atsitsina if he thought my prayers were of much use, since I was practicing Blackfoot ways but knew so little of the old language. He replied that the Creator made all things to be the way they are, including the ways he and I learned to speak. He said, "The Creator hears all prayers just the same, no matter what language they are spoken in." After that I felt more secure. I still wanted to learn how to pray in Blackfoot, but mainly so the elders would better understand what my prayers were about.

This kind of enlightened attitude about the world and its religions allowed the Blackfeet to accept the spiritual ways of others without feeling threatened about their own. Even the idea of the Sun Dance, which is the most important Blackfoot festival, is said to have come to them over the ages from the Aztec people in Mexico and South America. When Blackfoot leaders first saw the material accomplishments of Europeans, they apparently figured, "White men must pray to very good Spirits in order to have so much success." They willingly sat with the early priests and missionaries and learned how to address those Spirits, in addition to their own.

It is unfortunate that the Europeans did not also have such enlightened thoughts. Think of the beautiful society they might have created with the Nature-wise native people. But the missionaries came with one goal only, to "save the heathens from the devil." When men, women, and children went forward to receive the white men's sacrament of baptism (as they would come forward to have their faces painted!), the priests wrote back to their superiors: "The savages have recognized their evil ways and accepted God into their hearts instead." Nonsense! The idea of discarding tribal faith was then not even known to the Indians.

We have not heard a single Blackfoot elder deny the God of Christians, or the teachings of Christ. It is not unusual to hear Jesus mentioned in Blackfoot prayers, along with "Ninnai-Apista-dokee," or "Our Father who made us." Often they are mentioned in the same breath as Sun, Moon, Earth, and other natural elements. Along with Jesus are mentioned notable Blackfoot holy persons of the past.

Beverly's father is especially devout in the Catholic Church on the reserve. He has traveled to Rome to see the pope, as well as to Mexico to see ancient Indian shrines. He is training to become a deacon, yet he has also sung at medicine pipe ceremonies, and has often had his face painted. He likes to point out similarities between the two religions he knows best.

For instance, the symbol of the cross is considered very sacred and powerful in Blackfoot culture. It represents the Four Directions of the Universe, which reach out to all Creation. Christians and Blackfeet both like to use incense for purification, and to help their prayers. During a mass priests give out small bits of bread or wafers for communion, just as the sacred Sun Dance women give out pieces of buffalo tongue to the members of the tribe.

Because the Blackfoot people so readily adopted the Christian ways of my people, elders who came to know me also accepted that I could adopt Blackfoot ways. Ironically, unlike most of them, I have never been baptized into the Christian faith at all.

Around the time that Beverly's parents were growing up, the Catholic Church dealt very strictly with Indians who showed too

Visiting with Jim White Calf, or Last Gun, the last old buffalo hunter among the Blackfeet of Montana. Here he wears the three-braid hairstyle that once identified warriors of the Northern Plains. At this time he was the last known taker of an enemy scalp on Indian war trails. One night he lay down to sleep on this couch and never woke up again. When he died in 1970, it was said he had reached 116 years of age.

Willie Eagle Plume, or Atsitsina, and me on our way to a smoking ceremony on the Blood Reserve in 1971 (*Photo by Beverly Hungry Wolf*). *Below,* the "Old Folks," Louis and Maggie Bear Child, sharing a smoke in their reservation shack by the junkyard in Browning, Montana. The fringed container behind them contained Louis's sacred society headdress.

Joseph Young Eagle Child, or Makes Summer, wearing the fur hat he made from instructions received in a mystical dream.

Visiting with Louie Ninepipe of the Flathead Tribe, who taught me about Indian singing and dancing and told entertaining stories of his tribal past. *Below*, Wolf and me visiting with Jerome Vanderburg, an elderly Flathead Indian who took part in my first sweat bath.

Willie Scraping White, or Wolf Old Man, at the age of
ninety-five. He was then the leading medicine man and
ritualist among his Blood people, as well as the other
three Blackfoot divisions. *Below*, Wolf Old Man and
Wolf Child in the living room of our house on the reserve in 1971.

Willie Eagle Plume in the process of annihilating me in a game of pool, of which he was once a champion. *Below*, one of the last horse teams and wagons seen regularly around the Blood Reserve was owned by George Macdonald, who was a relative of Beverly's. Although he lived like a conservative Indian, George had several European ancestors who gave him not only his last name but also the only beard seen on an elderly Blood.

Willie Eagle Plume in the wall tent where we stayed as guests during our visit to Smallboy's breakaway band of Cree Indians living in the wilderness. The plywood wall inside this tent kept out cold winds when wintertime temperatures went way below zero. *Below*, Wolf Old Man and I share a joke while sitting in the shade of his little frame house in 1971. He was a strict traditionalist, yet he encouraged our modern attempts to make written and photographic records of the life and culture to which he belonged.

Atsitsina the first time he came to our new mountain land. He was telling an adventure story in which one of his forefathers came across the mountains to meet enemy tribes. We fried steaks on an open fire, which was his favorite way of cooking.

Beverly's father, Edward Little Bear, or Eagle Tailfeathers, dressed in the way of his forefathers. His eagle headdress is of a style adopted from the Sioux in the last century. Although considered essential for a complete "chief's outfit" worn by many elders, this kind of bonnet usually lacks the religious significance of the traditional Blackfoot feather headdresses, which stood straight up instead of sloping toward the back.

John Bird Earrings (*left*) and his last wife, "Princess Lexipar," (*below*) who claimed to be the granddaughter of Sioux chief Rain-in-the-Face, in their home on the Blackfoot Reservation of Montana in 1976.

Jerry Young Pine and his wife, our neighbors, hauling water for their household along the Bullhorn river bottom.

Joe Young Pine, a Blood Indian *and* cowboy, with his team of horses and his old, squeaking wagon.

Part of the tipi encampment for an Indian Ecumenical Conference held on the Stoney Indian Reserve at the edge of Banff National Park.

Horseback riding over ancient trails near our house along the Bullhorn River, which flows here in several small channels. Tops of the distant hills indicate the level of the surrounding prairie.

Pat Weasel Head puts the finishing touches on the sweat-lodge frame while Atsitsina helps prepare the hole that will later hold the hot stones. The ceremony was for our family as well as for our elders. Wolf (*playing on the right*) stayed outside with Beverly during the ceremony to raise and lower the lodge door and help with other ritual details.

Beverly, Wolf, and me outside a sweat lodge that we built behind our reserve home. Our neighbor's house is visible on the nearby hill. *Below,* Beverly and our uncle Atsitsina watch for the starting fire that will heat rocks for a sweat bath. The forked stick Atsitsina is holding was for carrying the hot stones into the lodge. Cold water poured over these stones by Wolf Old Man produced the steam that caused our sweating.

Pat Weasel Head, or Mokakin, guides Wolf Old Man to our newly constructed sweat lodge, where he led a special ceremony for our family. *Below,* Wolf Old Man and Pat Weasel Head ready to enter the sweat lodge with their ceremonial articles. Undressing comes as part of the special ritual inside the lodge. The clothes and blankets are passed out before the sweating begins.

much faith in their traditional ways. Among the Bloods, men and women who joined secret societies were subject to excommunication, as were bundle keepers. That was a serious punishment, since the Church controlled many important activities on the reserve, including the virtual upbringing of children!

Still, we have several times been to medicine bundle ceremonies on Sundays that were delayed while key participants attended church services first. Usually they show up neatly dressed in ties and suits, looking peaceful and happy. It is strange for me to see them thus, as they come from "the white man's church," while I sit in my moccasins and blanket on the floor.

The historian in me long tried to figure out which "era" of traditional life I should use as my model for learning. Blackfoot culture has always changed with the times and adapted to stronger influences. Even the strict and ancient ceremonies have lost some characteristics and gained others. Slowly I have come to realize that the ideal of a "good old days" is mostly romantic fantasy. The reality of life offers us only the chance to make each new day a good one. The challenge to learning ancient traditions is in combining them with beneficial modern ways, rather than wishing the world would go in reverse to make certain daydreams come true.

"Are you trying to be an Indian?" was a common question that helped me to think about what I was doing in the midst of a culture that I was not born into. Often Beverly was asked: "Is your husband an Indian," or "What kind of Indian is your husband?" Sometimes she wasn't sure how to answer. The question was frequently asked with respect, but sometimes an answer was defiantly expected. Most Blackfeet were simply curious to know about the newcomer in their tribe.

Apparently I was different from most newcomers, because I wanted only to live on the reserve with my new family. I wasn't interested in doing business or otherwise getting involved with the rapidly modernizing Indian society. I was not a government employee, nor a schoolteacher, cattle rancher, or spokesman for some scheme or another involving the tribe. I spent most of my time with a select handful of elders, and paid little attention to other things. I

didn't realize, then, that my behavior was threatening to some people, who saw my ways as "mysterious." Some said I must be "up
to something." These people were not directly involved in their
own tribal culture, and knew little of what went on with it.

I devoted myself so earnestly to our elders and their ways that I
soon lost touch with most people of my own generation, almost
including Beverly. After all the years of strict Catholic schooling
she wanted to exercise newfound freedoms and awareness. Instead,
I demanded that she now take up the equally strict ways of her own
ancestors, which no one else her age had done. I wanted her to wear
only long skirts and dresses, like Indian women of the past, even
though mini-skirts and jeans were then the fashion. I opposed her
efforts at hairstyling, and the use of makeup. When she wore her
hair loose, I talked like an elder and asked: "Whom are you mourning for?"

We both wore moccasins at home, but I began to insist that we
constantly wear them outside, as well. Since Beverly was still working as a teacher's aide at the old school nearby, her "new" traditional appearance caused attention and comments that were
sometimes embarrassing to her.

Even elders were surprised at my strict conduct. Some suggested that we were too young to cut ourselves off so completely
from our own generation. Still, Beverly now says she had too much
respect for my devotions to interrupt and point out how much I was
isolating her from friends and relatives. She grew accustomed to my
unusual demands, even if they did not please her. She is descended
from a long line of women used to having proud and strong men
dictate their way of life. I was too busy and too stubborn to realize
that this would eventually cause a conflict.

My writings also became affected by my strict devotions. I had a
small but faithful readership who were eager to hear about living
simply in nature, and learning the traditional ways and wisdom of
various native tribes. In my early books I talked about a new way of
life based on combining the past and present, but among the Blood
elders I slowly forgot about alternative lifestyles. Instead, I re-

treated into an archaic domain that offered very limited opportunities.

The elders to whom I was growing close did nothing to dissuade me from withdrawing into their conservative world. My strict European upbringing prepared me well for devotion to disciplines. When I talked to the Old Man about my future with his teachings, he replied simply: "I have shown you my footsteps; it will be up to you how you follow them." I think I decided to try growing old and living in the same way as he, though I'm sure he knew much better than I that my resemblance to him would always be more in spirit than in outward manners.

From the start I was made aware of deep and resentful feelings that many Indians have against 'the white man.' My regular presence within the tribal culture often made me the most obvious "white man" around. Defensively, I built an invisible shell around myself whenever I was near Indians whom I didn't know. When I passed people from the reserve at a powwow, or in town, I often pretended not to see them rather than take a chance at receiving their silent but painful stares. Without words, many people told me: "We know you are a white man, and we hate white men!"

The reasons most commonly given for this hatred are both real and imaginary. They are largely based on political and social problems that the average "white man" neither understands nor controls. "Stealing the land, breaking treaties, and crushing the culture and spirit of native people," would summarize the main accusations against "white men." I was not even born when most of these things happened, and I never felt complacent that they had occurred, but I often made a convenient scapegoat, nevertheless.

The prejudice I felt from Indian people seemed no different from that shown by most groups of people against others who are not like them. Even animals and plants express these feelings of distrust when they encounter each other wild in Nature. The modern world must somehow learn to accept and deal with these instinctive attitudes, since it appears that they can be neither legislated nor wished away.

Unfortunately, it took me a long time to learn that my silent shell was not working in my favor. While I walked around feeling guilty because of my race, many Indians thought I was too proud to be friendly. They were used to being looked down upon and regarded as lower-class people by whites. Many would have been glad to respond had I shown that I was seeking their friendship. But it appeared that my interest lay only with certain older people, which made some of the younger ones, especially, resent me.

However, even among those who resented me, some were led to wonder what hidden values the ways of their elders offered that would bring a young non-Indian from across the ocean to devote himself to them so earnestly. In the years since then some of these individuals have become close friends of ours. They may have been skeptical of me at first, but they learned from my example that it is possible to be young and still carry on with certain old traditions.

Among my earliest young friends were educated tribe members and liberal-minded "intellectuals." Usually they were friends of Beverly's who knew very little about their own tribal culture, and were amazed that she had become so deeply involved in it. One cousin of Beverly's told me: "I'm glad she married you, because in college she was getting too radical!" None of these friendly observers were interested in joining tribal cultural activities—most longed for advanced city schooling and modern-day living such as I had left behind. But they generally encouraged us in trying something different from the rest of our generation. They even thought our efforts might encourage other young people to renew nearly lost contacts with elders and Blackfoot traditions. One friend summed up my presence on the reserve by saying: "Now we can no longer blame 'the white man' for making us ashamed of our own culture and religion, since we have one right here, among us, who is practicing these things!"

I found it hard to understand the general disinterest shown by young Blackfeet for their tribal traditions, especially since those traditions were still being regularly practiced right around their homelands. Indians living away from reserves seemed much more aware of the value of such things. Many of them belonged to tribes that no longer existed except in name. They grew up as members of society's minority groups, without knowing tribal reservations or the keepers of tribal traditions. Compared to them, Blood youths were fortunate for having a strong tribal life to grow up with. It seemed that they should be in the forefront in any revival of Indian tradition and culture.

Ironically, when the "Indian movement" finally reached the Blackfoot Nation, around 1970, most of its followers came from the Montana divisions, which the other three considered most integrated with non-Indian society. Among Bloods the first real signs of cultural revival came, not from youths, but from a middle-aged man named Rufus Goodstriker. A former boxing champion and rodeo rider, he was an ideal person to set a cultural example for younger members of the tribe. For some time he had been the tribal policeman, and for one two-year term he served as the tribe's elected head chief. He was a modern-day warrior and hero.

Goodstriker's initial efforts were concerned less with culture than with encouraging young people to think about working together to improve their own lives and the general welfare of the tribe. He set up a youth camp on reserve land in the nearby Rocky Mountains, where participants learned the values of companionship and outdoor life. In those days there was little organized recreation for Blood youth outside of the strict boarding schools.

Since the original Goodstriker was a noted Blood warrior, as well as a participant in traditional ceremonies, it would have been easy for his popular and successful grandson to take a similar place in the tribe. The elders would have been glad for his presence. But for some reson he decided to take up the ceremonial ways of a neighboring group of Cree Indians, who were formerly enemies of the Blackfeet.

Most Crees live on various prairie reserves across Canada, and one in Montana, but this group had given up reserve life and moved to a wilderness area in the Rockies of Alberta. Government efforts to move them back out of the mountains brought much public attention, as well as the support and admiration of other Indians through-out North America. They were seen as a group of "Indian pioneers," and many wanted to visit or join them.

The leader of this group was an elderly chief named Robert Smallboy, who said he was tired of seeing his people spoiled and degraded by modern ways of life. He originally intended to move quietly into the wilderness, but in his group was a young medicine man who had a strong following and widespread popular appeal. Instead of taking up strict tribal beliefs and ceremonies, he practiced a form of "native spiritualism" that was then becoming a new inter-tribal religion and faith. Rufus Goodstriker became the first of many Bloods to express this new faith.

At first Beverly and I were disappointed that Blackfoot youths would prefer to be with former tribal enemies rather than with their own elders. However, we soon realized that the intertribal ceremonies were much more open for participation than the strict and de-fined ways we were learning. The Cree medicine man and his followers were young people experienced at modern living and able to relate to the problems and challenges faced by other youths. In comparison, Blackfoot traditions must have seemed tiring. The leaders of the ceremonies were old men and women who often dis-missed youths as being hopelessly spoiled and demanding. In order to participate with these elders the young faced a series of compli-cated initiations, each of which cost many transfer payments. It was difficult to arrange for these initiations, since elders were often slow about explaining the necessary preparations and even slower at get-ting involved in them.

In an effort to bridge the gap between his own people and his Cree friends, Goodstriker arranged for a cultural tour that included an intertribal visit to the Cree camp. When Atsitsina agreed to join other invited elders, Goodstriker said we could come along to help provide transportation. Others in the group included the ceremonial leader, John Many Chief (White Horn) and his wife, as well as his nephew, who was Beverly's father. In all there were nearly thirty Bloods traveling in a northbound caravan.

We found Smallboy's people in a new campsite to which they

had moved during the previous summer. It was a long, hard drive over rough dirt roads to get there. The nearest pillar of civilization was a combination store, post office, and gas station that sat alone in a deep forest. For the final part of the journey we had to drive through a half-frozen stream. Luckily, it was still early in the spring and the water ran low. I tried to imagine that crossing once the snows on high mountains sent down their melted torrents.

Smallboy originally led his people from their prairie reserve to a lovely meadow along the main highway leading into Jasper National Park. That place was so easy to reach that the camp was soon bothered by quantities of tourists, along with fellow Indians who sometimes came only to bring liquor and other troubles. When another Indian leader formed a rival band nearby, the potential problems grew and Smallboy decided it was time to move again.

We had romantic ideas of how his camp would look, based on stories told about it and its remote location. For one thing, we expected to park in the distance in order to avoid disturbing the tipi village. However, the road went right through the middle of a narrow meadow in which the camp was set up. Although sets of tipi poles could be seen leaning against trees in different locations, all the camp's people were living in white canvas tents. Our elders commented that the tents were set up without the circular order that they were used to seeing in tribal camps of the Blackfeet.

Cars and pickup trucks were parked all over, some of them without wheels and other vital pieces. Several horses wandered around the area, as well. Other horses could be seen inside corrals at the far end of the clearing, next to large stacks of hay. Tires, wheels, empty boxes, barrels, and many other things seemed to be lying about wherever they were last needed. Of courses, winter was just ending and snow was starting to melt. These objects were on top of the ground, so that their snow coverings melted first, making them stand out quite readily. Still, we had romantically thought such junk would have been left behind on the reserves in the first place.

An elderly man named Lazarus Roan greeted us on behalf of the camp's chief. He was the chief's main advisor—a man wise in both Indian ways and in methods for dealing with non-Indian governments. He sported a long white goatee, which our elders found very unusual. He divided us into small groups and brought us to stay with various camp families.

Beverly, Wolf, and I, along with Atsitsina, were brought to a vacant tent by an elderly woman and her teenage daughter. The woman explained that her husband had died during the winter and that she was staying with relatives during the period of mourning. His had been the first death in the camp, caused by complications resulting from pneumonia.

There was plenty of room for us in the tent, one of the larger ones in camp. Most of the back half was taken up by two metal-framed beds that stood side by side. In the middle of the tent stood two wood-burning stoves—a thin-walled one for heating, and a heavy, cast-iron one for cooking. They were connected to one chimney that went out through an asbestos-lined hole in the ceiling. We quickly lerned that the tent stayed quite warm as long as we kept wood burning in at least one of the stoves. As soon as both fires went out, the air in the tent became cool and damp.

The tent had a floor made of framed lumber covered with plywood sheets and topped by several old rugs. The inside walls were also framed and covered with plywood, which helped keep out cold winds. In the front part of the tent stood a small kitchen table, an old, overstuffed chair for relaxing, and an antique wooden dresser with a mirror on top. Between the large chair and the dresser was an assortment of trunks and suitcases that seemed to take the place of closets. Kerosene lamps provided lighting at night.

When Smallboy first led his people into the mountains, back in 1968, many critics said they would not make it through the winter. Temperatures get down to 40 degrees below zero regularly. Yet the people survived, and seemed to grow stronger in their convictions. There were 140 members in that original group. Some of these people had already gone and been replaced by others, but the group's size was still about the same when we visited. We were told that the number increased quite a bit during the nicer weather of summer.

Smallboy, as elected head chief of his prairie reserve, had petitioned the Canadian government for ten years to give his people a piece of wild land. He had earlier decided nothing good would ever come from life on the reserve, and he even offered to trade his rich ranching land there for a new and isolated home. He sat through many meetings with government officials, but all he got was lots of talk and red tape. After ten years he had enough talk and finally just made his move. Only his closest followers went with him.

The modern, conservative government of Alberta tried to prevent Smallboy and his people from settling on wild land by enacting a law to prohibit public camping in any one place for more than thirty days. The province's minister of lands and forests, Dr. J. Donovan Ross, publicly called Smallboy's group "squatters," which aroused the sympathy of other native people. He said: "Chief Smallboy is squatting now and has done so for some years. He has treaty rights on the Hobbema Reserve, and no claim whatsoever to any other land in the province."

Lesser government officials were more sympathetic, and thought, privately, that a compromise might eventually be worked out. However, when Smallboy said the Crees had traditional rights to the land, at least one neighboring tribe challenged his opinion. Nevertheless, he filed an official claim for an area made up of several "townships," which he said would suit the needs of his tribe. At this time the matter is still not settled.

Ironically some of Smallboy's harshest critics were other Indians, especially those back on his own reserve. Mostly they were progressive individuals who feared that the controversy might provoke negative feelings in the rest of society and endanger the process of turning Indians into ordinary, modern citizens. One wrote to local newspapers and said: "There are people behind the scenes using Smallboy as a puppet. He did not instigate the move to the mountains . . ." Non-Indian critics opposed the move because they feared Smallboy's example would cause hordes of other Indians to flock into what they considered public "recreational lands."

Throughout this controversy Smallboy was seen as a quiet and dignified chief who spoke softly and rarely. To one reporter he made the following statement: "I am not angry at any officials. I have no resentments and no quarrels with anyone. I don't want to cause trouble. But we will remain in the wilderness so long as this land exists. . . . It is as man was meant to live!''

Our own visiting group got to see this much-talked-about chief during a ceremony that was held the evening of our arrival. He was a stout-bodied, elderly man, who walked quietly in his moosehide moccasins. He sat down near the head of the gathering without speaking or otherwise calling attention to himself. At first I didn't even realize that he was the chief. Dressed in a new, long-sleeved shirt and a nice woolen sweater, he didn't appear like a wilderness man. He had on a pair of clean, modern trousers that were held up by a belt with a shiny cowboy buckle. He also wore ordinary, dark-rimmed glasses. His graying hair hung down past his shoulders in two thin braids. He showed evidence of European ancestry. In fact, without his braids and moccasins, he might have passed for a plain, gentle old man in any community.

There was an air about this man that indicated wisdom and good character. He acted much like old-time chiefs of whom I had heard and read. He reminded me of our own graying head chief back on the Blood Reserve. Unfortunately, many progressive Indians did not appreciate these traditional pillars of patience and quiet strength. They wanted leaders who would speak loudly and quickly.

During that evening's ceremony Smallboy sat quietly and watched. He seemed to have everyone's full respect without intruding into their activities. The real leader of the event was Wayne Roan, the camp's medicine man and a son of the advisor Lazarus. Handsome, fashionably dressed, and not at all shy, Wayne quickly united the gathered people with songs and prayers. It was said that some of his experience came from his earlier work as leader of a successful Indian rock and roll band. The unusual habit of wearing his long hair in one braid down the back caused our elders to give him the Blackfoot nickname ''Braid Behind,'' which is also their name for persons of Chinese descent.

The ceremony was held in a spacious new mobile home, which served as the camp's schoolhouse during the daytime. It was the only solid structure in the area, and looked totally out of place. It had been supplied by the government, along with a schoolteacher.

Even worse, it came equipped with a gasoline generator that provided power for light and other conveniences. The noise of its operation was heard clearly throughout the camp.

The windowless building was used because the ceremony required total darkness for some of its mysterious parts. A large, colorful tent had served the purpose before, though only late at night. It was still standing in the middle of the camp, where it seemed to await the coming of some Christian crusader who might have used one just like it.

The medicine man introduced his ceremony with a lengthy talk about prayers and religions. He had apparently been advised that the elderly Bloods would find his ways much different from their own. He relaxed tensions somewhat when he told everyone to pray however they wished—even if they happened to be Christians.

However, he was not so liberal when he mentioned "white men," though I was the only one of that kind present. He referred to my race a number of times, and insisted that we had been given our own religion, which required the use of a book. He proudly said: "My religion doesn't need a book, and it will never be found in a book." He had also been told of my work as a writer. In case I didn't get the hint, he added: "Those of you who are thinking of writing a story about what we do here tonight, let me warn you: It is too powerful to stay on paper! You won't be able to write it down!" Out of respect I didn't even try.

We had brought to the camp our own groceries, which we shared with our hosts. They, in turn, shared wild meat from elk and moose killed by their hunters. Most households seemed to have fresh meat drying in strips hung from lines near the roofs of the tents. Others had large chunks stored outdoors, up on high platforms that could not be reached by dogs. Raw hides from the animals hung from branches all over the camp, frozen until warmer weather would allow them to be tanned.

Hunting was perhaps the major topic of concern for Smallboy's people, as well as for their critics. Like other tribes, the Crees had long ago signed treaties with government agents, through which they gave up most of their traditional lands. Among the few rights left to them was the freedom to hunt anytime on unoccupied public lands, forever. Back in the 1800's, when these treaties were drawn up, there seemed to be endless numbers of wild animals, which the Indians were not expected to affect greatly with their relatively simple hunting methods. Besides, settlers and pioneers relished the thought of doing away with wildlife, some of which threatened their livestock and the rest of which competed for its grazing lands.

However, modern hunters have much more devastating weapons than did the treaty signers. Telescopes, high-powered bullets, and fast-shooting rifles tend to make some hunters careless. New roads and modern vehicles bring these hunters into the most remote regions. Most of Smallboy's men were equipped like modern hunters. No one could deny that their presence affected the area's wildlife.

Nevertheless, the Indians demanded to fully exercise their treaty rights. They said if wildlife became threatened the thing to do was take away hunting privileges from non-Indians, who are the real newcomers. The whites hunt mainly for sport and recreation, while the Indians said they do so to feed their families.

When he was asked his opinion about the conflict, Smallboy said he hoped that his people would learn to love and respect the wilderness so that no harm would come from their presence. He expected his young people to make their permanent homes there, which would cause them to learn how to live in harmony with their surroundings. He explained the matter quite well to a reporter when he said:

"That is the main purpose of us being here, for the young people. Not necessarily for us older folks, because we have knowledge of how the Indian lives in peace and harmony. We are here to teach them different things. We all know that many things attract them in today's society and that makes it difficult for them to understand, and many times they are led astray. At our camp, where everything is at a slower pace, they can be taught and they learn more about natural life. The parents and their families live a quiet life and as a result the children can reason things out by themselves. We welcome people to come to the camp, especially the younger generation, when they come with intentions of trying to learn something related to the Native way of life. We are grateful that they come to our camp. That is our main purpose for being out here.''

Interestingly, Smallboy began life on land claimed by other Indian people. He was born in 1898 along the banks of the Old Man River, near Fort Macleod, Alberta, not far from the Blood Reserve. Less than twenty years earlier the Bloods had given up rights to that area by signing a treaty of their own with the government. Although Cree leaders signed similar treaties, many Cree families preferred their simple roaming life until well into the present century. Smallboy's family did not settle on the Hobbema Reserve until 1915. He recalled:

"Before the white man came, the Indians made a good living in their own way. Now we are going back to that living. We would like to show the peoples of the world that it is possible to live peacefully, and develop contentment in our environment.

"White people want everything nice and easy—push-button and fancy. Their main goal is to gain money. They base everything on money, and they forget about the true meaning of God, or the Great Spirit.

"Yet I don't see where the white men can learn anything from me because they don't listen. They just say I am crazy. How can I teach them anything if they think I am a fool? White people already know there is a God, or Great Spirit, but they choose to value more highly the dollar. I have never heard a white man curse his dollars, but I've heard many curse their God.''

We met several of Smallboy's people during our stay in the camp. Among them was an elderly, heavyset man who was working under the hood of a large, modern car when we first saw him. He cursed at it, saying the vehicle had sat uselessly all winter, and that he only wanted to start it so he could drive it to the nearest town and sell it. Somewhat apologetically he explained that the automobile was left over from his city life, which he claimed to have permanently left behind. With it he had left a modern house, a good-paying job, and a non-Indian wife. Although he was evidently part European himself, he intended to start following the dreams and visions of his native ancestors. He still wore city-style clothing, along with a heavy pair of work boots, but his shoulder-length hair was a symbol of his new freedom and thinking.

We also spoke with a younger fellow, new to the camp from a home in the city. He had recently married a girl whose family was among Smallboy's original followers. He was an Indian—at least in part—but he said the members of his tribe had lost all touch with their own heritage. he had learned abut Smallboy's camp when it became a popular subject of discussion among his Indian friends in the city. He said at that time he was "just wasting life by drinking and chasing women." He came to the camp out of curiosity, expecting neither wife nor home there. Now that he had both, he admitted some doubts as to whether he could survive for long in such isolation. Also, he wasn't sure what to do with his time, or how to support his new family. He said most of the camp members were receiving some form of government aid for their subsistence, but he seemed determined not to accept any of it himself.

After a couple of days in the mountain camp Atsitsina began to hint that he was getting homesick. When I pressed him on the subject he said, first, that he was glad to have seen Indians trying to regain their free life in Nature, and joining together in a traditional manner. But then he complained of being too old to enjoy the camp's isolation, and the primitive living. Finally he admitted that his main concern was being so long in the camp of former enemies, against whom his own father had fought numerous times. He was especially uncomfortable during the ceremonies, which were held each evening, in the dark. He was suspicious of their nature, saying that his father had led every kind of Blackfoot ritual, but always with lights on so that they could be seen.

Our talk took place late in the evening, and I agreed that we would head back home the next day. Atsitsina seemed very relieved when he heard that. He asked me to get more wood for the fire, while he put on fresh water for tea. That meant he was in a mood to talk and tell stories.

Beverly and Wolf were already asleep by the time Atsitsina and

I got settled. Before we had a chance to start, two other members of our group came in to join us. First was Atsitsina's cousin and best friend, White Horn, the ceremonial leader. Right behind him came Pat Weasel Head, another noted Blood elder and participant in traditional events. Although not directly related to us, Pat took Beverly as a daughter after he adopted her father as a younger brother (they were about fifteen years apart). Since he was oldest of the three men, I did not then imagine that he would outlive them and end up as the last of our elders on whom Beverly and I would depend for traditional advice.

These two men were also lonesome for their homes and families on the reserve. I could tell that they had come over in search of company. Since they all spoke English well, I was able to take part in their conversations. I recall the next couple hours as an intimate sharing of companionship in a warm and dimly lit tent, while surrounded by a strange camp and a vast wilderness.

Near the beginning one of the elders prayed, and Atsitsina told me to get out a small pipe that he and I had been working on. Right there we gave it a smoking initiation. After that came little stories and anecdotes, lots of jokes, tea, and more tea, plus quiet times when our minds wandered outside, and back to the reserve. That was the first time I ever felt relaxed with a group of Indian elders. It seemed almost unreal to me, sitting in an outdoor camp with these wise men, and I wished it were *our* camp, so that we could remain there permanently.

The subject of medicine pipes came up several times during the evening. All three men were former keepers of such bundles—Atsitsina and Pat Weasel Head three times each. John Many Chief was considered one of the most competent leaders of their ceremonies. He mentioned having once been hired to open the bundle that we were planning to get. He said a museum representative and a collector of Indian relics had wanted to see the bundle's contents, in order to decide how much to pay for them. He did not know this when he was first hired, and he scolded the owner when the true purpose of the bundle-opening became known. He said mice jumped out from somewhere in the bundle, and the white men apparently decided it was not worth buying. It turned out later that the mice had done no damage.

White Horn also mentioned a bundle kept among the Bloods and known as the Cree Medicine Pipe. A well-known Blood chief of the late 1800's had taken this sacred pipe from a tipi during an attack on a Cree camp. Although the long pipestem was decorated and kept wrapped like medicine pipes of the Blackfeet, it lacked the many other articles that make up Blackfoot pipe bundles. Determined that the captured pipe should have its place in his tribe's ceremonial history, the proud chief hired wise and powerful elders to make up a set of accessories and complete the bundle.

White Horn wondered if any Cree person in the camp might know the original songs for this sacred pipe. The Bloods used their own medicine pipe songs and rituals for its ceremony, but it was said the Crees had a very different way of handling it. Later I learned that there are still persons left among the Crees who know these old songs, and even one who is still keeping a wrapped-up medicine pipe in his home. The custom of having special pipes was common to many tribes of the plains, and others, as well. There is still one among the Sioux, and another among the Arapaho. But it is widely thought that only the Blackfeet still perform the ancient ceremonies that go with them.

Our discussion about medicine bundles naturally led to the subject of museums—no serious view of Indian "religious" history could overlook their impact. Specifically there were then many more Blackfoot medicine bundles in museum collections than there were left among all the twenty thousand Blackfoot people. This, in a nation whose people still value such bundles as others value their religious writings, like the Bible.

On the trip to Smallboy's camp the elders had seen four or five medicine pipes in museum displays—nearly as many as there were left among the Bloods. In fact, one of these was the famous Long-time Medicine Pipe, the most ancient and revered of all the bundles. Its acquisition by Alberta's Provincial Museum was still a very sore point with the Bloods. One of their own number had secretly conspired with the museum to sell the bundle during his term as keeper. An unprecedented amount of money was spent by the museum in an effort to make the final transaction socially legitimate. That this failed was obvious from the tone of the three elders, if not from the general consensus back home on the reserve.

During a stop at the Provincial Museum, earlier on the trip, White Horn had been allowed to take the ancient and sacred pipe out of its glass display case and perform a brief ceremony with it. He prayed, then blessed all the persons present, who went up to him by turns. Each left a pinch of tobacco with the pipe, both as an offering and as a wish to have the bundle come back into their tribe. The elders talked with Rufus Goodstriker about the possibility of getting legal and federal government help to have the bundle returned. When museum officials were asked for an opinion, they tried to suggest it was so ancient and valuable that only a museum could safely look after it. To them, it was a valuable antique, but to the Bloods it was the missing link for a vital ancestral ceremony.

On that occasion museum officials did make one concession to Indian requests—they removed the sacred pipe from display and wrapped it back up in its bundle. Ordinarily this bundle would not have been opened except during the sacred ceremonies, and then only by qualified persons. The officials were obviously eager to avoid a possible confrontation, especially in dealing with Indian elders.

I was surprised when I first learned of the deep dislike that Indian people have for museums. I had grown up to think of them as respectable social institutions—almost sacred, like churches. But among Indians, churches and museums both share responsibility for causing permanent damage to traditional culture. In many instances, their condescending treatment of native people symbolized technological society's superior attitude toward other races and cultures around the world. Native artifacts have often hung in museums as though they were trophies of conquered lands and peoples.

At first, some people thought my reason for being among the tribe was to perform museum-related work, such as research or artifact-buying. Rumors circulated that this was the reason Beverly and I had gotten together. Sometimes I was offered tribal relics for sale. The sellers usually scoffed when I said I had no interest in acquiring such things, nor the money with which to pay for them.

By that time demand for Indian artifacts by museums and private collectors had driven their monetary values high. The man who handled negotiations for purchase of the Longtime Medicine Pipe was directly responsible for bringing a new economic system into Blackfoot ceremonialism. Fresh from a university in Europe, he brought a zealous desire to "capture" the remains of an ancient native religion for the benefit of future scholars. He had learned that Blackfoot ceremonial life was the most complete among tribes of the plains. He was able to convince Alberta's brand-new Provincial Museum of his theory. Backed by an oil-rich government, the museum was eager to be a showplace of the region's culture. Documenting and preserving the culture and religion of the province's native people seemed an ideal project.

This museum crusader initially found a lot of friends among Blackfoot elders. They had watched with dismay the declining interest in their culture among youths. Few young people came to the ceremonies, and fewer still were willing to become keepers of medicine bundles. It seemed that the current elders would be the last generation of traditional tribal elders. Many believed that soon their legends and ceremonies would be gone, and their bundles lost and scattered. The museum man offered to record their knowledge and preserve the bundles, along with other artifacts. Some elders agreed with his plans, and gave him the name Yellow Fly to make him feel closer to them.

Unfortunately, Yellow Fly was a zealot who knew nothing about "Indian time." The elders figured his idea could be put into action slowly. The articles could go to the museum as time went by, when their keepers died and no one offered to take over. Yellow Fly was eager to set up an impressive museum display right away. Privately he went around to the elders and offered them ever-increasing amounts of money until, one by one, they went along with him. For instance, it took three thousand dollars to convince the keeper of the

Longtime Medicine Pipe that he should give it up. Until then, that was an unheard-of price to pay an Indian for any artifact.

I recount these details to give you some idea of what influences "scientific studies" can have on natural activities. That is not to say the elders were innocent in this matter. During later research I saw evidence that even among the strict and conservative Bloods, most traditionally active persons had accepted payment for information or artifacts at one time or another. In some cases, such information included the deepest and most esoteric tribal secrets, known only to certain initiated members of the two most ancient societies for Blood men and women. One retired chief had sold a tribal medicine bundle even as a younger man was inquiring about taking it over. The man from the museum often promised no one would learn of the transactions. But in the world of Indian life such things always come out, eventually.

In spite of the discouraging things I learned about museums, Beverly and I found them to be invaluable resource centers for studying Indian history and culture. We came to know a few museum workers who agreed that changes in the methods of ethnological studies and interpretations should be made. The option we liked best was to instruct Indian tribes to build their own museums, so that cultural materials might be preserved closer to the homes of the people from whom they originated.

Even with their complaints, most elders seemed to be aware that museums are valuable assets. However, they, too, wished that the materials be made more easily accessible to their own people. They disliked having sacred resources of their own culture kept under lock and key by unknown "white men." A common criticism made by parents and grandparents of young Indians was that schoolbooks and other learning tools are filled with the accomplishments of Europeans, while making hardly any positive mention of native people. Museum artifacts and information could help make young Indians proud, and non-Indians more respectful. Beverly says: "From books and movies I learned to think that Indians had nothing worth contributing to history and society."

The lack of a written tribal history presented a tempting challenging to my training as a historian. Not that there weren't books about the tribe, but the specific knowledge of our own elders appeared in danger of being lost for all time after their passing. When Beverly and I discussed this with some of them, it soon became clear that we should produce a history book together. Not only did we have access to historical photographs and written materials from museums, but we were also in daily contact with people who could help us to make all this scholarly material come to life. I decided to try writing a book that would give a contemporary interpretation to traditional Blackfoot history and culture.

My own family background made me especially interested in working with historic photographs. My father's uncle had been an early-day photographer in Switzerland and southern Germany. My father often worked as his assistant—helping him to haul around cumbersome equipment, and to work in primitive darkrooms. From them I inherited a love for this art form. By the time I was fourteen I had my own darkroom for developing film and enlarging pictures.

Although a great many photographs of Indians exist, relatively few of them have been seen by the Indian people. Photographers generally traveled to reservations and camps from distant cities, took the pictures they wanted, and returned to where they came from. Few remained among the Indians, or even came back for return visits.

During my high school years I started spending spare money to acquire old photographs and postcards, scouring secondhand stores, flea markets, and estate sales to find them. I concentrated on scenes of western history, which also became the subject of my college major. I specialized in photos of Indians and trains. I never have figured out how I came to be fascinated with these two oddly matched historical topics. But I worked my way through college as a locomotive fireman on the Union Pacific Railroad, and I produced Indian craftwork in my spare time. I have written books about both.

By the time Beverly and I got together, I had in my collection nearly one thousand photographs of Blackfoot life alone. The desire to learn about them had already turned into an obsession that led me to spend countless hours with delighted elders. In my albums they frequently found not only photos of their forefathers and various notable persons of the tribe, but also their parents, grandparents, siblings, friends, and even themselves. These photos often inspired stories and information to come out that might never have been thought of in ordinary conversations.

I approached the plan for creating a tribal history book with the idea that I would help my adopted Indian people, while at the same time justifying myself among them in a way that was acceptable to modern society. The project began during talks with tribal elders who said they would be helping us with it. Thus, I could not imagine that anyone would want to criticize the work. Beverly may have known things would not go so smoothly, but she said nothing to dampen my enthusiasm.

However, I soon learned that written histories are not readily accepted among people who have always relied on oral interpretations of their own past. The lack of a written language has kept most Indian people from developing a sense of appreciation for good literature and historical writings. Reading materials in many Indian households consist primarily of comic books, newspapers, and current magazines. Indian parents and grandparents rightly claim that their youths have not been given good impressions about their people in many schoolbooks and classrooms. Many good books that have been written about Indians seldom make their way into Indian communities. We wanted to create an exception to this, though we had no samples for guidelines.

One reason why books about Indians have often been avoided by the very people they are about is because they are commonly thought to represent only "the white man's viewpoint." This attitude was probably formed in the days of early western novels, when Indians were "the bad guys" and "the savages." Some Indians feel that books about their people are written mostly to gain money and glory for their authors. One recent Indian militant leader said that such books are largely "heresy accounts of stories stolen from old Indians, which have angered and hurt many." Since money and fame are actually rare results from any book, aspiring modern authors might do well to reconsider any ideas they may have for writing about a subject so controversial as the life of Indians.

Back at Smallboy's camp, I suppose some members were glad when they heard the "white writer" who came with the Bloods was going to leave early. The rest of our group stayed for another day and night, taking part mostly in healing rituals. We had hoped to drive across the mountains for a short visit to the old homestead, where I still had some belongings. However, a heavy snowfall dimmed our enthusiasm for the long drive, and revived Atsitsina's eagerness to get back home. We compromised by spending the night in the mountain resort town of Banff, where color television and hot baths made us forget we were still surrounded by an immense region of wilderness. We had neither of these luxuries in our homes on the reserve.

Atsitsina had never been to Banff before, even though the world-famous place was less than four hours from his home by car. But he knew about it from his father, who went there once, in 1922. That year a large group of Bloods were invited to take part in an annual festival. Normally this honor went to Stoney Indians, whose reservation is just outside the boundary of Banff National Park. But after the previous year's celebration the Stoneys said they wanted a share of the festival's profits or they would not show up next time. So the Bloods were invited instead.

In a local library we found old photographs of this event. Among the well-dressed Blood chiefs and warriors was old Eagle Plume, riding a spectacular gray horse that had spots all over it. He carried a rifle and wore his fringed and beaded "war suit." Atsitsina mentioned that when his dad died some family member got hold of this buckskin costume and sold it to a museum in the U.S. before anyone realized it. He had wanted to take it for himself.

The Blood delegation had set up their tipi camp next to the palatial Banff Springs Hotel, and Atsitsina wanted to visit it. In the old photos he recognized the lodges of various families by their painted designs. He said they had traveled to the place by train, riding in two special cars. Half of the space was taken up by their camping gear and ceremonial clothing.

The hotel's long hallways, high ceilings, and ornate fixtures reminded Atsitsina of a church, and he spoke in appropriately low tones. But when we came upon a vintage pool table in a round-pillared lounge room, he stopped and looked at it as though he liked the idea of a game. Jokingly I challenged him to a couple of rounds, which he humbly accepted. He said nothing abut having once been a pool-hall champ until after he had beaten me unmercifully. He then said he used to make "pocket money" by playing pool back in his bachelor days, although he had troubles in some small ranch towns with losers who refused to pay an Indian. He said that at such times he was always outnumbered, so he marked those games off to experience.

As the leading medicine man with the delegation, Atsitsina's father was asked by the festival's officials to lead a Blood ceremony while in Banff. After consulting with the others, Eagle Plume agreed to perform a shortened version of the night-long smoking ceremony. While photos and recordings were made, the Bloods prayed for all the people, and for their own safe journey back home. They had agreed to sing only the "lighter" ceremonial songs, leaving out all those considered too private and sacred for such an occasion. The spectators, of course, didn't know the difference.

This was not the only time that a Blackfoot ceremony was performed away from the tribal home. We know of at least two medicine pipe bundle ceremonies that were held in faraway places—one aboard a train traveling through the eastern United States, the other in the movie capital of Hollywood. On the train was a delegation of tribal representatives, including a medicine pipe keeper who brought his bundle along. The group thought that its presence and power saved them from injury when their train got wrecked, so they performed the ceremony in appreciation.

The ceremony in Hollywood was performed to give strength and good cheer to a homesick bunch of elderly Montana Blackfeet who had gone there to star in a film with Shirley Temple. If the ceremony was recorded, it did not end up in the final show, called *Susanna and the Mounties,* when it was released in 1939. Both of these traveling groups were made up of friendly and traditional men from the

Blackfeet, some of whom traveled on other occasions across America, and even to Hawaii.

Atsitsina was especially eager to go to the hot mineral springs that are near the hotel in Banff. His dad had called them "Sacred Mountain Water," and brought back home some of the clay from the mineral pool to use as medicine. Now that Atsitsina was an old man, he suffered from some of the same ailments that his father had doctored with this clay. He wanted to see if a visit to the hot springs would help him in some way.

The hot springs were deserted, since it was a winter weekday. An old trail led us into the dimly lit bowels of its strong-smelling cavern. The inside air was thick, warm, and so moist that we were soon perspiring. Atsitsina mentioned that the place was probably just the same when his dad was there, fifty years earlier. The thought made us silent, while he sat down and pulled off his shoes and socks. After he had soaked his bare feet and legs in the mineral waters for a time, he said he could already feel its action working on his old bones. He frequently complained of soreness in his lower limbs, which he blamed on his years of rodeo riding and bronco busting.

Atsitsina took home a small bag full of the mineral clay and let it dry. After that he frequently mixed some of it into a tub of hot water in order to continue his soaking treatments. He said this made him feel better, and, alone, had been worth the whole trip.

Just a few days after we got back to the reserve, Atsitsina came with some important news for us. The man from whom we expected to get the medicine pipe bundle was up from Montana, staying with relatives on the reserve. He was seen in a local restaurant with the museum zealot Yellow Fly. The old man was sure he saw money changing between their hands. He said we should go and check into it right away.

The family that the keeper was said to be staying with were relatives of ours, too. We decided to look for him there first. We drove over several dirt roads to reach the other side of the reserve. Although the large family was fairly poor, they had managed to hold onto lands developed by their forebears when they first settled on the reserve. They lived mostly from their share of money made by a rich rancher from the nearby Mormon community, who leased rights to grow grains and hay on the family's land.

Outside their house two older cars were parked. One of them had Montana license plates, so we knew the keeper was there. Although cultivated fields stretched away from the place in every direction, the family had managed to preserve a little bit of the ancient prairie right around their house. Here, children rode their bikes and ran over trails used for countless ages by buffalo, and by those who hunted them. The children may have been reminded of this past if they were lucky enough to find arrowheads, broken spear points, or other indestructible relics.

The house of these relatives was a typical one of framed lumber, with two bedrooms and outdoor facilities. Its two-tone paint, although faded, made it appear like a home in most any suburb of the West. However, without the work opportunities found in such suburbs, the family seemed to lack money to fix a cracked front window, a noticeably damaged front door, and the peeling paint. Actually there were funds available for such purposes from the tribal administration, but paper work, waiting time, and general humility required to get that kind of assistance was often more than conservative Indian families wanted to put up with.

We felt guilty coming to the home of these relatives only to see someone else, but they seemed to understand. They must have known something about the purpose of our visit, since they directed us right to the back bedroom, where the bundle keeper and his wife were staying. When they saw us the wife went out of the room without speaking, and the man closed his eyes and pretended to sleep. From that we knew something was up.

For several uncomfortable minutes we stood just inside the door of his bedroom, wondering what we should do. When he realized we were not going to leave, he sat up without looking at us, and said: "I'm not supposed to see you. You shouldn't have come!" We knew he was referring to the traditional custom by which applicants for bundle ownership avoid the bundle's current keepers until the time for the transfer ceremony. Contacts should be made through a middleman, usually an elder hired by the applicants for this purpose. But nothing had been said about this rule on several other occasions, when Beverly and I either met the man and his wife somewhere, or when we went to see them at their home.

If I had been a traditional Indian, I would likely have avoided a confrontation by slowly beating around the bush. If he had refused to respond to my hints, I would have been forced to depart without even discussing the main subject. But in this case I decided to follow the examples of certain outspoken elders, so I asked the keeper if it was true that he had accepted money from a museum man for the bundle already promised to us. He shifted uncomfortably and looked surprised by my asking such a blunt question, but I could feel that he did not want to say "no," either.

After a time of silent debate he finally replied: "Well, now that you have asked me, I will tell you: So many white men are after that bundle that my wife and I have decided to have an auction. The one who pays the most can have it." I felt as though a fragile dream had suddenly been dropped and broken.

When I finally caught my breath I reminded him that he had already smoked my pipe, therefore the agreement between us was sealed. He replied that I had taken him by such surprise that he was afraid to refuse my pipe. I tried to tell him that I depended on him to help fulfill my vow, but he brushed my words aside and said he wished to talk no more about it. If we wanted to join the bidding, he would hear from us then.

I followed Beverly out of the room in a daze. Our relative was waiting outside to shake our hands in parting. Sympathetically he said: "I know what went on with him, and I think he is acting foolishly. Give him time, maybe he'll come around to doing this the right way." I nodded and made some reply, but without much thought. Beverly was upset that a traditional member of her people had treated our first efforts to maintain tradition so poorly.

We drove directly to the home of Wolf Old Man, hoping he

would be there to give us counsel and encouragement. When we told him what happened, he said for us to go and bring Atsitsina, so that he could join in the important discussion. Atsitsina's house was not very far away.

When we went through the whole story again with both of the old men, Wolf Old Man made the first reply. He said: "I know this man who has the bundle, and I also know the one who is going around buying all our sacred articles. I have been afraid that the two would get together before you could complete your transfer." When I asked if we should consider getting involved in the auction, he shook his head and said: "No, things are all mixed up now, but none of it is your fault, so don't worry. Forget about this medicine pipe and look around for another one. This man is going to have some troubles because of the things that he is doing, so it is best that you two stay away from him."

I felt sad about this abrupt ending to something that had held such wonderful promise for our lives. Yet I also felt relieved, since I still had not figured out how to get all the called-for transfer payments. In an auction I would surely have lost out.

Although I did not have much hope of finding another keeper who would be willing to give up his bundle to a white man, Atsitsina and Wolf Old Man talked seriously about it. They finally decided we should go and ask for the pipe bundle that Atsitsina had transferred to a middle-aged family a year or two earlier. It had once belonged to Atsitsina's father, Eagle Plume, which made me all the more eager to acquire it. Also, Atsitsina still claimed some rights to it, because the family had been too poor to make all the necessary payments. At the transfer, rather than fold the bundle up and call everything off, he told the new keepers to give it back after they felt their vow had been completed.

Wolf Old Man said he would speak to the elderly father of this keeper, who was a ceremonial leader like himself. But after a few days Atsitsina became impatient and told us to drive him directly to the keeper's house. When we got there he told us to wait outside while he went in to do the talking. Initially he had made us feel sure that this transfer would succeed, but I began to have some doubts when he told us: "Pray hard that the bundle is still here, and that they will let you have it!"

Our prayers must have lacked conviction, because he soon came back out with a grim face and bad news. The family had gotten so poor that the keeper had pawned his bundle to Yellow Fly, the museum representative, for nine hundred dollars. He was to get more money in the spring if he was willing to give the bundle up in a proper transfer ceremony, which would be filmed and taped. Otherwise he could buy the bundle back, if he wished.

Atsitsina was quite angry, because he himself had refused to sell the bundle to the same museum man several times while it was still his. What was more, he had made the new keeper promise not to let "white men" buy it for any price. He said other members of that family had sold medicine bundles before, and the possibility of it happening again had worried him at the transfer.

Wolf Old Man was equally angry when he heard the news, but for a different reason. He had finally run into the keeper's father, who told him that the bundle was fine with his son's family, and that they would not be willing to give it up yet. He wondered if the father could be so blind as not to notice the large bundle missing from over his son's bed, or if he had been deliberately misleading. I was feeling badly not only because of another missed opportunity, but also because my efforts were causing unhappiness for others. I began to despise this museum man named Yellow Fly, whom I privately renamed Manure Fly.

We finally decided to try the one remaining possibility, which was to provide the necessary money so that the keeper could buy his bundle back. When we went to see him about it he seemed to feel guilty, and immediately said he would help in any way possible. Before we came along, he must have thought Atsitsina was too old to ever ask for the bundle's return.

I regret to say that we never did get Atsitsina's medicine bundle back, although we really tried. When the keeper of it first went to see the museum man, he was told it had been brought to the Provincial Museum for safekeeping. However, a phone call there proved that story untrue. A museum official also told us that this representative had become so overzealous about acquisitions from Indians that they had terminated their relationship with him. That was bad news, because it meant Atsitsina's bundle had gone to some other place. When the keeper went back to ask for it again, he was given another false story. I finally learned that it had been sold to a wealthy art collector in Seattle, for nearly five times the amount given to the keeper. That week we saw Yellow Fly driving down the main street of town in a brand-new station wagon. Years later the same bundle was resold again, for an even higher amount, to a wealthy collector in Germany. He is not only missing the history and spiritual ceremony for this sacred bundle, but is no doubt ignorant of all the intrigue involved in getting it away from its rightful owners.

When Wolf Old Man learned that Atsitsina's medicine pipe was definitely gone, he said he had been thinking the matter over and that there seemed to be no other alternative than for us to ask for the pipe bundle that *he* once owned, even though its current keepers had only taken it over the year before themselves. He said that he would go and talk to them about it and that he would bring Atsitsina along, since the head of that houschold took him for an adopted brother.

The owner of this bundle was an elderly and successful Indian rancher named Stabs Down. Although he kept his hair cut short, wore modern clothes, and drove a late-model car, he was a traditional person in many ways, and spoke no English. His family had good ranching land, large herds of cattle, horses, a modern house, and the reserve's first color TV.

The pipe bundle had actually been transferred to the teenage children of Stabs Down, for whose benefit he made the original vow. I felt shy about asking them for such a great thing, even indirectly, through the Old Man, and I was doubtful that they would agree to give it to us. Without the Old Man and Atsitsina we would never have considered approaching them for it.

I was elected to drive the two old men to see Stabs Down. Before we left, Wolf Old Man prayed by his altar, and painted our faces for good luck. Unfortunately, by the time we reached his house the children said he had left on a trip to town, and they did not know when he would be back. They looked with curiosity at the painted faces of the old men who were standing on their doorstep, although they had certainly seen such painting before. When Atsitsina and Wolf Old Man came back out to my truck, those left in the house tried hard to figure out who I was, sitting behind the steering wheel, with my face also painted.

Wolf Old Man suggested we go away for a few hours before returning to see if Stabs Down was home. So I took them for a drive around the northern part of the reserve, where the original government agency buildings stood. The Bloods chose that area to resettle in during the late 1870's, around the time the Old Man was born. He told us ancedotes from his youth, about the years when the last wild buffalo were killed. Some years later most Bloods decided to move further south on the reserve, which is why Beverly and I knew that part best.

Our driving finally brought us to the prairie town of Fort Macleod, a historic place whose single main street still looked pretty much as it had when Atsitsina was born, seventy years earlier. I invited the old men to eat. Although the town had several restaurants, I knew Indians preferred the two run by local Chinese people. In fact, when traveling to strange towns, elders often considered their first business to be the finding of a Chinese restaurant where they could eat. There seemed to be some kind of kinship feeling among the elders toward Chinese people, though I will not say that this can be taken as evidence for the theory that the Indians came to America from Asia.

The Chinese who had restaurants seemed to treat elderly Indians quite well, too. In part, no doubt, this was due to the Orientals' own traditional custom of respect for old people. At the same time, they must have identified more closely with Indians than they did with Europeans. Prejudice on the prairie was so strong that a couple of steakhouses in Cardston, at the edge of the Blood Reserve, still refused service to Indians in the 1970's! I found this hard to believe when Beverly first told me abut it, but when I went there with her we got nothing but a few negative glances while waiting for service at one of the tables. I was considered the same as an Indian.

To my relief, the restaurant in Fort Macleod had no customers when we entered. I was used to being stared at in towns around the reserve because of my European features and Indian customs, especially whenever I was in the company of elders. On this day the red paint on our faces made us even more conspicuous. We took a table at the back, ordered soup and hot beef sandwiches, and spent the next hour or so visiting and eating.

Stabs Down was still not home when we got back to his house later, so Wolf Old Man left word that we had come on sacred business, and that we would return again in two mornings. It was late in the afternoon by the time we headed back home. A spectacular sunset lit up the vast western skies. We were traveling over the dirt road that runs through the reserve's sacred Belly Buttes, near where the tribe's annual Sun Dance encampment is held each summer. The steep, sandy, and fantastically eroded slopes of the Buttes face west, where they look out over the last flat ranges of the Great Plains and at the majestic Rocky Mountains beyond.

On this evening that ordinarily grand sight of prairie turning to mountains was made even more dramatic by the final sunlight, which painted everything in shades of red and orange. Atsitsina tried to describe it for the Old Man, whose eyesight was not so good. But after a while the Old Man chuckled and said: ''I am not completely blind yet. Even I can see the sun, and how it makes everything look very beautiful.''

When we passed the area of the sacred encampments, both old men looked silently toward it. They had been here every summer of their lives. Here, their mothers had carried them about in bead-decorated cradleboards. Later they had played in the gullies and bushes with friends, and after that they had ridden around on horseback and tried to make themselves look appealing to the girls of the tribe. Here, they had camped with their wives and their own children, and watched the circle of life continue. Now they were the elders, in charge of the encampment's ancient ceremonies that they had once watched with the innocence and curiosity of childhood.

Wolf Old Man pointed out that all medicine bundle owners were expected to take part in the annual encampment, which made me wonder if we would be among them in the coming summer. He said that he no longer camped there, since he had no wife and family. But someone would bring him up every day, and take him home before dark.

Two mornings later Atsitsina and I returned to the Old Man's house to try our sacred mission once more, but we learned that Stabs Down had already been there ahead of us. He had been curious to know why three people with painted faces wanted to see him. When he learned that we wished to ask for the medicine pipe, he agreed with Wolf Old Man to let us have it. He said he would soon set the date for the bundle's annual springtime opening after consulting with his family, and that we could have it anytime after that. The Old Man felt that our prayers and use of the sacred paint had worked.

The opening ceremony was held in a large tipi set up next to Stabs Down's house a couple of weeks later. There was a large crowd in attendance—perhaps more than one hundred people—and few places to sit because we arrived late. We had driven Atsitsina to town first, so that he could get the second in a series of radiation treatments for a spot on his face. Originally the spot had been a small, dark growth, just underneath one eye. When we finally talked him into having it removed, lab reports said it was malignant. The doctor said if he had waited much longer it would have entered his facial bones, after which there would have been little hope of stopping it.

The leader of the ceremony was the same elderly man that I had gone to visit one night with Beverly and her mother. We had hardly seen him since then, and did not know he had been casting jealous eyes on the growing relationship between Wolf Old Man and us. He seemed friendly enough on the day of the ceremony. As future keepers of the bundle it was necessary for us to be specially painted by him. While doing this he prayed that we should have luck with our upcoming duties and that we should take good care of the bundle. It was the same one he and his wife had cared for in their younger days.

Medicine pipe ceremonies consist basically of two parts, one serious and the other fairly lively. In between is a pause during which the participants go outside to stretch. Ancient legends account for the origins of the medicine pipes and the contents of their bundles. It is said that the very first such pipe was given to the people by the Spirit of Thunder, who appeared in the form of a person. The springtime ceremonies celebrate the return of Thunder, after winter's absence. This return signals the coming of warm weather and easy times. That was good news especially in the days of rugged outdoor life. Thus, the ceremonies also celebrate the reawakening of Nature.

These ceremonies always begin with a series of complex songs that accompany the untying of the sacred bundle. First, incense is made for purification. For this, coals are taken from the fire, which continually burns at the center of the tipi. The coals are placed on a decorated patch of earth, which is the altar. It lies between the fire and the sacred bundle. The ceremonial leader sits on one side of the altar, the bundle keeper on the other. Next to him sits his wife and one or two initiated children. Then comes the leader's wife, and beyond sit the other participants, men on the right and women on the left, looking from the doorway. Owners of important medicine bundles, along with chiefs and visiting dignitaries, are usually given seats closest to the altar. Others sit near the doorway, or in a second tipi, which faces the main one, and is left partly opened.

I had been to a number of medicine pipe ceremonies in Browning as an invited guest. But the one at Stabs Down's place was the first that I saw being held inside a tipi. It felt tremendously different from those that were in houses. There was a very sacred and mysterious atmosphere. Many of those present followed the traditional custom of wrapping themselves in blankets, and nearly all the talking was in Blackfoot.

Although we were late, the main part of the ceremony had not yet begun. The bundle still hung at the very back, across from the doorway, where it was tied to one of the tipi poles. A fringed, woolen shawl covered it. There followed many songs, prayers, and symbolic gestures that I had a hard time understanding, even though I had been studying this subject in books, papers, and photographs

Shadows of the Buffalo

for several years. I wondered if I could really learn this ceremony well enough to live by it, as Beverly and I hoped to do. At that point she began to realize there was a much greater seriousness to our planned undertaking than she had first thought.

After the bundle was untied—lying open and exposed between the keeper and the leader—there was the customary feast of sweetened wild-berry soup, followed by an assortment of other food. During a prayer over the soup, which is considered sacred, we each put one berry on the ground as an offering, and as a symbolic sharing with the Spirit World.

For the exciting part of the ceremony participants get up, one or two at a time, and dance with the medicine pipestem, or with other parts of the sacred bundle. To accompany them four men with strong voices sing special songs used only for this occasion. While singing, they beat on round hand drums, producing the dancing rhythm. The four singers on this occasion were quite old men, and I was surprised at the clearness and strength of their voices. The songs were in the form of chants, without words.

The time between this ceremony and the intended bundle transfer went quickly. We put together all the money that we owned, and spent a fair amount of it on blankets, dry goods, and horses. An older cousin had a good-sized herd from which he offered to sell us several head at a reasonable price. We also had to get new clothing and moccasins, to give away during the transfer in a symbolic re-dressing ritual.

When we went after the horses, the cousin's aged father—the brother of Beverly's grandmother—said he didn't think we would want them anymore. When we looked surprised he added: "Sure, didn't you hear that your transfer has been called off?" He had gotten the news from the ceremonial leader himself, the same man who had quietly been watching our growing dedication to Wolf Old Man.

We drove to the Old Man's house with heavy feelings again. If this opportunity failed, we were ready to give up our quest to be keepers of a medicine bundle. What then would given us the mental excuse and the spiritual power to resign from our youthful endeavors and take up the nearly lost traditional disciplines?

The Old Man had a message for us to go and see Stabs Down and his wife. When we got there they seemed apologetic for what they were about to tell us. It seemed that the ceremonial leader was their advisor—the same role that we originally asked him to take with us. He had lately come to them, saying that he could not sleep anymore because of what was about to happen to his sacred pipe bundle. In a dream he had been informed that I was actually a museum spy, and that I was with Beverly only to get near the old Indians and learn their secret ways. My first wife was waiting for me to get this information, as well as the bundle, after which she and I would disappear together and get rich by selling what I had gathered. He begged them to call off the transfer so that the bundle would not be lost.

My one season on the reserve, with Beverly, was certainly too short to make our side worth arguing, and I was ready to give up and leave. Then a casual comment by the couple brought out the fact that museum zealot Yellow Fly was again involved. He had been to see the ceremonial leader first, telling spurious tales to darken my image. Then he had gone to Stabs Down and asked how much we were planning to pay at the transfer. He seemed to think that we were playing his game—buying the bundle for its relic value—and he offered to pay double. The couple said they had made no decision in any direction, and they seemed to be sincerely confused. We agreed to wait and let them settle the matter.

The settling didn't take very long at all. Pat Weasel Head and his wife, Ponah, heard about our problem from Beverly's parents. They were respected traditional leaders, having gone through many sacred transfers. As three-time keepers of medicine pipe bundles, their opinions on the subject were usually accepted by everyone. They also happened to be aunt and uncle to Stabs Down's wife, Agnes. With a tremendous gesture of faith in Beverly and me, they placed their own reputations on the line and promised that we would take proper care of the bundle, and that we would transfer it to another Indian family whenever the time came to do so. Stabs Down and his wife accepted that promise, so the transfer went ahead as first scheduled.

It is for the retiring bundle keepers to select a leader for the transfer ceremony. In this case, Stabs Down hired our relative, White Horn, since his usual advisor refused to have anything to do with the matter. He was criticized by other elders, who said he should not have painted us and given his blessings in the first place if he felt that way. He avoided us for the next couple of years, and occasionally made other charges that proved groundless. Time eventually healed the wounds this caused, so that he and I became quite good friends after all.

The first part of the transfer ceremony is held in the lodge of the retiring keepers. During that time we were left to sit alone in our own tipi, which was pitched some distance away. Atsitsina helped us to put it up the previous afternoon, and we spent the night in it. We used a very old canvas cover that was said to have been hand-sewn back in the early 1900's. Two sons of the woman who sewed it were still alive, both of them elderly men. We got the tipi from one of them, who also transferred to us the rights to its painted design. It is red all over, with circles of yellow around the top and bottom to represent various stars and constellations. At the back is a lone yellow circle in honor of the moon. The tipi cover was mainly used during the tribe's annual summer ceremonies. From these it carries a great deal of good Spirit, along with a minimum of physical wear for its age.

We tried to relax while we sat in the tipi, awaiting our part of the ceremony. It was hard to believe that this ancient ritual was to be for us. We could hear distant sounds of talking and laughter, then drumming and singing as time went on. Beverly, Wolf, and I were alone, and we could see nothing outside. Beverly's parents had put up a large white tent next to our tipi to serve as a cookhouse, but even they were gone to see the events in the distance.

Back during the buffalo days strict duties for keepers of medicine pipes required so much time and energy that some families tired before anyone made vows to take their places. In such instances there was an interesting alternative. The keeper could "hire" several noted warriors and leaders, all of whom had to be former keepers, as well. It was their job to "capture" someone for the sacred duty. The head of this group carried the sacred pipestem with him, hidden beneath his blanket. If he found the intended new keeper inside his own lodge, the man could not refuse to accept the sacred pipe when it was handed to him.

This "capturing" of a new keeper is symbolically reenacted at every transfer, even if everyone involved has known and planned for the event for months. It was this capturing group that we awaited while we sat in our tipi. For me, that was a time of true reckoning, with myself and with my childhood dreams. I knew I was about to enter a spiritual door to a lifetime of mystery and power, and that there would be no more turning back. For Beverly, the door led to a deepening relationship with her own tribal past, which she had never imagined happening.

The capturing party finally arrived, to the tune of many little jingling bells. They were attached to the sacred pipestem and to other articles from the bundle that the men carried with them. White Horn was in the lead, wrapped in a white blanket with colored stripes. The men behind him were barely recognizable as they wore their blankets right up over their heads, with only parts of their faces showing. One by one they handed me the sacred articles and made blessing gestures over our heads. They did all this silently, while above us the tipi canvas flapped loudly in the wind.

Then they spread a large blanket on the ground and had me sit on it, holding the sacred articles in the crook of my arm. With the help of two younger men they picked me up and carried me out of our tipi and toward the place of the ceremony. Beverly and Wolf walked along behind.

Atsitsina appeared by our side, singing loudly the ancient honoring song of our family clan, the Many Children Band. He followed each rendition of the tune by calling out our names in loud, singsong fashion: "Natosina, *Ah-hey* . . . Sikskiaki, *Ah-hey* . . . Makwi

Poka, *Ah-hey . . ."* Then he announced the sacred duty we were
about to take over, prayed for our good luck, and called out words
of encouragement.

In the near distance we could hear Wolf Old Man's voice boom-
ing above three other drummers who were singing in Stabs Down's
tipi. Three times White Horn called a halt so that the carriers could
rest. He prayed for us continually, and in a loud voice. The wind
and our movements made the bells jingle from the sacred things in
my arms. Around us the wind rushed noisily through fresh green
prairie grass.

We made a fourth stop inside the tipi, which was again
crowded. I was placed at the back on the seat of the bundle keeper,
which was already vacant. Beverly sat down at my right, with Wolf
in between us. White Horn then sat down across from me and instructed me to place the sacred articles back with the rest of the
bundle. It lay open between him and me.

Wolf Old Man's red-painted face stood out among the crowd.
He beamed with pleasure, evidently glad that everything was finally
working out so well. He seemed especially proud because the event
concerned the sacred pipe of which he had once been keeper. For
many winters and summers it hung over the head of his own bed.
Now it was to be transferred to his adopted "grandchildren"—the
young ones who said they would try to learn his ways. He sang a
rousing honoring song that silenced everyone in the tipi. When he
finished he took up his drum and beat a rolling introduction to one of
the dance songs with his wooden drumstick.

As the other singers joined him, members of the capturing party
got back up and danced with the same sacred objects they had
brought to me. White Horn again led the group, followed by Arthur
Healy and Jim Red Crow, both of whom were former keepers of this
bundle, and Henry Standing Alone, a relative of ours who once had
the revered Longtime Pipe. The dancers demonstrated their spiritual
enthusiasm with rhythmic movements symbolic of Nature.

Perhaps the most important moment of a transfer ceremony is
when the retiring keeper dances out of the tipi with the sacred
pipestem to inspect the horses and other payments that should be

placed in front of his door. If he considers them good enough, he comes back in, dances to the new keeper, and hands him the sacred pipe. However, if he is not satisfied, he can tell the drummers to sing a special song during which he may request some additional sacrifice. In the past this was often a favorite and valuable horse. If the retiring owner considered the showing of payments a mockery he could put the pipe back in its bundle and call the whole affair off.

Stabs Down's teenage son, Wallace, as initiated keeper, danced outside to inspect our goods. Our main payment was to have been seven head of horses, some of which we already had. But before we managed to buy them all, Stabs Down sent word that a misfortune in his family required money, and that he would prefer cash rather than the additional horses. Besides, he already had a herd of his own that he hardly used. The best of our offerings was a thoroughbred quarterhorse, more valuable than any horse I had ever owned. In addition, we had a good riding mare and colt, plus a large number of twenty-dollar bills sewn to a costly Hudson's Bay woolen blanket, according to custom. For transfers held during the tribal encampment, such money-covered blankets are usually paraded around the camp circle on the backs of horses, so that everyone can see what is being paid. Besides horses and money, we had quite a pile of blankets, clothing, and other goods that Beverly's parents piled by the door for us.

We held our breaths when young Wallace danced out, hoping that all our spiritual hopes and prayers would not be obliterated at this final moment for lack of sufficient material payments. But after only a brief glance at everything, the boy came back in and danced toward us. At the end of the fourth song he handed the sacred object to me, saying in a low voice: "You got yourself this holy pipe!" Then he turned around and walked to a seat by the door.

With that simple gesture we received the key to our spiritual door. During the ceremony that followed, we were painted in the peculiar style of medicine pipe keepers, given new clothing and blankets, as well as special shell necklaces and bead wristlets to wear. Each step had symbolism and meaning that we were expected to learn in the seasons ahead.

A transfer within the transfer took place when the little grand-daughter of the elderly Weasel Heads gave up her rights to wear the sacred "topknot" from the bundle. This strip of otterskin is an ancient symbol of medicine pipe keepers, who used to wear it wrapped around a queue of hair formed over their foreheads. Nowadays this symbol is usually transferred to a child of the family, who is then considered something like assistant keeper. In this case, the strip was ritually wound around a small queue that Beverly had made for Wolf. We gave up another thoroughbred quarterhorse, plus another pile of blankets, dry goods, and moccasins in payment for this.

When the transfer rituals were completed the whole crowd got up and headed for our red-painted tipi. White Horn got the bundle tied up and placed on Beverly's back, where she held it by a sturdy strap passed around her shoulders. Then he led the way to our lodge while continually praying. Beverly followed behind him with the bundle, while Wolf and I came last. It has always been a woman's duty to handle medicine pipe bundles, and to look after their daily care, including morning and evening incense. For camp moving in the past, an especially tame horse was kept for carrying nothing but the bundle.

It was evening by the time we finally finished the last of the ceremony, which consisted of more praying and dancing. By that time the gathering had a joyous feeling of unity that I wished would last forever. I did not think about the sadness of seeing those same happy elders slowly passing away in the following years.

When everything was over Atsitsina came up and gave me a hug—our first one—and said that he wished I were his son. Out of happiness I handed him my new blanket coat, which Beverly and her mother had made for me out of a Hudson Bay blanket the previous Christmas. He admired it from the moment I got it, and I knew he would be thrilled to wear it as his own. In those few moments our feelings for each other reached new heights. We discovered a deep bond of love and respect that transcended our many outer differences.

3

EXCITING NEWS WAS HEARD during the day of the transfer ceremony. A Sun Dance, or medicine lodge ceremony, was going to be held among the Montana Blackfeet in the coming summer. Earlier, rumors had hinted of this possibility, but now the story was confirmed by Mrs. Rides-at-the-Door, the elderly Sun Dance woman of the Bloods. She said that a young Blackfoot man had gone to war, in Vietnam, and during a battle received supernatural instructions to sponsor this powerful ceremony if he wished to get back to his people alive.

No one at our ceremony seemed to know the young man in question. It was said that he was a mixed-blood, and that his wife, who would be the "holy woman," was a mixed-blood from another tribe. Since she could speak no Blackfoot, the elders wondered who would instruct her in English. Such a thing had never been done in Blackfoot history.

Later, when more specific plans for this important event were announced, Makes Summer sent word for us to be there. He had not forgotten his promise to teach me the sacred duties within the medicine lodge. I wondered what the old folks thought about all this, since they had been so convinced that there would never be a Blackfoot Sun Dance again.

Back in the buffalo days the whole tribe camped together only once a year, during the Sun Dance. The rest of the time the people scattered out across their domain according to family bands, who kept in close touch with each other. When the whole tribe camped in one place it did not take long to use up the area's firewood and grazing, or for the buffalo herds to move away. Each of the four Blackfoot divisions had its own Sun Dance, which members from the others often attended. These were favorite occasions for visiting friends and relatives. There is no record of a time when all the divisions camped together. That would have made an impressive sight, since around the end of the last century the circle camps of the Montana Blackfeet alone were more than a mile in circumference.

In our photo collection we have scenes showing hundreds of Blackfoot tipis gathered for Sun Dances, even though the people were already well settled on their reservations, and spending most of their time in log cabins and houses. The summer celebrations reasserted tribal faith, which missionaries and government agents wanted to stamp out.

Lengthy tribal legends tell of a young man whose love for a beautiful girl caused him to seek the home of Sun. The girl said she was promised to Sun in a vision, and that she could have no man without Sun's permission. After facing many trials and challenges the young man reached his goal, and eventually found favor with Sun, who appeared in mystical human form. The young man not only got permission to marry the girl, but also instructions for his people to perform Sun's favorite ceremony. He was told that the ceremony always required a woman as true as the beautiful girl he married.

Missionaries condemned the Blackfoot faith in Nature as "Sun worship." Outsiders often thought the people considered Sun as God, which is only partly true. In Blackfoot belief *everything* is a part of God, who is called the Creator. Sun is only the most obvious symbol of that Creator. Most Nature-oriented people agree with this.

Sun Dance is a term that more accurately describes the summer festivals of other Plains tribes. Blackfoot people use it to describe their own ceremonies only when speaking in English. Dancing in honor of Sun is one of the many rituals they perform at that time. The most important ritual is the erection of a log-and-pole structure said to resemble the place where the long-ago youth found Sun during his mystical journey. This whole matter is so complex that it has been the subject of several thick, scholarly volumes. In the past it called for the participation of every member in the tribe.

Our photo collection documents the sad decline of interest in this tribal celebration. Over the years the camp circle grew continually smaller, even while the Blackfoot people increased three- and fourfold in population. Changing lifestyles and modern influences brought about a tribal disinterest more devastating than the many ultimatums and efforts by government agents and Christian missionaries.

So it was at this Sun Dance that we attended among the Montana Blackfeet, the summer after our bundle transfer. Elders said it was the smallest ever of such gatherings. Ceremonial leaders and "holy women" from three divisions worked together in order to complete the sacred rites. The main holy woman was nearly one hundred years old. With a few more years of waiting she would have been gone, taking with her the rights to perform this ceremony.

Not just any woman can qualify for the Sun Dance, or the medicine lodge ceremonies. She must be an honest and virtuous woman—a virgin, or one who has been totally faithful to her husband throughout life. Blackfoot customs stress these virtues, although many women have succumbed to other temptations. But even among the truly virtuous few are eager to put themselves through this ceremonial test. If anyone in the tribe doubts her honesty, the holy woman may be publicly shamed. Even worse, if anything goes wrong during the ceremony, or if any relative of the woman has an unusual accident in the seasons after, that will be taken as evidence that she lied about her virtue. This was the main reason why tribal elders felt there would be no more Sun Dance ceremonies in our modern days.

In spite of the small camp and poor attendance, the elders were pleased that this young soldier and his wife were willing to take on such an important challenge and duty. She would be the first young "holy woman" in many years. It was ironic that for the second time in a short period the future outlook for important Blackfoot ceremonies improved because of the involvement of "newcomers" to the tribe.

Mrs. Rides-at-the-Door asked us to bring her to the sacred campground in Montana. She took Beverly as a "granddaughter," as she did all the girls in the tribe. Besides sponsoring the tribal Sun Dances, she and her late husband had also been keepers of a medicine pipe bundle, as well as other sacred articles. While traveling with us she talked about them, and gave Beverly valuable advice.

The old woman was friendly to everyone, and always greeted me with a heartwarming smile. However, as I was her "grandson-in-law," she avoided direct communication with me, even when we were in the same house or car. One time she told Beverly of an embarrassing incident in this regard. One of her real granddaughters had moved to a city where she married a black man, who was said to be a friendly fellow. When the two came to the Reserve for a visit, he was introduced to his grandmother-in-law. Out of apparent enthusiasm the young man gave the old woman an unexpected hug and kiss, which upset her traditional conscience a great deal. She said the black man felt very badly about it when informed of his breach of customs.

Although the season was still early and cool, Browning was already experiencing the added dust caused by summer traffic. The nearby mountains were still covered with snow, and the prairie grasses had not begun to turn yellow from the seasonal heat. The Sun Dance was being held a little ahead of the ancient schedule, which called for the time "when berries are ripe," or "when Sun is closest to Earth."

We drove through the mountains on our way to Browning from the Blood Reserve, skirting the borders of Glacier National Park. The Sun Dance camp was to form on a flat above Cutbank Creek, just a few miles from where it flowed out of the park. This was the site of the Starr School Community, one of several villages around the reservation. They were originally settled by the various family bands. The young Sun Dance couple lived at Starr School, which was named in honor of George Starr, a well-liked mixed-blood of the early reservation period.

We had gone to Starr School first, thinking to set up our tipi and help others with starting the encampment, but we found the proposed site deserted. Unsure of the cause, we drove into Browning to find out.

Browning is the last of several sites used by the government for its agencies to serve the Blackfeet of Montana. It has always been a reservation town, dusty and underdeveloped. Tourists drive through in large numbers during the summer season, since it straddles the main highway approaching Glacier Park from the east. Basic tourist services are available, but most travelers find the stark simplicity of Indian life around Browning much less glamorous than their romantic imaginations care to experience. At best, they may stop at the end of town to visit the government-run Museum of the Plains Indian, where the most colorful parts of native life are safely on display.

To find out about the Sun Dance camp we went to Browning's largest grocery store. There, the "moccasin telegraph" would provide us with the latest news. Most anyone can be a link in this traditional system. It did not take long for us to hear that the encampment would not be starting until the next day. Unfortunately, because of the vague nature of this kind of reporting, we could not be sure that the information was fully correct. We decided to pass some time in the town and then head back out to look at the campsite once more.

Mrs. Rides-at-the-Door seemed glad when I suggested we go look through the museum. I don't know if she had seen it before, but most members of the Blackfoot Nation are familiar with its public displays. The family heirlooms of many are housed there, having been sold mostly by elders who thought the interest for their old ways was otherwise gone. Unfortunately, most of these relics are stored elsewhere, out of sight.

The old holy woman seemed to enjoy the displays that we saw after first entering the fortresslike building. She made comments about some of the clothing and other articles from the past. But I had forgotten about the contents of one glass display case until I saw a pained look on her face that told me it was too late to keep her away from it. Mounted on a blank-faced plaster head was an old headdress of plumes and feathers, with many little symbols attached to its rawhide headband. It was a Natoas—the sacred headdress of the Sun Dance. Traditionally it should be brought out only with the proper ritual, and only during the medicine lodge ceremonies. It can be worn by none but the initiated holy women. It was almost identical to the one Mrs. Rides-at-the-Door kept hanging over her own bed, protected by a well-worn bag of thick rawhide. It was out in our truck, right then, waiting to be used at the upcoming ceremonial. This one at the museum was simply displayed like a fifty-dollar Stetson hat.

Mrs. Rides-at-the-Door muttered something in Blackfoot as she sadly shook her head. Then she said, out loud and to no one in particular: "Do they not consider anything sacred?" At that she hobbled from the museum in disgust, holding her wooden cane almost as though she would have liked to knock it against something. When we got to our truck she turned and said to Beverly: "I have a good mind to come back here and take that Natoas from this place!" We were not sure how serious she was about trying.

By the time we got back out to the Starr School area, a wind was blowing across the prairies so strongly that I didn't think we'd be able to set up our tipi, even if the time for starting the encampment had arrived. However, the proposed site was still vacant, and I had a hard time imagining that in a few days a real Sun Dance might be taking place there.

By a nearby log house we encountered an elderly woman named Katie Home Gun. She appeared younger than Mrs. Rides-at-the-Door, and was dressed in more modern fashion. Yet the old lady surprised us not only by saying Katie was her friend, but also that the younger woman had been a Sun Dance holy woman in her younger days. Since that time Katie Home Gun had remarried and given up the strict vows of her office. She assured us that there was going to be a Sun Dance, and said that the soldier who made the vow for it was her grandson. We asked her to guide us to his home.

We were brought to a meager little house that sat next door to the community's Baptist Church, which consisted of a small white wooden building. We wanted to know the plans for the encampment, but no one at the house knew them. The pledging couple seemed unfamiliar with the whole procedure, and their grandmother had been away from it for so long that she had uncertain recollections.

Mrs. Rides-at-the-Door spoke with Katie Home Gun in Blackfoot, which was translated into English for the vow-maker and his wife. She tried to tell them to go ahead and get their tipi set up, but they preferred to wait for the very aged holy woman, Mrs. Many Guns, who was going to do the ritual transferring.

The vow-maker was about my age, somewhat heavyset, with shoulder-length hair and tinted glasses. His wife was light-skinned, and shy. Somehow she immediately impressed me as being the kind of person that a young Sun Lodge woman should be. She discreetly nursed a newborn baby in her arms.

We finally decided to drive back to Browning, where old Mrs. Many Guns was said to be staying with relatives. We found her, and she was relieved to hear that Mrs. Rides-at-the-Door had arrived. She was depending on her to help with much of the ritual work, since her old-age blindness was a severe handicap. When she found out that Beverly was also there, she cheerfully called her "granddaughter," and asked about her grandmother, Hilda, who was her own relative and a lifelong friend.

Mrs. Many Guns was quite a talkative and humorous woman. She was small and very thin, but spoke with a loud and clear voice. Her hair was neatly braided and absolutely white. Soon after we got there she asked: "And where is our son-in-law, your husband?" Beverly jokingly replied: "He is sitting near you and you are looking right at him!" She squealed with concern, thinking she was violating the old customs. But when she learned that it was not so, she laughed merrily with the rest.

The two old women then discussed the sacred ceremony and the encampment for it. Mrs. Many Guns said that she was too scared to go camping during the terrible windstorm, but she insisted the others should go ahead as soon as it was possible to set up the tipis. They could come and get her when everything was prepared.

It was getting late in the day by the time we made our third visit to the campsite. Nothing had been done yet, even though the wind was finally slowing down. We gave the waiting party the old woman's message, but they were still hesitant about going ahead without her. It was finally agreed that we should at least take a load of tipi poles to the site and mark out the general area.

As though word of our activity had gone out on the "moccasin telegraph" a heavy-duty farm truck showed up with a big load of tipi poles that belonged to the tribe. A husky middle-aged man named "Buster" Yellow Kidney was the driver. He smiled, gave a cheerful greeting, and said he had come to help. Although he had the look of a progressive Indian and wore the badge of a tribal policeman, he had learned the old tribal traditions as a boy, while growing up in the home of his grandfather, Yellow Kidney, who was a leading elder.

Within a short time other people showed up, mostly from the surrounding homes of the Starr School community. Their presence was important, since tipi-raising often requires several persons. That may be one reason why the vow-maker hesitated to get started earlier. We soon had the tipi up for him and his wife, although they did not stay in it that first night. Ours was put up next, but by that time there were so many helpers that we ended up with too many "chiefs," each one giving slightly different instructions. As a result our tipi went up poorly and looked so lopsided that the first strong wind would have blown it back down. In the gathering darkness we decided to leave it for the night and come back the next day to try again. With some disappointment we drove back to town and stayed in a motel. So much for our first night in a real Sun Lodge encampment!

The following morning we got back to the campground early. We immediately took the tipi back down, before anyone else could see it and laugh at us. Beverly and Mrs. Rides-at-the-Door returned to town to bring Mrs. Many Guns, while I sat on the dismantled tipi, feeling forlorn, hoping someone would come by to help me put it up properly.

Before long my friends George and Molly Kicking Woman

drove up in their new truck. They were among the elders who had welcomed me during my very first visit to the reservation, at the time of the Indian Days powwow. I knew they were experienced at setting up tipis. In no time they measured the canvas cover against some of the long, slim poles. Tying some ropes here and there, they soon showed me how to lift it with only three persons. By the time Beverly came back with the old women the tipi was ready to be furnished inside.

After Beverly tied up the draft-stopping curtains and arranged our rugs and sleeping places, Mrs. Rides-at-the-Door brought in her own bedding, which she arranged near the door. She said she would stay with us until the sacred ceremonies were ready to start, after which she would remain with the young Sun Dance couple. Her grandsons brought in their own blankets and pillows, on which they spent a lot of time sleeping and reading comic books.

We were both new at tipi camping, and at being part of a traditional camp. Besides that, it was our first time of staying in a tipi with our new medicine pipe bundle. Mrs. Rides-at-the-Door instructed Beverly in hanging it over our bed, making its altar for incense, and bringing it outside each morning and back in at night. During the daytime, in good weather, it was kept suspended from a special stick over the doorway.

Every morning and evening she joined us while we made incense and prayed. Sometimes I sang one or two sacred songs, as well. I was just learning to do these things, and my inexperience must have been very noticeable, but the old lady was kind about it and made only encouraging remarks. Back home on the reserve, some weeks later, we heard rumors that I had been performing "mysterious ceremonies" during the encampment, and that the old lady had been so "overpowered" by them that she finally moved out and left us. I don't know how many persons the story went through before it became so imaginative, but the old lady thought it was very funny. However, some people took it seriously and said that I was possessed of magical powers.

The camp grew very slowly at first, as is the custom with events operated on so-called "Indian time." By the following weekend there were only a half-dozen tipis, and about the same number of canvas "wall tents." Among the people who drove by to visit, several said they would come and camp "as soon as things get going." I was somewhat annoyed by this attitude, thinking that if everyone else felt the same way nothing would get going at all.

During one of the first nights a tremendous thunderstorm passed by and nearly blew the camp out of existence. Tipi poles and canvas covers rattled and flapped so hard that I was sure they could not hold up long. I had not yet learned to have much faith in this ancient form of dwelling. Rain followed wind and drenched everyone, inside and out. Part of the campground was left standing in water, but we had been lucky in selecting a higher spot for our tipi, so we remained fairly dry.

While the storm was raging, a bearded man with his head well covered peeked through our doorway and asked if he could come in for shelter. We had to motion for him to do so, since the bundle's regulations did not allow us to speak with someone outside. When he got settled he told us he was seeking advice. He had read the book *Black Elk Speaks* (the story of a Sioux holy man from the past), and now he was on the road looking for an old Indian like Black Elk.

My first response was to suggest that if the bearded man wanted to make friends with old Indians he should shave his beard. This seemed to take him aback. He replied that the kind of wise man he was looking for would not judge him by appearance. But I explained that most Plains Indian men have no facial hair and often react unfavorably to the sight of it. To their forefathers beards were often symbols of strangers and enemies.

During the discussion that followed, our visitor made it clear that he was looking for a "guru," like many others at that time. We tried to tell him that he was among the wrong Indians—the ones he should visit were on another continent. The native people of North America have generally been too involved with life's daily struggles to follow gurus. Their spiritual wisdom has grown from a life of hunting wild animals, fighting human enemies, and surviving harsh environments. Their spiritual leaders were principally people of action, not of meditation.

We nicknamed the bearded man "Don Juan," after he said that Carlos Castaneda's popular book by that name was his favorite. I tried to suggest that he had read too many such books. They tend to make Indian people and their lives seem overly ideal. But then I realized that I was guilty of doing the same thing in my own writings.

After the storm was over "Don Juan" set up a little nylon tent for himself, out on the prairie at the edge of the camp. He seemed to have no trouble making friends in the following days, especially among the adolescents, who were attracted to his flashy motorcycle. It was a German-made BMW, the same kind that attracted my childhood friends and me back in Europe. The soft purr of its high-powered motor, not far from our tipi, made me recall some of those times of my earlier life.

One result of being first to get settled in the camp was that I was available to help others set up their tents and tipis. Among these was an elderly Blood couple—Albert Chief Calf and his wife—who were brought by younger relatives too busy to stay. The old fellow was a big man, and still quite strong for his age, although he was practically blind. When I saw him he was on his hands and knees, trying to fit together the wooden posts for the frame of their tent. His wife—who could see well—was calling out the directions. But she was partly crippled, so she could not help with the physical work.

When I went over and told them that I would help, the old man smiled and reached out for my hand. He said he had already measured the poles and sawed them to the proper lengths. All that needed to be done was to nail them together and lift them up, along with the canvas cover. I told him that we would have it done in no time.

Nearby were two large families putting up similar tents, but they must have been too busy unpacking to notice this old couple's plight. They paid no attention until we tried to lift the nailed-together poles into place. At that point a couple of them came to lend a hand, and the others stopped to watch. Shortly the whole crowd broke out laughing. The old man's eyesight had been too poor to measure the poles correctly. The upright ones should have been much shorter. When the tent was up, it looked fine, except that the bottom of it was a couple of feet off the ground all around. It looked so ridiculous that I had to laugh, too, even though I was embarrassed at the same time. But when his wife told the old man the problem, even he started laughing. He bent down so that he could see the light in the space underneath.

It only took a few minutes to saw the posts off to the correct length and get the tent set back up properly. After I got their bedding and meager belongings stacked inside, I left these old folks and went to help another family put up their painted tipi. By evening of that day—about the fifth or sixth since we arrived—the camp had grown from a few scattered tents and tipis into a small village of several dozen homes. From them came the cheerful sounds of children, laughing and playing. Smoke could be seen rising from openings at the tops of the tipis, and from metal chimneys protruding out of tents. Within these canvas dwellings there were sounds of cooking and conversation. At last there was life in this, our first Sun Lodge camp!

We never learned just why things took so long to get started during that encampment. Nearly a full week went by with nothing more exciting than the setting up of lodges, although rumors regularly had us believing that ceremonies would start "tomorrow." Not even Mrs. Rides-at-the-Door was sure about the ceremonial plans, but she didn't seem to be in a hurry about them, either. Since Indian culture has neither watches nor written calendars, it has a history of time that feels very "timeless." Non-Indians often find this frustrating, especially when they are having business dealings with Indian people, or when they expect something within a specified period. Of course, many modern Indians carry watches, and have learned how to guide their daily lives with them. The "Indian time" of more relaxed and traditional neighbors sometimes annoys them, as well.

When the sacred ceremonies finally began in the vowing couple's tipi, the news traveled quickly through the "moccasin telegraph." By the next day the camp's population grew from about one hundred people to three or four times that many. In fact, for a while it seemed as though a major event was under way, although we had been told that there would be nothing for the public to see until the fourth day. We soon learned the cause of all the interest from relatives who stopped by our tipi for a visit. They said the reservation's tribal council was contributing several thousand dollars toward the costs of the ceremonial, mainly in the form of food that was to be handed out as rations.

"Don Juan" soon came by and confirmed this story, telling us that he had been requested to help set up a row of tables on which the food was to be placed. The tables were unloaded from a large truck, which also brought the rations. Included were boxes of apples and bananas, sacks of potatoes, and crates of canned goods. In addition, there seemed to be enough loaves of bread to completely fill a tipi, and several cases of soda pop. Unfortunately, the bread was the common, store-bought white stuff, which our kids called "air bread." Squeezed together it might only have taken up half a tipi, or even less!

Rations were brought to all the tents and tipis first. The balance, which seemed to be the larger share, was given out to those who had come to the camp expressly for that purpose. Some of it was consumed right away, especially the pop, bananas, and other "snack foods." By the time this visiting crowd left, the camp had lost its appeal as a clean village on an untrampled prairie. Luckily, winds later blew much of the trash away.

Beverly looked forward to a special initiation that Mrs. Rides-at-the-Door said she would perform for her during the Sun Lodge ceremonies. She was to receive a certain necklace representing these sacred rites. One night, while she stayed with us in our tipi, she rummaged through a small suitcase and showed it to us. It had a soft buckskin strap on which were beads, seashells, and a small, braided hairlock. It was coated with sacred red paint and kept in a small sack.

The initiation for this necklace took place in the tipi of the vow-makers during the final day of their private rituals. Shortly after that they came out to attend the public raising of the sacred Sun Lodge. The new "holy woman" wore the Natoas headdress as she walked in a procession with her husband and the elders who had attended them. Quite a large crowd came to the encampment to witness this highlight of the ceremonies. All stood quietly as the procession went from private tipis to the sacred lodge.

The time of raising the Sun Lodge is also the only occasion on which medicine pipes can be smoked. This is considered a special blessing for the pipes, their keepers, and all those who take part. It was a blessing that we wanted to experience, and for which Wolf Old Man had given us instructions. He had come down to visit us at the camp one day with his cousin and chauffeur, Mike Yellow Bull.

We wished the Old Man would camp with us during this Sun Dance, but he said he was too old to do so. Actually there was another reason, though he did not speak about it. He was a known leader of certain Sun Dance functions. By Blackfoot customs he should have been personally invited to take part in this ceremony. Since he was not, it would have been a breach of those customs for him to show up anyway. He didn't seem hurt by this slight, knowing that the leaders of the ceremony probably thought his participation would be too much strain for him. When he arrived in Mike's car he got out and came directly into our tipi. When we finished visiting he got right back into the car with Mike, and left.

Wolf Old Man was not around when it came time for us to bring out the medicine pipe. However, the elder who had talked against our getting the bundle in the first place was in camp, and he began to talk against us. He complained that the bundle belonged to the Bloods and should not be opened during a ceremony of the Piegans, as the Montana Blackfeet were originally called. He seemed to forget that these same bundles were often transferred back and forth among the four Blackfoot divisions in the past. He also ignored the fact that the "holy women" inside the sacred lodge were from three of those divisions. Nevertheless, his talking made us lose courage, so we decided to pass up this special chance.

Albert Chief Calf, the almost-blind old man whose tent I had helped put up, was one of the leaders of medicine pipe ceremonies among the Bloods. We had talked to him about bringing our pipe out for smoking, and he agreed to unbundle it for us. Now he sent Pat Weasel Head to ask if we were ready to start. When we told Pat how we felt he scoffed and said we should not let "the idle talk of others" interfere with our intentions. He added that gossip and mean criticisms have no place in sacred events like the Sun Dance. He cheered us up until we agreed to go ahead with our original plans.

For the next couple hours we seemed to be in another world from the modern one around us. The sacred Sun Lodge stood in the center of the tipi camp, as had countless others like it in ages past. Although the crowd was largely dressed in modern clothing, there was a tribal spirit and unity of sacred purpose that seemed to transcend historical changes. Pat Weasel Head walked ahead of us when we left our tipi, clearing the way to where the holy party sat, waiting. We had our faces painted, and were wearing moccasins and blankets. In my hands I held the long and elaborately decorated sacred pipe. It was the only one in the camp.

The ceremonial leader of the Sun Dance was first to smoke the pipe, after he made a special prayer. He was followed by the others of the sacred party, and then by a number of elders in the nearby crowd. As I held the mouthpiece from one person to the next, I felt humble and nervous, and also unusually strange. I was a misplaced European, acting as bearer of this most sacred article handed down from the forefathers of these same people. There seemed to be hundreds of faces waiting eagerly for an opportunity to receive the pipe's blessings, but Pat Weasel Head soon led us away and back to our tipi. There is a special way for nonkeepers to behave in front of medicine pipes, and many of these people did not seem to know about it. The old man was afraid that someone might violate the strict rules of protocol, especially after one stone-faced, elderly man refused to smoke the pipe at all. We later learned that he was a devout follower of the Full Gospel faith, which considers traditional ceremonies to be "heathen ways." He was probably at the camp out of nostalgia, since his father had been both a Sun Dance leader and keeper of a medicine pipe.

The single most exciting event of each Sun Dance is the raising of the sacred lodge's "Center Pole," a heavy, forked tree that represents the center of the universe. This event was ready to begin by the time we had the pipe closed back up in its bundle. We quickly went out and joined the crowd, which was still growing larger. It is well known that the raising of this pole usually comes just about at sunset.

The Sun Lodge consists of a circular framework of forked posts connected to each other by long poles. A large hole is dug in the space at their center. With its butt-end near that hole, the large Center Pole was already lying in place, waiting to be lifted, when we got there. Some men were attaching ropes to its forked upper end, while others were gathering spare tipi poles and tying them together in pairs near their tips. When these were ready they were held up by pairs of men, who stood in a loose circle around the edge of the camp. Suddenly they begin singing—a hauntingly beautiful song that was taken up by the rest of the crowd. It has been called the tribal anthem, since it is the only Blackfoot song sung by so many people at once.

During a pause in the singing the men with their paired poles moved forward. After another round of the same song they moved forward again. During the fourth round they were right at the edge of the sacred lodge, after which they rapidly converged on the still-lying Center Pole. Some began to pull the Center Pole upward with ropes, while others struggled to get their paired poles into the forks of the big pole in order to help lift it up.

For a few moments there was an immense silence, while everyone concentrated on the task. At first the pole slid along the ground until its butt reached the hole and went partway into it. The crowd seemed nearly breathless as the pole swayed and wobbled. A mistake at that point would not only have caused many injuries, but would have been taken as a very bad omen by the whole tribe. Suddenly the butt-end jarred loose and slid way down into the hole, leaving the forked end standing tall and straight. The crowd went wild—men and women shouted and screamed as though they had just accomplished a major victory in battle. In fact, the event does symbolize a tribal victory over the many challenges that face the people in their yearly rounds. Even those who probably knew little about these traditional meanings seemed caught up by the enthusiasm. There was a brief feeling of group ecstasy that I, for one, had never experienced before. I can only try to imagine how this might have felt a hundred years earlier, when the whole tribe took part in this wonderful festival every year.

After the Center Pole was raised, loose earth and rocks were quickly thrown into the hole to fill up the extra space and make it stand firmly. A number of long, thin poles were pushed up into the Center Pole's fork, their other ends resting on the circular lodge framework, where they were tied tightly with strips of fresh rawhide. From a bird's-eye view the completed lodge would have looked like a large, spoked wheel. At that point the vows of the holy woman and her husband were considered completed. While the last rays of Sun came down over the nearby mountains, visitors and spectators drove away from the camp, leaving wind-blown clouds of dust to settle on the tents and tipis. I found myself wondering if such a powerful tribal event would happen again.

The next morning dawned cloudy and cool. Mountain peaks lay hidden under swirling mists, and the possibility of a storm during the day appeared likely. It was an auspicious time to be initiated by Makes Summer for the role of Weather Dancer. Makes Summer had come by for a brief visit the evening before, warning of the possibility of a storm. The people were to gather within the newly completed Sun Lodge for a day of dancing and other festivities. It would be our job to see that they had pleasant weather.

On that cloudy morning Makes Summer brought me to the now-vacant tipi used by the Sun Dance party during their four days of private ceremonies. There, he painted my face and gave me an introduction to the mysterious ways of his weather-making office. I was instructed to wear nothing but a white shirt, white breach-cloth, and white, undecorated moccasins. My face, legs, and arms were all coated with red paint. Over my shoulders I wore a cape of thin white cloth, and my hair was unbraided and left to hang down. For each of these things Makes Summer had an explanation, although he dressed himself to appear different than I. He also brought out several small, symbolic objects, some of which he and I wore, and others we carried. He said it would take time to gain faith in the mystical powers represented by these things, in order to succeed with their purpose.

He was still explaining things to me when another old man from the camp looked in through the doorway and asked if we were ready to go. Makes Summer led the way out, where we found four elderly men with hand drums, waiting to accompany us to the Sun Lodge. Makes Summer hummed the start of a certain song that he wanted them to use. After they caught on to it they began singing and beating their drums.

We paused four times on our way to the lodge, dancing up and down on our feet at each stop. We kept time to the drumming by blowing on small whistles made from the wing bones of eagles. Eagles are considered the most noble of birds, and these whistles symbolized both their power and a call for the Spirit World to join us.

By the time we made our fourth and final stop, inside the sacred lodge, the vow-making couple and their elders joined us. They went to a prepared place near the back of the lodge and sat down, while we went into a specially constructed booth next to them. It was at the extreme back of the Sun Lodge—the place of honor. Directly in front of us stood the Center Pole. Our booth was made of leaf-covered branches piled on a framework of posts and poles. As the rest of the Sun Lodge filled with people, no one entered our booth, or even walked in front of it.

After a while the drummers began to sing again. This time they were joined by several others who knew the songs. They were seated on logs next to our booth, on the other side from the holy party. Makes Summer and I got up to dance, standing in one place and facing the Center Pole, gazing up into its fork and at the vast universe beyond. At first I felt conspicuous as the only non-Indian participant, but soon I forgot all about it. The crowd kept growing, along with a feeling of respect and sacredness that I sensed in the air.

Across the way from our booth was a large opening in the walls of the Sun Lodge, which was otherwise covered by leafy branches. After the lodge was filled with people, many more gathered around this opening to watch. A few of the people came up to our booth seeking blessings of facial paintings and prayers, for which I again felt humbled. If they had any dubious feelings about my ancestry they did not show it.

About the middle of the day dark clouds began rolling over the encampment. Rain threatened to interrupt the activities at any moment, and I began to feel concerned. Makes Summer said we must concentrate even harder to keep the storm away, although the situation seemed nearly hopeless to me. There are published accounts by respected ethnologists who witnessed the scattering of impending storms by earlier Weather Dancers, on similar occasions. In this case, after Makes Summer performed a brief ritual with the hat he had given to me, several hundred people watched in awe as the clouds suddenly broke and allowed sunshine to stream down on us. The experience amazed me, and gave me a surge of faith that sent me even deeper into these ancient and mysterious ways.

By the time the final dancing and ceremonies were completed, dark clouds again covered the skies. A thick gray mass spread from the mountains eastward, out into the open prairie as far as our eyes could see. We hurriedly took down our tipi, packed up our gear, and loaded everything into the camper box on the back of our truck. By the time we pulled out of camp, huge raindrops pelted our windshield. As the wipers went back and forth, Mrs. Rides-at-the-Door sat quietly (by the door) and looked out the passenger window. A smile of contentment caused creases and wrinkles to move upward on her face. She said nothing, but it was obvious that she was immensely pleased with the success of her sacred tribal work.

Later that same summer we joined another sacred encampment, this time the "Sun Dance" of the Bloods. They are the only Blackfoot division who have never missed a year of this annual tribal encampment, although an actual Sun Lodge was not always vowed or built. This summer was one of those times when there was no sacred lodge.

The Blood camp was near the Belly River, underneath the buttes by the same name that Atsitsina, Wolf Old Man, and I drove past during our journey to ask for the medicine pipe. The site is an ancient one in Blood history, and regarded as being so sacred that it may not be fenced or cultivated. Although only a small percentage of the tribe's six thousand people actually came to camp there, most of the others still had faith in benefits from the various ceremonies and prayers that were to be made. That is why Wolf Old Man said we must go there and bring the medicine pipe bundle. Other keepers also brought theirs.

We would like to have used our old, handsewn, red-painted tipi, but it seemed too frail to be safe in strong winds. During our pipe transfer ceremony some of the spectators leaned too heavily on its doorway and caused several of the seams to rip. Since Beverly's mother was a noted tipi maker, we asked her to help make us a new lodge. For a hundred dollars and a couple of days' sewing (with an ordinary treadle machine) we ended up with a sturdy, new, Blackfoot-style tipi large enough to house our family and several guests. Beverly's grandmother aided our efforts to have a traditional home by giving us her rights to paint it yellow, with black otters and other symbols drawn around it. Atsitsina performed the ritual in which these rights were transferred.

Atsitsina himself owned the famous and highly regarded Buffalo-painted tipi design of the Bloods, which he eventually gave to us. But at this time he still wished to use the design himself, so we gladly accepted what was commonly called the Yellow-Otter Lodge from Beverly's grandmother.

The Blood Sun Dance camp was still sparsely populated when we set up our new, yellow-painted tipi, with the help of Beverly's father and Pat Weasel Head. Pat and his wife also owned a Yellow-Otter Lodge, although its designs were slightly different from ours, indicating that it originated from a separate mystical encounter. It had been transferred to them many years before by an elderly couple of the northernmost division, who are known as the Siksika, which means "Blackfoot." Somehow history has given the name of this division to all four groups, although in their native language the other three groups never called themselves that at all.

The Blood encampment lasted for nearly three weeks—twice as long as the one in Montana. In addition, at least twice as many people camped there, and they were practically all Bloods. Since the Montana reservation was nearly twice as populous, the camp sizes symbolized great differences in cultural survival between the two groups.

Although there was no Sun Lodge put up during the encampment at the Belly Buttes, many other traditional activities took place. Most important among these were secret meetings and public dances of the tribe's two leading societies—the Horns of the men, and the Motokiks of the women. Since Beverly and I had nothing to do with either of them, we had much time to rest and enjoy the old-time tribal style of life. Relatives frequently came to visit us, along with friends, both old and new. For many Bloods it was the first opportunity to see the "white man" whose traditional efforts had been topics of several "moccasin telegrams."

Almost every night during this encampment we went to sleep to sounds of drumming and singing. Sometimes we heard lively music performed mainly for social enjoyment, other times the tunes were ancient and sacred-sounding ones coming from special lodges used by the societies. In the middle of the night we were likely to hear still different songs from the strong throats of hardy "serenade singers." These self-appointed individuals are the night owls of traditional Blackfoot encampments, often covering themselves with blankets to remain anonymous, as well. Their hauntingly beautiful songs must have been heard by many enemy raiders in the past, when these singers also served as night guards.

Traditionally, serenade singers go around in small groups, usually riding horses. Young couples double up on single mounts, covering themselves with one big blanket. Unmarried girls sometimes waited for the voices of their sweethearts, then tried to sneak outside to join them. That may be why the custom of remaining anonymous got started!

Atsitsina said that in the days of his youth most girls were carefully watched by their parents. It was difficult to meet alone with them, especially after dark. But, he added, there were always some young women who risked punishment and social disgrace for a few private moments with one or another of the young men. Such girls were often from families whose reputations were not particularly good in the tribe anyway. This was perhaps because the parents frequently quarreled, gambled, or acted stingy. Sometimes they were girls living with widowed mothers and longing for affection. He said chiefs and other notable men never married such girls, and often they faced lives lacking in honor. It was not unusual for such women to commit suicide.

But that is not to say that only girls who remained virtuous found respect in life. We have heard several elders talking about their days of "tipi creeping," yet none of them thought the participants had committed the worst of crimes. One close elder told me how he used to sneak into family lodges to be with his girlfriends, one of whom later became a noted leader in the tribe one of the first women to do so. He said sometimes his luck was not too good. One mother expected his visit and placed a row of pans and dishes across the doorway. He had a hard time to get out of the dark tipi after he stumbled into the trap and made enough racket to wake everyone in the neighborhood!

Ben Calf Robe told us several "tipi-creeping" ancedotes from the time of his youth, in the 1890's. He said: "One time I was with my best friend. We were singing around the Sun Dance camp, late at night, as was our custom. We stopped by this white tent that belonged to a visiting family. Inside there was a real pretty girl—we were all after her, she was so nice. My friend and I crawled under a wagon, by this tent, to take a rest. Pretty soon two other fellows came along. They were older than us. They didn't see us resting in the dark. The one fellow told the other: 'I'll go in first, and you watch for me. Scratch on the tent if anybody comes along.'

"It was a new white tent that the girl was living in, and it had a picket rope that went down the front. These fellows pulled the picket pin up from the ground so that they could put the rope out of the way, in case they had to make a run for it. But the one who was staying outside tied the end of that rope to his friend's overalls, who didn't know anything about it. He went on in and found a tin stove in the way. It was dark, and he tripped over something. Pretty soon we heard the stove rattle. A dog jumped up and started barking. The fellow threw himself out the door and started running. Then the rope gave out and it looked just like somebody threw him back into the tent. He jumped up again and started running, and the same thing happened. By this time the dog was really barking and everybody in the tent was awake. My friend and I were laughing like crazy. Finally he noticed that the rope was tied to his overalls, so he tore it off and ran away. All the dogs in the camp were barking and neighbors were calling out to see what was going on.

"Another time two friends of mine went to a tipi where their girlfriend lived. One stayed outside and watched, while the other one snuck in. He knew where the girl was sleeping, but he didn't know that she had a small hawk for a pet. Sometimes the people of the past trained wild birds and animals. This hawk was perched on one of the back rests by the girl's bed. When the boy got close, the bird made a sound, like 'hagh, hagh.' The boy thought it was his sweetheart calling to him and he went closer. 'Hagh, hagh,' the bird said. The boy whispered, 'What are you saying?' The bird just kept going 'hagh, hagh.' Finally the boy put his hand on the back rest, to lean down, and the bird scratched him and bit him on the hand. The boy got scared and jumped up, the bird screamed loudly and flapped its wings, and everybody in the tipi woke up. The boy ran out real quick!"

One night we heard a group of serenade singers going around the camp accompanied by the low rumble of a motor, instead of the thudding of horses' hooves. When they paused from singing we could hear them talking quite loudly, and with slurred speech. They were apparently celebrating the summer evening in their own way, although liquor is forbidden in the camp. But from their music you would not have known they were drunk. They sang loud and clear, and in good harmony. One of them shook a string of sleigh bells in time to the singing. These tunes can be compared to the sounds of a very musically talented pack of wolves serenading on a moonlit night.

In addition to the singing, our camp was filled with all kinds of other inspirational sounds. Most emotional were the early morning songs and prayers of the elders. These were usually addressed to Sun, Moon, Earth, and the Creator, who made us all. They were reminders to everyone that a new day was beginning. The elders wanted us to be thankful just to see each day arrive.

Sometimes certain individuals walked around the camp slowly, calling out news of interest, as well as invitations for feasts or ceremonies to be held later on. Those who heard their names called usually found themselves advised to "bring along a bowl," for eating. Strong-voiced elders, like Pat Weasel Head, were most often hired to make these announcements. For this service they were given tobacco, money, or blankets.

Unlike the camp in Montana, nearly everyone here spoke Blackfoot, even the children. Sometimes this made me feel very alienated, especially when I understood enough of a nearby conversation to know that it concerned me. I grew to despise being called a *napikwan,* or white man. I wished I could somehow change myself so that I would no longer be one. I wondered why fate had placed so much spirit and dedication for Indian ways into a body with no Indian ancestry. It took a long time for me to realize that the challenges I faced because of my ancestry gave me added strength and determination to learn the faith that I follow by choice, instead of by birth.

During the seasons that followed these first summer encampments we spent a lot of time wondering in what direction our family life should grow. The duties and obligations as medicine pipe keepers were beyond question, and we knew they would have to come first. We also knew that we wanted to be close to Wolf Old Man for as long as he lived, and to learn all we could from him. But after that, what? There was no future for me on the reserve, where I couldn't own a home and needed a permit just to live.

One part of my childhood dream still waited to be fulfilled—I still yearned to practice the traditional ways in some primitive and peaceful part of Nature. If Smallboy's group had been Blackfoot we might have joined them. But our dedication to Blackfoot traditions made it impossible to consider living with another tribe. In fact, it even made my ideas for forming a "new tribe" seem unlikely to succeed. It did not seem right to consider bringing the bundle into a group who might question its status.

If Beverly had been born on a reservation in the United States our dilemma would have had other possible solutions. There, we could have bought reservation land either from Indian or non-Indian owners, and thus remained close to the tribe. The U.S. government long ago allowed Indians to take full and individual title to parts of their reservation lands. For the sake of Indian people I'm glad this didn't happen in Canada. A lot of Indians in the U.S. lost their individually owned lands through poorly planned sales and outright swindles. Some reservations now have populations whose majority are non-Indians. This has been an important factor in the decline of cultural traditions, as among the Montana Blackfeet.

An older cousin of Beverly's once offered to sell us her eighty acres of partly wild reserve land, down in a treelined riverbottom full of deer and other wildlife. The price she asked was very low, since the offer included an older house. The transaction would have been made in Beverly's name, to keep it legal. It was tempting, but we turned it down to avoid controversy and an uncertain future. Not long afterward there was an official drive to remove all non-Indians from the reserve, but by that time we were already gone.

The realization that we would eventually have to find a home off the reserve led us to explore the nearby foothill region of the Rockies for a possible homestead and permanent campsite. However, that search was made difficult by the fact that most private lands in the region consisted of large ranches for which we had no money. But we finally found a rancher willing to sell one of his summer grazing pastures, which consisted of wild mountainside, with a forest of huge trees. From a clearing near the top of it we could see the lights of the Blood Reserve at night. The rancher was in no hurry to sell, and I told him that it might take a while before we could even afford a down payment. We went there frequently after that, to walk over the land and make plans . . .

Meanwhile, continuing sales of our small booklets provided enough income for us to live simply, down in our house on the Bullhorn. The booklets also brought a lot of mail from all kinds of people, especially young ones seeking to get closer to Nature. Some of these seekers wrote and said they hoped I would take leadership and invite them to build an Indian-style camp, or a tribal community. I generally replied that it was hard enough getting my own family back to the land, and that I did not feel competent to try it with a larger group.

But not everybody took my word for it. In fact, some didn't even write before they showed up at our door to see what might happen. We made a practice of having a rented mailbox away from our home, but some people found this only one more step along their wanderings.

In the latter part of our first summer a young couple from California found us on the reserve. They said they were looking for Indian "parents" to adopt them and teach them a good way of life. They seemed sincere, romantic, and full of ideals. Their initial Indian contacts had been with some of the same friendly people in Montana who had first encouraged me a few years earlier. It was from them that they learned our whereabouts.

We were having supper with Beverly's parents when the California couple drove up in an old white sports car. Such cars were rare on the rough roads of the reserve, and even more so among Indian drivers, so we knew they were visitors. One of Beverly's nephews looked outside and called out: "Hippies!" At that everyone rushed to the windows to see a young fellow with long hair and a mustache, and a pretty, long-haired girl.

The couple introduced themselves and said they were looking for us. We invited them to join us for supper, which was a typical reserve meal of meat and potatoes. The young man blushed, as he said in a gentle voice: "I hope you're not offended, but we don't eat meat." Several of those in the house stared with disbelief. Belonging to a tribe of former buffalo hunters, they had not imagined anyone could live without meat of some kind. Strange to say, among the many so-called "hippie ideals" that eventually made the rounds of Indian reserves, vegetarianism was never one of them. The practice seems to run against nearly all Indian cultural customs that remain.

We went ahead with our meal, feeling somewhat awkward, while our visitors sat quietly and watched. When the girl asked us if we lived somewhere else, I noticed that she was obviously bra less underneath her thin blouse. This added embarrassment to the situation. The house was full of relatives, and that kind of personal freedom was not yet very common in our part of the country. The eyes of a couple younger fellows were already twinkling. I knew word of the "hippie" visit would hit the reserve's teenage telegraph before nightfall.

Still, we sympathized with this young couple's search for a peaceful life, since we were wishing for that ourselves. They spoke of spiritual enlightenment in a way that many hoped would bring universal freedom and understanding. Beverly and I had missed such talk since we began our involvement with tribal elders, who knew little of such worldly philosophies.

The young couple stayed at our house and visited for a few days, while the weather was very hot. With their peaceful thoughts they went around wearing little clothing, which made us worry that someone might come to visit and see them, or that one of our neighbors might ride by quietly and observe them from horseback. Sure enough, a middle-aged couple chose a hot afternoon to stop by and ask for the legal papers to one of the quarterhorses we had given in payment for our pipe bundle. The woman's father was an old former member of the Horns Society. He had transferred his membership during the Sun Dance encampment, and the horse was among the payments he received. It had been given by Stabs Down and his wife to help her brother, who took over the membership.

The Indian couple stood by our door and said they had no time to come in for a visit. As we talked the man glanced several times toward the California couple lying in the sunshine, while his wife pretended she did not see them. They were close enough that it must have been obvious the young woman wore only a very brief, two-piece bathing suit, the top of which was so loosely knitted that it barely concealed what was underneath it.

The young couple acted as though they enjoyed their stay so well that they were in no hurry to leave. But they were understanding when we explained some of the problems created by their presence. We told them that we wanted to move elsewhere eventually, and they said they would like to move with us and help. We agreed to meet again the following summer.

The search for peace and understanding was carried on by Indian groups and individuals as well as by youths from the mainstream of modern society. Some people got together and began holding what they called Indian Ecumenical Conferences. These were intertribal gatherings of elders and traditional leaders, sponsored by the United Council of Churches. Indian cultural survival and revival was obviously becoming acceptable to modern society when leading Christians willingly financed encampments of Indian medicine men and women!

That summer the Indian Ecumenical Conference was held on the Stoney Indian Reserve, in a serene little tipi camp that lay hidden in a quiet meadow underneath the towering crags of the Rocky Mountains. John Snow was a chief of that tribe, and also an ordained minister. He arranged with his people to make this idyllic tribal campsite available. "Religious" Indians came from all over Canada and the United States. Some were Christian ministers and preachers, others were native ceremonialists and traditional doctors who worked with rituals and herbs. They all met to exchange knowledge and inspiration. Their main hope was to help reawaken spiritual feelings in all Indians, no matter from what tribe or religion.

Young people who heard about this gathering went there hoping to learn ancestral ways. Many came from distant cities, with no experiences in camping and tribal living, and little knowledge about approaching the traditional elders for advice and wisdom. The "generation gap" discovered by the rest of society was equally noticeable in that Indian spiritual camp.

A number of "old-time Indians" showed up. There were several elderly men with braids, who spoke little or no English and carried a strong presence of humble wisdom. They walked around quietly, or else they sat together in small groups and visited with each other. Seldom did they mingle with any of the young.

Beverly and I met a young Cree fellow who introduced himself as Blue Dog. His grandfather was an Anglican minister back home, on their prairie reserve. At the conference the grandfather was on the committee of elders. Blue Dog said he lived with his grandparents in their reserve home, along with his little son, who quickly became Wolf's friend. Blue Dog's grandparents had encouraged him to learn about old tribal ways. He wore long braids—long enough to indicate that he was not one of the recent converts to the "traditional Indian look," which was just coming into style. We sensed something deep and sincere about Blue Dog, who was one of the first young Indians we met who seemed to be devoted to the culture of his people.

Blue Dog introduced a pretty, dark-skinned young lady as his girlfriend. She lived in Smallboy's camp, and had come with a group of others from there. Blue Dog said he was planning to move to the camp himself, to work and learn for a year. Then he wanted to go somewhere else and start a new camp. He said that the girl, and his little son, would go with him. Also that there were five or six others of his tribe who were planning to join, including one long-haired boy named Weasel Tail, who was with him. When we told him that we were planning a similar move, he suggested we join forces.

Our talk was overheard by some other young people, who moved closer so they could listen to us. The idea of going out into the woods and learning to live with Nature appealed to them, as well. In fact, several of them already lived in various wilderness camps around the country.

After we talked for a while an Indian rock band set up their equipment near us and began to play. The electronic sounds quickly caught the attention of many youths in the camp, as though they were ants who had learned of a fresh pantry. Blue Dog and his friend watched with disgust. Finally they got up to seek a more peaceful location. We agreed to continue our talk on a nearby hill. We said we would stop at our tent for a pipe, and another said he would go and get his drum.

Blue Dog said his main concerns were getting land for the proposed campsite, and food for the people. He thought we should select an appropriate place in the wilderness, as Smallboy had done, and simply settle on it. He said we could later file with the government to receive a deed for it. He knew the difficulties an organized group like Smallboy's was having in getting rights to such land, but he felt the government would eventually give in, and he seemed thrilled by the potential challenge. But he changed his mind when we told him about our series of little books, and how they could be used to pay for a piece of private land. He agreed to try it that way, so we could save our energy for positive growth, rather than using it to fight bureaucracy.

There were no Blackfoot people at the Ecumenical Conference, which disappointed us. The place was not far, since the Stoneys are Blackfoot neighbors. Some of the Indian elders and leaders had come from as far as the Yukon, Great Lakes, Pacific Coast, and the deserts of Arizona. Even Blackfoot elders admit that their people have always been aloof, and very proud of their own heritage.

During the last evening one middle-aged Blackfoot did show up, by himself. He was a noted individual, yearning to become a medicine man. He was also a member of the tribal secret society, which made his visit to the spiritual gathering more noteworthy. He didn't know we were there. His business was limited to the committee tipi, which was off-limits to ordinary participants like ourselves.

We were very surprised when it was publicly announced in camp that this man was going to perform an ancient Blackfoot ceremony for the blessing of buffalo tongues. The Stoneys owned a herd of buffalo near the camp, and two had been butchered earlier.

Several elders in the spiritual encampment had sacred medicine bags and bundles with them. A few of these were opened for participants to see and be blessed with. Our medicine pipe bundle was with us, too, but we said nothing about it to anyone. We were not allowed to do anything but take care of it, very carefully. I wondered what Blackfoot ceremony this man had been given that he could share so openly with strangers. The ceremony was held inside the committee tipi, which had a guard outside to keep uninvited persons away. We walked to a nearby tipi and sat down in its shadows, so we would be able to hear what was going on.

We had not long to wait. There was a brief introductory talk in English, some praying, and then the singing of songs. Canvas tipi covers don't hold back sounds from inside, so we heard everything very clearly. We were astounded when we realized the Blackfoot's songs were those of the secret society! They were to be sung only at formal gatherings of the group, especially during the Sun Dance encampment. This man was singing them for a very different purpose. In addition, he clearly told the other people to sing along with him. Among his own people none but initiated members dared join in these songs.

We walked away feeling saddened and troubled. Was this an indication of the future for revival of old tribal ceremonies? Would similar things be done that the elders would not approve of? Without giving details, we later asked Pat Weasel Head what he thought about the singing of those songs. He said the matter was hardly to be discussed with nonmembers, and that none but the foolish would misuse the songs. The man who did this never knew that we heard him. As far as we know he never did it again. Perhaps by now he has realized his mistake and is thankful that no one from the tribe was around to hear.

Before the Ecumenical Conference was over Blue Dog and I submitted a written statement to the committee stating our belief that more effort should be made in future gatherings to get elders and youths directly in touch with each other. Blue Dog's grandfather had suggested making the written statement. He agreed with our views, and said others should be able to see the statement as a future reminder. It was later published in the conference newsletter, which was given out to participants.

During the next winter we corresponded frequently with people like Blue Dog and his friends. Some were readers of our books who said they were determined to make major changes in their lives and planned to move in our general direction. Although I continued to insist that I was not interested in being a leader, or "chief," I slowly found myself organizing a group.

Blue Dog made a visit to our home on the reserve, along with his friend Weasel Tail. They were still eager to start the camp, although Blue Dog was looking for a new girlfriend. Weasel Tail had been searching for the right one all along. Now he said he was looking for two women, one of whom was to live with his father, who had left his mother and said that he would join us in the wilderness camp.

We introduced our friends to a few elders, especially Atsitsina, who said he might also come to live in our camp. We had already talked to Wolf Old Man to see what he thought of our plans. He said he was too old to join us, but that he liked the idea very well. He encouraged us, not only because he thought it would be good for young people to step away from the rapid pace of modern life, but also because he realized that I, as a non-Indian, would find more peace away from the reserve.

As the reality of this intertribal wilderness camp seemed to come closer, we were particularly bothered by one thing—our devotion to the specific initiations and ceremonies gotten from Blood elders meant we were following a primitive form of nationalism. Our ways were specifically the Blackfoot ways. How would others in the camp feel about that? Especially those from different tribes, who were perhaps just as devoted to their own ways. Would modern-day friends be able to overcome the bitter feelings their forefathers had against each other? Blue Dog must have wondered about this, too, especially after his visit to the reserve. He must have noticed the depth of our tribal dedication, which may have surprised him. At any rate, before we ever reached the proposed camp together, our trails quietly separated. Blue Dog remained on his own reserve, where he has since become one of his people's spiritual leaders.

During our second winter together on the Blood Reserve, I became totally immersed in compiling a photo history of the tribe, as we had discussed with the elders. Every day I sat at my typewriter and turned out a dozen pages. When I wasn't writing I was reading ethnological books and papers, or showing my collection of tribal photographs to people who could identify them. I spent so much time thinking and talking about events and people from the past that I began to feel as though I knew them almost as well as I know the present. Frequently I dreamed about them—good things, though sometimes mysterious things, as well. More than once I woke up in the morning and wondered in which era I was actually living.

As my work became known to other people on the reserve, some of them asked me for photos and stories of their own families. Elders sometimes asked me to clear up historical details about which they were uncertain. They considered written records to be valuable, even though they and their forefathers seemed to have done well without them. Only with ethnological interpretations of spiritual matters did they frequently disagree. But they didn't agree on these things with each other, either. I had to learn how to blend their opinions with information that was sometimes recorded even before they were born.

My favorite diversions from cultural learning and writing were hunting and horseback riding, both of which were easy to do where we lived. Countless trails crisscrossed the brush-lined riverbottom, over which wild birds and small mammals constantly roamed. Deer lived in great quantities not far away, although I never saw anything but their tracks near our home. One snowy day a whole flock of plump prairie chickens settled in the bushes growing in front of our house. I was able to open our front door without scaring them away, but I knew they would leave if I opened the screen door. Instead, I fired both barrels of my twelve-gauge shotgun right through the screen, hitting and knocking down most of the birds. For several days we enjoyed them in our meals, even though the remains of our screen door looked as though someone had been thrown through it headfirst!

The husband of one of the numerous cousins was my regular hunting partner. He read a lot, and he loved to discuss his thoughts. In return for my ideas and companionship he showed me the wildest and most remote places on the reserve. His favorite hunt was along the shores of Belly River, where it formed the reserve's northern boundary. Here, neither plow nor tractor had disturbed the land. Huge cottonwood trees stood in groves, just as they had when Bloods still pitched tipis in their shelter a century earlier. Under a few of the trees he pointed out bleached bones and rusty metal objects that remained from the days when dead people were bundled with their favorite belongings and tied into the tree branches.

There were always fresh signs of deer in this isolated place, though they were wary from being continually hunted. There is no closed season on the reserve, or on public lands off the reserve, for Indians whose forefathers signed government treaties. A dedicated hunter could still supply all his family's meat needs that way, although I have not been in a household where this was the case. Most of the people we knew regularly bought their groceries in supermarkets and ate wild meat only as a special treat.

One morning this partner and I headed across the open prairie in my pickup truck, bound for a deep coulee where he felt sure we would find deer. We talked about the stamina of deer hunters among some southwest tribes, who chase their quarry on foot until they are able to run it down. He mentioned that as a boy he had been quite a runner himself. I later found a photo and other evidence that he was the fastest in his time. He said the elders he knew were more impressed by his speed and endurance than by his high marks in school.

On our way we passed grain fields planted on reserve land by non-Indian ranchers who had leases from the tribe. For many years these leases provided the tribe with its main cash income. The grain fields also provided feed for a great many wild deer. They would hide all day in the riverbottoms and in steep coulees that led down to them, coming up to the flat fields mostly at night. That morning we surprised a herd of ten or twelve that was a bit late in getting down to its hideout.

My partner knew the area well. He quickly noted that there was no place for the deer to find shelter in over a mile, and said we should chase them in the truck. He instructed me to leave the well-worn wagon trail we had been following and to head straight across the prairie in an attempt to head the deer off from the distant coulee that they would surely try to reach. Had the deer turned back into the grain fields they could have easily disappeared from our sight. Their instincts must have told them it was daylight and time to get into shelter below.

I drove as fast as I dared, following the bounding creatures who were making a desperate effort to escape. My partner grabbed a rifle and rolled down his window, ready to shoot when we got near enough. There was not much hope for him to take good aim, since we were bouncing so much I had to watch that my head did not hit the ceiling. Frequently I had to dodge rocks and, even more dangerous, various-sized holes made by gophers, foxes, and badgers. One of these could have easily broken a wheel or an axle—just as they used to break the legs of speeding horses and the necks of their buffalo-chasing riders in the old days.

We finally got so close to the deer that I wondered if I should try running them down instead of waiting for my partner to shoot them. I considered this even more seriously after he opened fire and I realized that, in his hurry, he had grabbed the small .22-caliber rifle. We had brought it only in case we saw birds. To kill deer with such a rifle the bullet would have to hit a vital area, which was not likely under these conditions. In fact, the only reason he hoped to hit them at all was that the whole herd was quite closely bunched up.

By this time we were so near the coulee that I had to quit following the deer and pass on their left side. I could barely hear the "pop, pop, pop" of the rifle, although I saw dust flying up from the ground several times to show where some of the bullets hit. Had my friend grabbed the double-barreled shotgun, which we also had along, he might have knocked the whole herd down, after which we could have finished off the wounded with little problem. Many elders and poor families would have been glad for some of the meat. Instead, the whole bunch disappeared down into the coulee, leaving us emptyhanded and feeling very foolish.

Later that morning we separated and hunted on foot through the dense willow brush along the riverbottom, as we had originally intended. Along my way I saw a lone porcupine sitting still on a tree branch, and a couple of beavers working on a small dam. Overhead there was a steady procession of hawks, crows, and magpies. At one point I saw the slow, circling form of an eagle high in the sky. A strong feeling of timelessness accompanied me on that trail.

That same morning, while I was still at home and getting ready for the hunt, I had accidentally walked into an open door in the dark. The result was a deep, oozing gash right over one eyelid. The wound swelled up and looked ugly, but otherwise didn't bother me. It certainly didn't keep me from aiming correctly at a sturdy doe that stood in my path later on. I knocked her down instantly with just one shot. When I got to her she was already dead. My bullet had left a similar oozing hole over one eyelid, which astounded me quite a bit.

My partner joined me after he heard the shot, and helped to skin the deer. I was dismayed to find three .22 caliber bullets in its body. I wished that they were from our earlier foolishness, so that I could think I had saved this animal from further suffering. However, at least one of the bullets was of a type that we had not used. My partner said it was not unusual for youngsters from poor families to try getting meat by hunting, even if they could afford no better weapons than the almost useless .22. Later, while eating the meat, I also found shotgun pellets in it. I have often found these in wild ducks, as well. Having grown up quite removed from the so-called "sport" of hunting, I always assumed this to be a very honorable pursuit. It shocked me to realize that living targets frequently become wounded survivors of careless hunters.

During that second winter we were invited to bring Atsitsina to a "prayer meeting" on the neighboring reserve of the North Piegans. Based on a somewhat similar theme as the Intertribal Ecumenical

Conference, this meeting was planned as a gathering of Blackfoot youths and elders.

Atsitsina agreed to go with us, but when we went to pick him up he made all manner of excuses not to come. He was a conservative Blood, and as such he remained aloof even from the other Blackfoot divisions. In our years together we were seldom able to persuade him to attend ceremonies off the reserve like this one.

The event lasted all day and evening, and included meals, prayers, talks, as well as several small rituals. Atsitsina was given the honor of singing medicine pipe songs for the leading elder among the North Piegans, a popular man named Joe Crow Shoe, who was the keeper of that division's only medicine pipe bundle. Several elderly members of the Siksika division came and performed the sacred Blacktail Deer Dance, which Atsitsina had not seen since the days of his youth.

A very unexpected offer came to us during this gathering. A young fellow with a mustache said he represented the renowned Smithsonian Institution, in Washington, D.C. He asked if Atsitsina and I would go there to participate in an annual affair called the Festival of American Folklife. Joe Crow Shoe and his wife, Josephine, had already agreed to go, along with several people from the Montana Blackfeet.

Atsitsina and I had often talked about making a long trip somewhere together. In the 1930's he went to visit a branch of the Sioux people in South Dakota, which had been the biggest trip in his lifetime. He went there with his half-brothers and some cousins. For driving and guiding they hired a likable half-breed who was a good friend of theirs and also owned one of the first automobiles among the Bloods. Atsitsina said they had a great time on this trip, and won first prize for Indian singing during a big powwow. They met friends and relatives of old Eagle Plume, who had gone there many years before.

The old man knew that Washington, D.C., was more than twice as far away as Sioux country, and that our trip would be a completely different kind of adventure. It meant flying on an airplane, which he had never done. It also meant seeing the home of the "Great White Father," a romantic goal for many Indian elders, even in Canada. Not that governments and politicians were particularly important in Atsitsina's life. He basically distrusted both, and generally stayed away from them (although he once painted the face of Canada's Governor-General Roland Michener and presented him with a headdress in a public ceremony that tribe leaders asked him to perform). But to see a place so famous in North American history as Washington, D.C.—where countless great chiefs and warriors have traveled on behalf of their tribes—that was an opportunity without equal in his mind. We agreed that we would go.

The man from the Smithsonian was at the prayer meeting by invitation from a friend, who was its organizer. This fellow had come to live near the Blackfoot people and establish friendships with some of them. He became director of a "Native Friendship Center," which had been set up in one of the larger towns near the reserves. The center, and others like it, existed to provide welcome for native people who felt lonely and depressed, or simply wished for the companionship of their own kind of people. Previously, such people often turned to bars for lack of any other social place where they were welcome.

This same fellow had asked Atsitsina and me to get up before the people at the meeting and pray. Atsitsina went first, speaking in Blackfoot, and I followed, in English. The organizer's friend later said he thought this symbolized a transition from old to new in Indian culture, which was something he wanted to bring out at the Smithsonian's Folklife Festival.

It was our understanding that at that festival we were to give daily workshops to groups of people interested in learning how the old was being passed on to the new. The representative from the Smithsonian said my lack of Indian ancestry would be no problem, and might place an "interesting accent" on the theme of cultural revival. He said that for ten days of doing this our round-trip flight would be paid and we would get room and board, plus a small honorarium afterward.

The trip grew in Atsitsina's mind during the months that fol-

lowed our invitation. We concluded we would demonstrate the
making of pipes, rattles, and other crafts that we regularly made
together at home. The work would give us something to do besides
answering questions and holding discussions in workshops. We began to accumulate the tools and materials we would need. Atsitsina
kept these in a little suitcase underneath his bed. He frequently
showed this to friends and relatives, who found it hard to believe that he was going so far away in his old age. Perhaps they
didn't know that his real dream was to visit France and Germany,
from where his only non-Indian blood came (through one far-back
ancestor).

I continued to work on my book of Blood history, hoping to
have it far enough along to show publishers while we were on the
East Coast. Every day my work ended with a list of questions that I
saved for Atsitsina, with whom I met often. When he didn't have
the answers—which was rarely—I saved the questions for the next
smoking ceremony, where I presented them to other elders. In addition, Beverly went around for me to collect stories and anecdotes,
for which I gave her outlines. Sometimes she brought elders back
home with her, to share a meal and to discuss things with me in
more detail.

Wolf Old Man was back in the hospital again, for the season. He
told us: "The doctor says it is safer for me to stay within reach, even
though I am feeling fine. Come and get me any time the weather is
good." We brought him to our house at least once a week, mainly
to sing medicine pipe songs and to teach us about the bundle's ceremony. The winter passed quickly, and soon we found ourselves
preparing for the return of Thunder, and for the summer festivals.

One announced change of summer plans caused us some concern—the Blood encampment by the Belly Buttes, usually held in
August, was to be held earlier this year. Those who were in charge
of the encampment said its purpose was sacred, so it should precede
all the powwows and other social events of the summer. We wondered if it would also conflict with our trip to Washington, D.C.,
which was to begin in June. We also thought the encampment might
coincide with the birth of our first child, which Beverly was then

carrying. As it turned out, all three important events blended nicely together.

I had not been eager to father more children when Beverly and I first got together. I wanted to make a full-time effort at learning the traditional and natural life that I envisioned, and I wanted Beverly's full-time help. Besides, she and I were already responsible for two sons, and I had a daughter who lived with my first wife. I firmly believed that there were enough children in the world, and that over-population lies at the base of most modern troubles. I still agree with this view. But having children—like falling in love—is not something readily controlled by logical thoughts.

Beverly grew up in a society that places heavy emphasis on a woman's maternal role. She agrees that there are too many people on this earth, but she also feels that a deep, basic instinct exists in all women to give birth to offspring. She thinks many women today try so hard to deny this instinct that modern psychological problems often result. Together we have come to feel that Nature will soon use one of her many available methods to control overpopulation among humans. While we would like to protect our family from any catastrophe that might occur because of overpopulation, we decided that having more children is as natural as worrying about their possible futures.

When we first learned that Beverly was pregnant we wished to be living in our tipi by the time of the birth. We wanted the child to be born outdoors, even if I had to do the delivering myself. But when Beverly's mother heard about this she opposed it so strongly that we soon gave up our plans. In Blackfoot customs men have nothing to do with childbirth— except in the first place, of course! Looking back, I'm glad we heeded my mother-in-law's wisdom. I'm sure I was not qualified to take such a heavy responsibility for two human lives.

The family doctor sympathized with our desires for a natural childbirth, so he allowed me to stay with Beverly throughout the event. It was enlightening and, for me, deeply moving. It brought me much closer to both mother and child. The doctor explained all that he did. He pointed out potential difficulties, and possible solutions, in case I should have to do the delivering myself, some other time.

We had hoped all along that the childbirth would happen during the Sun Dance encampment. That seemed like an auspicious beginning for a child's life. Secretly, I still hoped somehow the child could be born in our tipi—perhaps with the help of some skilled old woman. But this hope faded when I realized Beverly was frightened by the experience of her own grandmother, whose first child died after birth due to a mistake made by the midwife. The umbilical cord got cut off too close to the baby's body. In addition, Beverly's grandfather lost his mother right after she gave birth to him, because the midwife could not get her to pass the afterbirth.

We had been postponing our medicine pipe ceremony, which was to celebrate the return of Thunder, while we waited for this child to be born. Someone told us that a traditional woman needs a ritual purification after giving birth before she can have anything to do with a bundle. Just before we moved to the Sun Dance camp we learned our misunderstanding—the restriction did not mean a pregnant woman had to wait until after birth to attend a ceremony. Since other bundle keepers had already completed their ceremonies, Wolf Old Man said we should have ours at the start of the tribal gathering. He was going to lead the ceremony, and he seemed pleased with the idea of having it at such a special time and place.

Just a couple days before our ceremony we received several unexpected visitors. First was the young "seeker" from California who had been to see us the previous year. He was back with longer hair, which he now wore in braids. He also drove a different small car, and he had a new girlfriend. This young lady was as pleasant and quiet as the other one, but no more modest. In addition, she had bright blond hair, which really made her stand out in camp. She did not feel nearly as uncomfortable being there as I did in having her. We offered them the use of our house during the encampment, which they later accepted. But they had come a long way to see the Sun Dance camp, and I did not have the heart to chase them away.

The next day a stereotype "hippie" showed up, complete with backpack, army jacket, whiskers, and scraggly, long hair. He had written to us during the winter and said that we should meet. In our reply we had tried to accommodate him, but we clearly stated that we would be busy during the time of the Sun Dance. That had evidently just whetted his appetite to come a little earlier. Even worse, he was brought to the encampment by an "intellectual" young woman from New York, who said she was "just out seeing the country." At the Sun Dance camp that phrase described a tourist, especially since she came in a bright-colored VW and brought along a big, weird, skinny dog. She said she liked the looks of the camp and intended to "stick around."

Beverly tried to be hostess to the visitors, as tradition taught her. But I felt unpleasant with so many conspicuous strangers around our tipi. Beverly said I was acting prejudiced about them. But she knew that my own presence in camp caused discomfort enough, for us as well as to others. I did not want to be the cause of any more outside distractions in the conservative tribal camp.

I tried to explain the situation to our visitors, who seemed to understand. The tourist woman naively replied: "Don't worry, we won't bother anyone." She had no way of understanding the tribal pride that was being "bothered" simply by her out-of-place presence there. The camp was under the strict control of the ancient Horns Society, and the leader of it soon came around to check on the strangers. I explained that two were friends who would be leaving after our ceremony, which was agreeable to him. I said nothing about the other two, but they later said he gave them permission to put up their tent at the edge of the camp. He must have said something explicit to them, since they packed up and drove off early the next morning, and were never heard from again.

Another visitor came to see us from within the tribe or, at least, from one of the Blackfoot divisions. I had seen this young man before, watching quietly in the background at some of the medicine pipe ceremonies. He had been seeing an elder in his division for traditional guidance and advice. When he introduced himself to us he said he wanted to learn some other things about his ancestors. He had heard about our plans to move into the wilderness, and he was willing to come along.

Meanwhile, the location of our intended camp had finally become clear—we had paid a deposit on a place away from the prairie, on the other side of the mountains. We missed out buying the rancher's mountainside, with its virgin timber, by just a few days. When we finally got money for a down payment, the rancher said he had already sold it to his next-door neighbor. He was glad, because he wanted someone who would love the big forest and not go in with machines to log the trees.

At first our failure to get this place was disappointing. Through our visits we had grown quite fond of it. Now we realize that our loss was not bad, after all. Within a couple of years roads were carved into the nearby mountain wilderness for the laying of huge, shining ribbons of natural gas pipelines, which the rancher had thought he was successfully fighting against. In addition, he was dismayed when the neighbor hired a logging contractor who went up and stripped the whole ridge of its primitive forest.

After that incident we decided to search for land on the British Columbia side of the Rockies, where large, commercial ranches are less common. We wanted just a little piece of wilderness, untrampled by domestic cows. We wished for neighbors who would see more in Nature than just a place to raise cows and horses.

Our finances for land seemed more secure after two publishers liked my writing and offered cash for it. Unfortunately, those who wanted to move to the land with us were not familiar with the struggles we had finding that land and getting the necessary money. They thought it was all there just to be used. Later this caused disappointments for us all.

Our land search brought us to a little town where I knew a realtor who specialized in finding the kind of land we wanted. He was an ambitious immigrant from Germany who had a weakness for fishing. He used his search for isolated properties as an excuse to try out new fishing waters. When he found an old fence, or an abandoned cabin, he went to government agencies to learn who the owners were, so he could ask them if they'd like to sell. When I gave him an idea of what we had in mind, he said right away that he had just such a place.

It did not even take us a full day of looking before we found our new and permanent home in British Columbia. We left the reserve one morning, and that afternoon we followed the realtor's map to an isolated corner of a narrow river valley that is now our home. The only thing that bothered us right off about the place was that it included 320 acres, which was five or ten times more than we wanted. Yet the price was far less than we'd have paid for another place half as big but less remote. The exact amount we paid no longer matters, as land prices have changed drastically since then. The funds that we had were enough for us to make a down payment.

We got back from our successful land search just a few days before moving to the Sun Dance camp. When we had our medicine pipe ceremony there, Wolf Old Man prayed earnestly that we should find a good life in our new mountain home. He painted our faces, as well as those of our friends and relatives. He and other elders said that we would be missed, even though we would make frequent visits back for ceremonies and other gatherings.

Ours was to be the only medicine pipe ceremony held at that year's encampment, but—much to everyone's surprise—the highly revered Longtime Pipe was brought from its dark closet in the Provincial Muscum. This event was the beginning of an interesting and complicated affair in which we became so involved that I ended up being threatened with jail by government officials!

It all started in camp when White Horn, the ceremonialist, came to our tipi and said I was invited to an important conference, right away. It was evening, and I had no idea what the meeting would be about. I was directed to a yellow lodge with otters on it, somewhat different from ours. It stood not far away, in our part of the camp circle. When I got there and went inside I was startled to see the bearded, light-skinned face of Yellow Fly, the ethnologist. He was surrounded by several elders whom I knew well.

I was given a vacant seat near the head of the lodge. Shortly afterward White Horn came in and sat down beside me. The discussion that followed was mainly in English, and Yellow Fly did most of the talking. He said he no longer worked for the Provincial Museum, and that he wanted to have the Longtime Pipe removed from the museum's keeping. He claimed he wanted it brought back to the Blood Reserve.

He failed to mention a recent falling-out he'd had with museum officials, which added a revenge motive to his seemingly helpful offer to bring the bundle back. Nevertheless, he said he was willing to give up the traditional rights for the bundle, which had been transferred to him during a filmed and taped ceremony for which the museum hired several elders. By tribal traditions the bundle was his, so we took his words and offer very seriously.

He had previously made arrangements for the ancient bundle to be brought to the camp for a ceremonial opening. Museum officials had approved this when he told them the elders requested it. That was one of the stipulations made upon sale of the bundle by its previous keeper. The officials had no idea that Yellow Fly would transfer his rights to a new keeper from among the Bloods while the bundle was out of their hands.

The ethnologist said he had other business, so he left as soon as he finished telling us his intentions. We agreed on a day for the opening ceremony, and said we would make further plans at that time. When he was gone the elders expressed great pleasure that their prayers had been heard for the bundle to be among them again.

A large crowd showed up for the opening ceremony a few days later. White Horn and his oldest son, Ray Many Chief, provided their otter-painted tipi for the purpose. Ray was a leader in the Horns Society, and a minor chief of the tribe. He let it be known that he was thinking of becoming the new traditional keeper of the Longtime Pipe, as well.

White Horn led the opening ceremony, and his cousin, Atsit-sina, was the head drummer. We helped by providing a smoking pipe for the occasion, along with our tobacco-cutting-board and to-bacco from our own bundle, since Yellow Fly had forgotten to bring these important accessories from the museum. Many people reacted suspiciously when they first heard that Yellow Fly was bringing the bundle to be opened at the encampment. They thought he wanted to make further recordings, or even movies. But the rumors proved incorrect, and there was no ethnological work done.

During the ceremony Ray Many Chief's face was painted by his father, who added a prayer of good wishes for success as the bundle's next keeper. However, in spite of that, a conservative old man named Many Gray Horses announced at the end of the ceremony that the Longtime Pipe would be transferred to him and his wife. He explained that the bundle had previously belonged to his wife's late father, a noted ceremonialist named Bobtail Chief. He had been the half-breed son of a Blood woman and a white trapper. Many Gray Horses said he still had the four special drums belonging to the bundle, and that he was going to reunite the two once again.

The announcement took the crowd completely by surprise, but no one said anything. Many Gray Horses was known for having a strong will, and he was traditionally well qualified to speak up whenever he wanted. Not only was he of an age that made him respected, but he had also been owner of many medicine bundles, as well as the leader of the Horns. He had a status that allowed him to speak virtually unchallenged—unless someone in the group felt his status was even higher. When Many Gray Horses picked up the bundle and left, everyone knew that it was in safe hands.

The ceremony for the Longtime Pipe was the last event that Beverly and I were able to attend together during that Sun Dance encampment. A couple of days later she gave birth to our child. She woke up one morning in our otter tipi, and by that night she was in a hospital bed with our new baby boy. On my way from the hospital back to camp I met an adopted grandmother from Browning, old Mary Ground. When I told her news of the birth she said the timing was perfect, since the sacred camp was just reaching its annual climax. She predicted the child would grow up feeling especially close to his ancestors. As a blessing she gave him the name ''Natoapi-Sachkum-Api,'' or ''Holy Medicine Boy.'' We shortened this name to Okan, which is the Blackfoot name of the Sun Lodge ceremony, or Sun Dance. We surprised the nurses at the hospital by writing on our son's birth certificate that this was his official first name.

Beverly came home with me less than two days after the birth, because we wanted to take the new child out of the hospital as soon as possible. Besides, I wanted to spend some time with him and his mother before Atsitsina and I left for Washington, D.C., in just three more days. On the way home we stopped by the Sun Dance camp so that Wolf Old Man could meet the boy, as well. He had become quite anxious himself about the birth in the final weeks of Beverly's pregnancy. He was at the Sun Dance to observe a sacred performance of the Horns Society, of which he was once leader. When he first saw Okan he beamed with happiness and said he would also give him a name for good luck, which he did later.

Those three days at home seemed short, and I had a hard time leaving. The infant was just a tiny little dark-haired thing, almost completely swaddled in a soft bag made from hand-tanned deerskin that laced up in front. I wanted to stay near him and watch him start to grow. It must have been hard for Beverly to see me go at that time, too, although she said nothing. She was stoic about insisting that the trip with Atsitsina was a rare opportunity that might not come again. It turned out that she was right.

Atsitsina was still camped at the Sun Dance, which was ready to break up. I had already brought home our tipi and camping gear the previous day, and others were starting to pack theirs. It was early evening when I arrived at the encampment to get Atsitsina. The camp was crowded and lively, in part from the many visitors who usually come by at the end of each day to enjoy the tribal atmosphere. Around the outside of the camp circle stood rows of cars and pickup trucks, in some places three and four deep. Only the tops of the camp's tipis were visible from a distance because of the many parked vehicles.

Atsitsina's tent was crowded with friends and relatives who had come by to see him leave. Some were crying, and others had tears in their eyes. Somehow I felt kind of guilty when I looked in the door and asked if he was ready. He nodded his head and looked sheepish, as though he were embarrassed by all the attention. He seemed to be having a hard time packing his suitcase.

I went inside to help get the old man out of his fix. Several relatives reached out to shake my hand as a gesture of farewell. The smell of liquor was in the air, although no one appeared to have had too much. Atsitsina said he had turned down the offer of a farewell drink altogether.

The obvious love and concern for the old man by all these people took me by surprise, and made me more aware of my upcoming responsibility. When we got outside, the crowd gathered around us and began to sing the ancient "Victory Song" of our Many Children family band. Countless times in the past that same song bid farewell to Atsitsina's forefathers—who were also those of my new son—as they set out on their many trails of danger and excitement.

The farewell song was poignantly beautiful and gave us extra courage. It brought tears to my eyes, and a lump in my chest. It came with love from the two dozen voices of those relatives and friends. Several were women with voices so high and clear that chills went up my back, besides. For an instant I imagined us getting on horses and riding out of the camp in a cloud of dust, although it was exciting enough to know that we were about to soar high through the air in a jet.

With our car windows rolled down we drove away to the fading sounds of the singing. Last, we heard the general, timeless hubbub of the crowded camp. The Belly Buttes were again bathed in the orange glow of sunset, as were the tipis of the camp, while we drove away on a dusty gravel road to the highway. Atsitsina was quiet, but several times I sensed he was swallowing hard. He must have been wondering if it might be his last view of the ancestral camp.

When we reached the pavement and left the reserve, our mood quickly became cheerful. We talked and sang all the way to the airport in Calgary, which made the two- or three-hour drive seem fast. We got quiet again as we neared the terminal, and Atsitsina got nervous when he finally saw the jets. Before we left the truck we performed a short ritual that cheered him quite a bit.

Aboard the plane Atsitsina reminded me of a little boy afraid to make a wrong move. He watched me out of the corner of one eye, and the rest of the people out of the other. Following my example, he buckled up, and then leaned back to await our takeoff. When the plane started rolling he made the sign of the cross on his chest, and prayed quietly in Blackfoot. By the time he was finished and opened his eyes, we were already way up in the air. After that he acted much like any other air traveler, eating, talking, and dozing. He was surprised when I told him we had arrived in New York, just a few hours later, and he was eager to get a glimpse of this famous city.

We spent a couple hours waiting for a connecting flight at Kennedy Airport. I wanted to take Atsitsina for a stroll around the huge terminal, but he said he was afraid the plane might leave without us, so we stayed near the departing gate. He spent part of the time napping, and the rest telling me all kinds of jokes. He was acting very happy.

The long journey apparently tired his old body, since he kept falling asleep, although he had also been up late with relatives during his final night at the Sun Dance. He dozed again during the short flight down to Washington, D.C., so I had to wake him when we got ready to land. The plane was just banking sharply to the right when he opened his eyes. Since he was sitting in a window seat on the far right, he awoke to an instant bird's-eye view of buildings and autos not far below. He was so startled that he nearly banged his head in an effort to jump back from the long fall that he thought was about to take place. I apologized when I realized that I had not been very thoughtful.

The worst thing about Washington, D.C., on a hot day near July must be the humid climate. It was the first thing we noticed when we got off the plane. The airport terminal seemed grubby and crowded, not at all what I expected for America's capital city. The place did have an interesting 1940's vintage decor, but when I mentioned it to Atsitsina he said he was more impressed by the modern airport in New York.

We were met by the same fellow who had invited us to the festival at the Piegan Prayer Meeting. Atsitsina was glad to see a familiar face amid the flow of countless strangers. He acted nervous because so many of the strangers stared openly at us. Atsitsina never got used to all this attention. Back in Calgary—the largest city near the reserve—there are many Indians with braids, so they cause little interest among other people. But during our weeks in the East the only other men we saw with braids were fellow participants at the festival.

Our friend from the museum said we were the last to arrive. The other participants traveled together on the same plane from Denver, where they all gathered. He said several of those who had been invited changed their minds at the last minute and stayed home. We came separately because we paid our own way, while the others still had theirs paid by the Smithsonian, as originally agreed. A couple of weeks before our departure the same fellow had sent us a message saying that because of a funding shortage he had to withdraw our invitation. By that time Atsitsina would have been greatly disappointed to miss the festival, since he thought of little else but the big trip to Washington, D.C. We kept our invitation only by agreeing to pay the plane fare.

From the airport we were driven to the campus of Marymount College, in nearby Arlington. Dormitories served as our homes during the festival. Every morning we got breakfast in the cafeteria, after which charter buses drove us straight to the festival grounds, on the lawns near the White House. The dormitories, built of cement blocks, were ugly and square, and we were glad each morning to get away.

The Festival of American Folklife turned out to be America's official cultural event to celebrate the national holiday on the Fourth of July. It was part theater and part living museum—intended to symbolize the nation's population of diverse people, and to show how they were free to practice their own ways. It was a noble idea, though many of the spectators acted as they might at a zoo or a circus.

The so called Indian Village shared Washington's sprawling, treelined promenade with other invited groups, including hillbillies, union carpenters, Yugoslavians, tobacco growers, and bluegrass musicians. Not far from the village sat what must be the ultimate symbol of the "Great White Father"—the monstrous-sized, sculpted form of Abraham Lincoln, inside his tomblike memorial. The irony of it occurred to me one time when I saw Atsitsina staring toward it from the tipis.

In our section of the festival there were about fifty Indians, mostly of middle age and older. That year the festival honored Indian people of the Northern Plains cultural area, so all the participants were from tribes living near the Blackfeet. Atsitsina's father had considered most of them enemies, and met them on his numerous war trails. Atsitsina was aware of this, and it made him somewhat leery. Fortunately, there were others who belonged to the Montana Blackfeet, and there were our friends the Crow Shoes, so he didn't feel completely as though among strangers. As time went by he made several new friends, besides.

Each participant was expected to share tribal and cultural activities with the festival's many visitors. For instance, there were beadworkers from the Sioux, feather workers from the Arapaho, a flute-maker from the Crow, and singers from the Cree. One Sioux woman from South Dakota came with her young daughter to demonstrate the ancient technique of porcupine-quill embroidery.

Atsitsina and I had along two suitcases full of materials. There were stones for carving into pipe bowls; sticks for making pipe-stems; rawhide for making rattles; as well as buckskin, sinew, feathers, beads, scissors, saws, drills, and files for whatever else we might be inspired to make. It was an awkward and heavy load to haul back and forth from the reserve to Washington, and from the dormitory to the festival grounds. We envied those who had come just to demonstrate Indian singing. All they carried was their wooden drumsticks.

The Indian Village was made up of brightly colored canvas booths and several small white tipis. We were supposed to sit in one of the booths and perform our work. Each booth had a long table and several chairs, set up on a wooden platform, so that spectators could watch the work at eye-level. The booths had awnings that gave shade in the already hot sunshine of our first morning. But otherwise they seemed crass and tasteless. Atsitsina wandered away from them and looked at the tipi materials piled under some trees.

There was a large bunch of poles and several canvas tipi covers, but when we asked about using them we were told that they were for display only. There were to have been daily tipi-building demonstrations, but the tipi-making women were among those who had decided not to come. We would have to ask higher authorities if we could set up a tipi to use for our work. Knowing that such authorities could take a long time responding, we decided to set up a tipi and see what would happen.

When we began our unofficial tipi-raising we didn't expect the attention of inquisitive tourists, who already roamed the festival grounds in large numbers. As soon as they saw us unrolling a tipi cover and picking up poles, they surrounded us and made our intentions very plain to everyone else. By then, however, none of the festival staff dared to come and stop us!

In the days that followed we were glad we had taken matters into our own hands. The little tipi gave us more pleasant and familiar feelings than the rest of the village. As it was, there seemed to be a remoteness between most participants and spectators. We thought our crafts would be part of a workshop situation. Instead, we felt like living displays in front of constantly changing masses of strangers.

One side of our tipi cover was rolled up and left open so that people could see us work. At first we thought to keep the tipi closed up, visiting only with whoever wanted to come in. But the canvas cover had been sewn in New York, and it didn't fit our method of setting up a tipi, even though we tried a number of variations in front of the curious crowd. We finally gave up and pretended the tipi was supposed to be partway undone so that we could be seen inside. We were too embarrassed to admit that the odd cover had us stumped, and kept us from setting up the lodge properly.

The open front and bottom of our tipi were useful in keeping us from suffocating in the thick, hot air, which otherwise stuck to our bodies and clothing. I had brought an old eagle wing for a feather-work project, but the old man quickly laid claim to it. He spent much of his time and energy using that wing as a primitive fan, in the manner of his ancestors.

In some ways our situation reminded me of stories about Buffalo Bill's famous Wild West Show many years earlier—the challenges for reservation Indians to survive being objects of curiosity in far-away cities. The father of one Sioux participant at the festival had come to New York and Washington, D.C., with Buffalo Bill in the 1890's. After a couple of days of the crowded festival the son of the Sioux man said he finally understood why his father had been so glad to get back home to his quiet prairie land.

There was, however, at least one old Indian at the festival with us who liked crowds and attention. Several times a day he got up on a little podium behind our tipi and started drumming and singing out loud, until he was surrounded by listeners. His long black hair streamed loosely past his shoulders. A handsome, hawklike nose was the highlight of his dark brown face. More than the rest of us, I think, he gave the crowd what they wanted—a real Indian song-and-dance. Very subtly, he also gave them witty and sarcastic lectures on social justice!

This old man was a Sioux spiritual leader named Henry Crow Dog. He was a captivating Indian orator and actor. Even without his intriguing personality he would have been an attraction, at least for those familiar with Plains Indian history. His grandfather made the Crow Dog name famous by assassinating the government-appointed Sioux chief Spotted Tail, back around the time of Sitting Bull. In addition, the Crow Dog name had been in worldwide news not long before the festival when Henry's son, Leonard Crow Dog, served as medicine man for the militant American Indian Movement (AIM) group that took over the Sioux reservation town of Wounded Knee at gunpoint.

Henry Crow Dog's lectures went far beyond the typical Indian complaints about losing land and getting cheated by "the white man." He had some interesting thoughts on the course of current world events, as well as past history. He was an unusually aware old Indian. He combined his abilities to speak and write good English with a touch of artistry to give illustrated talks that used up huge sheets of drawing paper. Among the conclusions he reached was that Germans are "too damned smart," that Hitler was a "spider man" (which related to a lengthy Sioux myth that he told), and that hippies and Indians have something mysterious in common. In front of his podium hung one of his signs, which read: "Crow Dog's Paradise."

Crow Dog started his impromptu sessions by singing Sioux songs while beating on a hand drum. We learned to know when he considered the crowd large enough because he then always sang a peculiar tune of his own composition. It had a standard Indian melody and sound, plus the English words: "Mister Indian, sing me a love song so that I will learn to love you, *hey-yah, hey-yah, ha.*" It was a cynical social statement based on the original purpose of Indian love songs, which is to make two people grow closer to each other. Many of the casual listeners probably thought they were hearing an ancient tribal tune.

The Indian Village officially closed each day at five in the afternoon. Chartered buses then took us back to our dormitory homes. As far as the Smithsonian staff was concerned, when "show time" was over we were on our own. This was unfortunate, since the Marymount College appeared to be miles from anything worth doing or seeing. Most of the Indian participants had never been in Washington, D.C., and wanted to do some sightseeing. We spoke to staff members about this after a couple days of boredom. Later they came back and said an "after-showtime" bus trip to the National Cemetery had been approved.

Atsitsina and I decided to pass up the chance of seeing America's most distinguished graveyard. Blackfoot people are not very fond of places where the dead are laid to rest, anyway. That may be one reason why graves in the two official cemeteries on the Blood Reserve often appear anonymous and indistinguishable from surrounding prairie land within a few years after burial. Until the turn of the century most Blackfoot corpses were wrapped in blankets and left outdoors to decompose back to Nature. Originally they were tied on scaffolds, or in forked branches of big trees. When government agents objected to open disposal of the dead, after the tribe got settled on their reserve, families built small huts of lumber and placed their dead inside of these, within flimsy wooden caskets.

Atsitsina was eager to see the famous Smithsonian Museum, of

Our first two boys, Wolf and Shane, wearing traditional dance costumes made by their mother. Here they were on their way out to the dance arena for the first time. For this event we had a "giveaway dance" during which we and other relatives gave money and presents to visitors and friends in honor of the boys.

Louie Ninepipe, a well-known Flathead Indian singer and dancer of the early 1900's, singing and drumming inside his one-room log house on the Flathead Indian Reservation in 1968. On the wall are letters and pictures sent by various people Louie corresponded with, including several fans who heard his singing on a long-playing folk album he helped record many years ago. With his brothers, Louie recorded one of the first long-playing albums of American Indian music.

The fairy-tale marriage of old Louie Ninepipe to a young British fan, Vivien, made newspaper headlines in 1974. Louie claimed his magical Indian "love medicine" lured the pretty lass clear across the ocean to him after they had corresponded by mail for a few years.

Atsitsina recalls a serious moment in the adventures of an ancestor whose history and legends he was exceptionally knowledgeable about.

A scene in the Browning Indian Days encampment of 1967 showing a costumed man in head-dress leading his three young sons toward the tribal parade.

Beverly in front of our mountain home, which we slowly and simply put together ourselves without any plans or training. Since we could not drive close to the house, snowshoes and toboggans became important for traveling and hauling. *Below,* ''Grandma'' Ruth Little Bear, Beverly's mother, with her pet boy, Shane. After raising her many own children and several others, she would not be content without having kids in her household.

An elder of the neighboring Stoney tribe looks over the tipi camp set up by his people while hosting an Indian Ecumenical Conference. Indian church leaders met here with medicine men and women from many tribes to exchange knowledge and inspiration. *Below*, presenting the flags of the U.S.A. and Canada at the Smithsonian's Folklife Festival in Washington, D.C., in 1973. Piegan tribal elder Joe Crow Shoe stands between Atsitsina and me and tells me what traditional Blackfoot song we are about to sing. Two participants from the Montana Blackfeet flank us.

Mary Ann Coombs, who inspired my family by the traditional way she lived all alone in a little log house. She became our "grandma" and told us about her kind of outdoor family life. When she was a girl, her Flathead people were forced to leave their ancestral homeland and settle on a reservation. She never gave up the ways she learned in the wilderness.

Dancers exhibit their traditional pride and heritage during the annual Indian Days celebration at which friends and relatives from many tribes camp together each summer.

Many wise tribal elders passed their time sitting quietly in town, almost unnoticed in the modern rush that went on around them. Here, Blood medicine man and ceremonialist Albert Chief Calf sits in front of a store on the main street of Cardston, a dusty little prairie town along the edge of the Blood Reserve.

"Grandma" Mary Ground already had great numbers of grandchildren and great-grandchildren by the time I met her. At the opening ceremony for the medicine pipe bundle that she long had in her household, she announced that I was a "faraway grandchild." She was proud of her own European characteristics, including light skin and blue eyes, which took nothing from the respect she was shown in the tribe for her traditional wisdom and knowledge. Here she is by her front porch in Browning, Montana, in 1971.

Sioux medicine man Henry Crow Dog surprised
many visitors to the Smithsonian's Folklife Festival in Washington, D.C., with his unusual interpretations of human history, which he
illustrated with large felt-pen drawings. His
grandfather assassinated famous Sioux head
chief Spotted Tail.

Eagle Plume, or Natosina, the father of our
friend and uncle Atsitsina, or Willie Eagle
Plume. A noted warrior who captured many enemy horses and scalps, Eagle Plume became a
peaceful rancher and renowned medicine man in
his later years when this photo was taken. He
died in the 1930's. *(Photo by Hileman, Glacier
Studio)*

Willie Eagle Plume, who encouraged us to learn the traditional ways of his forefathers, during one of his many visits at our mountain home. He is wearing a Hudson's Bay-blanket coat first brought to the Blackfeet by early traders.

Singing some of the many medicine pipe bundle songs with Wolf Old Man was a regular practice each time he came to visit us.

A sacred Sun Dance encampment pitched on the open prairie in the summertime, just as it has been for ages past. Our otter tipi is the center one with the darkest top.

A pause during the opening ceremony of the ancient and highly revered Longtime Pipe of the Blood Tribe after we brought it back from its museum captivity. The bundle's traditional keepers, Mr. and Mrs. Many Gray Horses, sit at the left. The open bundle lies between them and the ceremonial leader, Bob Black Plume, who is at my right. In the foreground is the stone-encircled lodge fire with an earthen altar for incense between it and the bundle. The sack at left contains four hand drums used to accompany some of the ceremonial's many songs.

With some of our elders inside our tipi. Tom Morning Owl, a member of our family, was about to transfer ceremonial rights to me for a traditional weasel-decorated shirt that he owned. It hangs on a wooden stake between us. Atsitsina and Bob Black Plume drummed and sang the ceremonial songs. Next to Tom sit Many Gray Horses, then Laurie Plume, who transferred a similar shirt he had owned as a boy to young Wolf. Pat Weasel Head sits by him and our medicine pipe bundle hangs at its usual place in the back.

At home with three of our boys shortly after the death of Wolf Old Man. Iniskim is firmly wrapped in a cradleboard, Okan stands next to him, and Wolf holds his bow and arrows. Low clouds hang on the mountains behind us.

Louis and Maggie Bear Child in their tipi.

During a pause in the dancing at Browning's North American Indian Days, summer of 1971.

which even old prairie Indians have heard. We arranged for a visit there with several others from the festival, all of whom wanted to see relics from their own tribes. Instead of being guided around the public displays, we were taken right through the staff entrance and brought to the museum's storage rooms. Closets and drawers were opened for us, where everyone readily located collections pertaining to their own tribes.

Atsitsina looked first at pipes, searching for ideas to use on those he was making. We were told that the best pipes were then being studied somewhere else by an ethnologist who was writing a book on the subject. Atsitsina asked what the purpose of the book would be, but the museum person did not know. The old man said he wondered why an educated white man would want to spend time studying something as impractical as Indian pipes. He thought more important things in the world needed studying—things of value to masses of people, not just a few. It was a topic he brought up again at other museums.

After seeing the pipes, we were shown some Blackfoot medicine bundles. One of these contained a sacred headdress that signified membership in the ancient women's society of the Bloods known as the Motokiks. Back home Atsitsina had just been asked to remake such a headdress, one that had been lost by an old woman who was still alive. It was presumed that one of her young relatives had sold it to Yellow Fly.

Atsitsina looked long and quietly at the intricate details of this sacred item. It consisted of a soft buckskin headband, stuffed and decorated to look like a small snake. Several tall, feathered plumes were made to stand up on its top. Now and then Atsitsina looked at the museum guide out of the corner of his eye. Finally he said to me, in Blackfoot: "I will steal this!" He sounded serious, and I became alarmed. Thoughts of federal prisons rushed through my mind. I could not see any possible way to get the bulky bundle past the many guards and sentries without being caught.

Luckily, Atsitsina shared my hesitancy and wrapped the sacred bundle back up. But for some days afterward the missed opportunity bothered him, and he said so. It was his opinion that the headdress had been made by Blood Indians to be prayed and danced with, and that there were still Blood women wanting to pray and dance with it. There were not enough headdresses left in the tribe to fill all the requests for society memberships. For lack of such headdresses there was always a line of women waiting to join.

The college dormitory buildings were ugly, but we found our room within one of them even more unbearable. It was a sterile little box, with cement-block walls and two modern, roll-out beds. Atsitsina called it "our cell." It had absolutely nothing to entertain us. The only place of interest, after dark, was the campus snack bar, where beer was served in paper cups to quench thirst created by the humid weather. Bluegrass musicians went there to "jam" with champion fiddle players from around the country, while folk singers and dancers from Yugoslavia twirled next to square dancers. Only the Indians seemed too shy to dance and sing. They sat in little cliques and visited, or watched the entertainment and drank beer.

One night a bunch of "good ole boys" from the South decided to get some of the Indians involved in their merriment. They had several bottles of Kentucky bourbon in their instrument cases. These they offered to share with the quiet natives. The liquor was potent stuff, especially when compared to the cheap wine that is most common on reservations. Soon a couple of the Indians were becoming noticeably drunk. From the talk, I gathered that these same southerners normally look down on Indians in part because of their problems with drinking. They didn't seem aware of their own guilt in this case.

Fortunately, the drinking party turned out all right. Crow Dog asked a well-known folk singer, who was with the group, for his guitar. It was handed over among snickers and guffaws, which quickly stopped when the old man started strumming a fancy tune and singing one of his creations of wit and sarcasm. He improvised words to suit the occasion, making subtle fun of the shallowness of his would-be tormentors.

The performance reached a climax when one of the bystanders called out: "Hey, Crow Dog, now that you drank up my liquor I'm gonna steal the rest of your land!" Crow Dog didn't change his expression at all, but he cast a wily glance toward the other man's fancily dressed wife, and replied calmly: "I don't give a damn about the land; I'll steal your woman!" While everyone laughed he again began strumming the guitar, only much harder than before. The owner of it winced as if in pain, no doubt thinking the old Indian would destroy it. By then he was probably wishing he had left the quiet natives alone.

Later Atsitsina got a chance to take part in the fun, as well. He and I went to one end of the long, rectangular-shaped lounge to watch a group of Kentucky dancers having a lively hoedown. The leader of the group spotted the old man, with his silver-gray braids and moccasin-covered feet, and decided to get him into their action. He went up to Atsitsina and said: "Hey, old-timer, why don't you step out here and give it a try? There's nothin' to it!" He probably thought Atsitsina's efforts would be good for a few laughs.

The old man acted shy, and pretended complete ignorance of what he was expected to do, but he stepped into the dance circle. While he stood there and smiled, the professional dancers whirled around him, hollering and whooping. He never let on that he was at one time perhaps the only Indian champion at hoedown dances in rural Alberta towns. In fact, in his younger days he was even a square-dance caller. Sometimes, when he was staying with us, he would delight in startling our visitors by suddenly bursting out with some of his fast calling, accompanied by his imitation of a western drawl.

Atsitsina stood and acted dumb just long enough to let the lively Kentucky music bring his old bones and joints into rhythm, then he cut loose. From there on them-there Kentucky folks was all eyes, and their mouths was just-a-hangin' wide open while old Uncle Willie Eagle Plume clicked his moccasin heels and stomped that shiny linoleum darn near through the floorboards. I stood and watched quietly, hoping that his old heart would stay inside his chest and his braids on his head, while he slapped himself silly on the legs and the behind. Those Kentucky folks sure seemed to have a lot more respect when they whooped and hollered to applaud his finish. By the time we left Washington, D.C., he had a bunch of names and addresses of true blue Southerners who said they would be proud to have him come and visit in their homes.

Toward the end of the ten-day festival Atsitsina became noticeably worn out from heat, loneliness, and the constant stream of staring people. Many asked questions that seemed shallow, and they didn't appear to think about our answers. It was as if they only wanted to hear us talk. The uncomfortably humid weather seemed better suited to lying back quietly and fanning oneself than to serving as objects of curiosity.

We had with us some traditional Blackfoot clothing, both for display and to wear during the "powwows" that were held several times as part of the festival. In our tipi we hung these items along a rope tied up behind us. Sometimes Atsitsina arranged the displayed clothing so that he could work behind it and remain almost hidden. At other times he would go for walks, alone or with one of the other old Indians, especially Henry Crow Dog. He usually came back from these outings feeling more cheerful.

Many of the spectators appeared to have had no previous experiences with Indians, nor any knowledge of Indian life. We tried to give honest and forthright answers to their questions, but sometimes their conversations with us made little sense. At those times Atsitsina would play "dumb," pretending he could speak no English. Some of the other participants became so frustrated that they turned to drinking. Two men were gone for several days before they returned, still drunk. They barely showed up in time to catch their homebound plane.

Since we were the only participants using a tipi, a lot of questions had to do with such Indian dwellings. Children often thought Atsitsina and I had brought ours with us, and they asked if we lived in it at home, as well. Others wondered if it would not be awfully cold in the winter to have the tipi so open in front. A few wondered how it was to sleep in a tipi while camped so close to the White House. To all of them we said: "This is not our tipi," and explained that back home tipis are used mainly for festivals and ceremonies.

Often spectators stopped for a moment in front of our open workplace, looked inside, and called out: "What are you making?"

In most cases, the answers would have been self-evident if they had stood and watched us for a little while. There was much to see at the festival, and few seemed to have time for more than momentary glances at our work. If we were making pipes, someone invariably asked what we planned to smoke in them. Some were glassy-eyed longhairs who no doubt hoped that we would say "pot." Instead, we pointed out that smoking mixtures vary with tribes and individuals, and that the Blackfeet most commonly use a blend of bearberry leaves and commercial tobacco.

During the festival Atsitsina added several new words to my Blackfoot vocabulary, including a few that would have surprised those romantic writers and historians who have insisted that Indian languages are without profanity. Atsitsina used a few strong words and expressions when certain people intentionally tried to annoy us. He didn't care for remarks made about "redskins," "savages," "squatting in a wigwam," and "wearing pigtails like women," though we heard all of these, and more. Several times we heard taunting war-whoops, usually made by teenagers going around in groups. A few times we heard small children asking their parents if we were going to scalp them.

Atsitsina became happy whenever someone took time to actually get acquainted with us. We made a number of new friends. One middle-aged woman watched us one day for several hours. The next day she came back and brought a home-cooked meal, which was a pleasant change from the catered lunch of chicken and salad that was normally served to us on paper plates. This woman called herself a gypsy, and said that she got very good "spiritual readings" from us. When she got ready to leave she kissed us on our cheeks.

I thought Atsitsina would be taken aback by such emotional behavior from a total stranger, but he was quite moved. He surprised me by saying: "Gosh, that was a nice lady. She don't even know us, but she comes here and feeds us, and then kisses us good-bye. There should be more people like her!"

Thinking now of this incident makes me realize that most Indian elders we've known were happy to be friends with anyone who showed respect for them and interest in what they were doing. Per-

228 *Shadows of the Buffalo*

haps the stereotype of cold and unfriendly Indians came from people who were themselves that way? On the other hand, some elders act so friendly to strangers that they appear to be overly humble. This is especially true of people who belong to tribes used to being dominated—both by white society and by stronger tribes before that. Many tribes were so repressed that their members gave up the struggle to keep their own identities and allowed history to swallow them up.

Bloods and other Blackfeet have always ruled the lands on which they lived, so their personal pride and tribal identity are still relatively strong. Except for one uncalled-for massacre of a Montana band by an army troop, the Blackfeet people have never fought government soldiers, nor been defeated by them. This is an important factor in their outlook on life. For instance, the Bloods feel quite independent from many worldly problems on their own reserve. They are proud to show off their land to friends, and appear ready to fight for it in case of challenges by enemies, including federal government officials. Many other tribes have humbly given up all their lands, or else allowed themselves to be pushed around even in their own homes.

One afternoon Atsitsina and I got into a discussion with two blacks who wore African turbans and said they belonged to some sect whose name I have forgotten. They had been talking to Henry Crow Dog for an hour, or more, before they came to us. We had heard their earnest—almost demanding—voices out behind our tipi, where Crow Dog often sat. During occasional pauses he gave quiet replies, using far fewer words than they.

The blacks wanted to know if American Indians were willing to accept members of the transplanted African race as "brothers and sisters of Nature," and if they would join them to drive the "white man" back to Europe. Before starting with us they asked me if I was a "real Indian." Atsitsina must have sensed what they were getting at, so he told them, matter-of-factly: "He's my grandson!" They looked silently at him, then at me, and their eyes told me they didn't believe him. Yet they must have decided that arguing about it would not further their efforts at promoting an interracial alliance, so they let the matter drop.

They wanted to know if our people in Canada owned land. I told them that the Blood Tribe has the largest Indian reserve in Canada and that the old man farmed some of it, which he considered his own. I also explained that he was not allowed to sell any land to "white men," nor could outsiders come and take any of the land away. They asked if he had enough land so that other people could find room on it to live—other people like dispossessed "black brothers of Nature," for instance. Would Atsitsina allow such "brothers" to come to him, if in need, and settle on some of that land?

I don't think the old man understood the purpose of their conversation, and the blacks seemed unwilling to have me explain, or to answer in his place. I gathered that their sect was looking for a land base where they could live near other "anti-Europeans," with whom they could begin their proposed drive to rid the country of the "white man." They seemed to have no concept of tribal reserves, especially Canadian ones, or of the strict laws limiting access to anyone but members of the tribes.

The main difficulty these blacks had in speaking to an old Indian like Atsitsina was their apparent intellectual background. They seemed to be well educated, and spoke knowingly of worldly events and movements that Atsitsina knew little or nothing about. They backed their comments with philosophical theories that were completely foreign to him. They spoke of a united front of dark-skinned peoples against those with lighter skins— "the enemies." They did not realize that Indians who still dream of getting back a native America want to see the country rid of *all* races but their own. The blacks also did not seem to realize that recent Indian militancy—of which they had heard—was a response to specific Indian problems, rather than part of an international racial conspiracy.

The blacks finally left, obviously displeased with the encounter. Atsitsina asked me to explain what they had talked about, but he knew little more about their social conditions, and their reasons for complaint, than they did about his. He said he felt sorry for blacks because they had been brought away from their country as slaves, but he also admitted that these young men had frightened him. He had seen and heard news reports of black violence and riots in the cities. The lack of black people within his own small world at home had led him to adopt stereotyped opinions about them from what others said.

Atsitsina found one favorite among the visitors who came and spent time with us in our tipi. This was a small and pretty young lady with long black hair. Among her ancestors were some Chinese, so he frequently asked me: "Where is my girlfriend, that Braid-Behind girl?" She usually wore her hair loose, but the Blackfoot name for a Chinese person is Braid Behind. She was an artist interested in cultural things, so she spent many hours sitting quietly inside our tipi, making pen-and-ink sketches. She also studied the language of her Chinese ancestors, for which she found unexpected use right at our tipi. One afternoon the ambassador from mainland China came by, wanting to see something of American Indian life. He must have been quite startled, as he stood by our tipi, to have a young lady come out and speak to him in his own tongue.

Atsitsina and this young lady wrote letters to each other after the festival ended. She finally came for a visit to our home in Canada, during which time he gave her the name Pipe Woman, in memory of our meeting while making pipes. For a while it looked like more might come of the relationship between them, but distance and age interfered. He carried her picture with him for a long time.

One thing that worried us during the festival was how to get back home, since we had no money or return tickets. We had used Atsitsina's pension check to pay for our plane tickets to Washington intending to replace it with the two hundred dollars we were each promised as an honorarium. But when the festival came near its end, we were told that this money was not immediately available. In fact, it didn't reach us until some time after we got back home. We asked the Smithsonian people for two of the travel tickets left over from those who didn't show up, and they promised to look into that possibility, but nothing came of it. We were disappointed, since we did our "folklife" work diligently every day from morning till suppertime, while some of the other participants took lengthy breaks, or did relatively little to help the festival.

When the festival staff finally realized that we might get stuck in their city, they came up with two train tickets to New York, which was the cheapest way to get us out of town. Once there, I had hopes of getting more funds from one of the two publishers who were bringing out my books. An editor there had become a family friend, and she eventually loaned us the money for our fare, after we were guests in her home.

Our train ride to New York City might have been pleasant if the air conditioning had not broken down during the 100-degree weather. Since there were no windows to open, we had a very uncomfortable ride. Atsitsina unbuttoned the front of his shirt and fanned himself furiously with the old eagle wing. He finally gave up and fell asleep, so that he never saw most of the people who got on and off that train. But every one of them saw him—a sweating, long-haired, old Indian man, with his shirt hanging open and a bird's wing lying across his brown chest, passed out on the hot afternoon train from Washington to New York. No one made a remark, but many stared as long as they dared. In comparison to him they all looked so uncomfortable, wearing their business suits and carrying briefcases.

We finally arrived at New York's Penn Station and changed from the train to a subway. On the way we had to walk through dingy, dusty, underground caves that felt hot enough for baking bread. Our five bags and suitcases were filled with sufficient weight in clothing, tools, and craft materials to burden four people. They nearly killed the two of us. After countless stairways, stops for breath, and stares from strangers, we finally ended up aboard a subway train that took us the final stage to Brooklyn's Borough Hall, near the editor's home.

If Atsitsina had ridden that hot, stuffy, and speeding subway train on the first day of our journey away from the reserve, I'm sure he would have turned around and gone back home. He looked tired, pale, and frightened as we raced through the dark underground from one station to the next. Yet he never said a word. By this time I think he had resigned himself to have faith in our ability to get back home safely.

We happened to be in the subway about the time that summer school classes ended for the day. Great mobs of city kids crowded aboard the train—mostly blacks, with Afro hairstyles and wild clothing. They completely surrounded the old man, who had taken the last empty seat, near where I stood. He held tightly to his eagle wing and didn't even dare to fan himself with it. He kept looking at me for reassurance, but I was busy holding onto one of the metal center posts, while guarding our baggage and working hard to keep myself from falling over onto other people, as the hot train swayed and bucked under New York City.

At Borough Hall we got off the train and wearily climbed yet another long flight of stairs to reach the scorching sidewalks. As we made our above-ground appearance in the city, I quickly realized that we would not have attracted any more attention on the crowded street if two naked girls had been walking with us. It was like a continuation of the festival mobs, and I couldn't believe that we were *that* unusual in everyone's eyes. I was tempted to sit down with the old man and take out our tools to make pipes, so that the throngs of people would really have something to stare at. Instead, I tried to hail a taxi to save us from walking four long and crowded blocks to Sidney Place, where we were bound.

Can you imagine what it was like for two conspicuous men, wearing hair in braids and carrying five suitcases, to hail a taxicab for a simple four-block ride through Brooklyn, New York? Impossible! Most of the drivers pretended not to see us, what with all the luggage they would have had to load and unload. Of those who stopped, two said they could not accept fares to such a nearby destination, one said he couldn't accept passengers unless they were headed out of Brooklyn, and the last one said he didn't know where Sidney Place was, and he didn't want me to show him. We finally gave up and decided to walk there instead.

There is a certain amount of risk involved in bringing a seventy-year-old man from his simple and quiet life on the prairie into the continent's largest and most crowded city, especially during one of its hottest afternoons. Among the sufferings we had to endure were the hot sidewalks, which burnt easily through the thin leather soles of our moccasins and tired our feet with their concrete hardness. I finally told Atsitsina to sit down on a bench while I went ahead with part of the luggage. When I came back I carried the rest, so that he could walk with less strain.

At the house of our editor-friend we barely managed to climb four more flights of stairs that brought us to a room of cool comfort, where we collapsed for the rest of the day. We talked about plans for seeing the city, although Atsitsina had little knowledge about it or what there was to do. His main interest was in seeing Madison Square Garden, because in his younger days as a rodeo cowboy it had been the goal of every rider to perform there. He was disappointed when I took him to the Garden, because the present building was newly constructed and didn't offer much for him to look at.

There was a fireplace in the home where we stayed, and this surprised the old man greatly. He had thought all cities were too modern for such seemingly primitive things as open fires. He was even more startled, a few days later, when I brought him to a neighborhood grocery store, where firewood sold for three and four dollars per bundle of half a dozen pieces. Back home he thought times were getting tough when a nearby lumber mill quit giving away its scrap wood for free and began charging ten dollars for it—by the truckload!

At the same grocery store he saw small steaks selling for several dollars each, and Atsitsina shook his head in amazement. On the reserve a family of ten ate their whole dinner for that amount of money. Besides, he liked his steaks large, with plenty of fat, and the little connoisseur pieces in New York seemed to him hardly deserving of recognition. In a clothing store window he saw a man's suit priced at several hundred dollars. That was more money than he was used to spending to dress his entire family for a whole year!

Of course, the subject of money was of prime interest to an old man who had never had much of it. In New York it was obvious that great quantities of money were being spent all around us. Atsitsina talked about it the way a peasant child would talk about a big toy store. When he saw the Empire State Building his first comment was: "Must be lots of money in there!" When he saw a museum full of Indian relics, he remarked: "This old stuff must be worth lots of money!" Commenting on the rush-hour crowd in the subway station one afternoon, he said: "Must be lots of millionaires here."

Yet in spite of all the glamor and attraction of the big city, he didn't forget to humble himself in prayers to the Great Spirits of Nature, every morning and night. Sometimes he did it by himself, often we did it together, and one night we sat by the fireplace with our hostess and made sweet-smelling incense, just like at home. He always prayed for the family we stayed with, along with our own families. He always addressed our Earth Mother, underneath us, even though in this case she was covered by a five-story house and subway tracks far below.

One of the most memorable events during our stay in New York happened when our hostess took us to eat at a very high-class restaurant. Atsitsina had never seen such a fancy place, and I had never eaten in one, especially not with a tribal elder.

Atsitsina was still carrying the old eagle fan when we went for our meal. The French waiter looked dismayed as he brought us to one of the ornately set tables among the apparently well-heeled patrons of the restaurant. We both wore jeans and moccasins, and I wonder that we weren't asked to leave for lack of proper attire.

Although Atsitsina could read and write quite well, he only took a quick glance inside the restaurant's menu before he turned to me and said, somewhat sheepishly, "Just order me some meat." He later said he thought the menu was written in another language, because he had never heard the unusual entrée titles before.

When the waiter arrived to take our order I turned to the Old man and said, in Blackfoot; "You wanted to eat some cooked guts?" Cooked guts are a delicacy among the Blackfoot people. When done properly, stuffed with wild berries and soft meat, they taste much more appetizing than they sound. Atsitsina would have been glad to have some guts right then, fresh from the campfire. Taking my question as a joke, he replied, also in Blackfoot: "Yes, indeed, some cooked guts!'' I turned to the French waiter and said clearly: "He wants to know if you have any cooked guts.'' The waiter looked at me with disbelief. In a few moments he recovered himself and said, hastily: "Cooked oatmeal, sir?'' "No,'' I told him, "cooked *guts!*''

For some moments no one moved, or said anything. The waiter just stared at his notepad as though he had not heard me. I finally looked into the menu and said that a sirloin steak would do. He heard that, and quickly wrote it down. It was a good steak, and I had one, too. Atsitsina's eyes grew big when I told him the whole meal had cost nearly forty dollars, with the two of us having done most of the ordering. It would have been very difficult for us to eat all the food that so much money would buy in any restaurant he had ever been in previously.

That evening, when we got back to our Brooklyn home, Atsitsina gave me hell! The episode with the cooked guts didn't please him any better than it had the waiter. He said: "By gosh, I'm pretty mad at you! You made a fool out of me back there, where all those fancy rich people eat. You told that man, 'This fellow wants some guts!' ''

4

THE TRIP TO THE EAST COAST with Willie Eagle Plume was like a symbolic divider between our family's life on the modernizing reserve and our move to the wilderness, which followed right after. From overcrowded buildings and streets I went to forests and mountains where animal trails are seldom disturbed by people.

During the trip old Atsitsina made me realize more clearly than ever before that my ways of looking at life frequently differed from those of most of my Indian relatives. Our social and material goals were often not the same. For instance, Atsitsina longed for money when he saw luxury, while I was disgusted by the evidence of greed and power that I thought it represented. I had grown to dislike these qualities during my years of living in cities, which the old man had never experienced. He knew only the simple life and spiritual ways that I wanted to learn. He yearned to sample the material comforts that I was already tired of, but that he'd never had. We seemed to be on the same path, but going in different directions!

Fortunately, Beverly and I had fairly similar ideas about wanting to live with a minimum of money and material goods. We did have occasional conflicts over the subject, as many married couples do, but we solved most of these by using her ancestors as examples. That meant doing without a number of modern, expensive commodities. However, there were other aspects of the simple lifestyle I had planned that did conflict with Beverly's ideas, and with the general customs of Indian society. Most important of these was my

237

longing to be isolated from public life. This did not go well with the close-knit family and tribal life that she grew up with.

In the past, few members of the tribe took their families and camped away from others. There were isolated cases, but they risked being attacked or even wiped out by wandering enemies. If their luck was good, and they survived, other tribe members often moved out and joined them, until they found themselves surrounded by a new band within the tribe. One way or another, it was not part of tribal custom to live alone for too long.

When we moved to our newly acquired mountain land, initially we were too busy to think much about being lonesome. We had to prepare a cabin in which to live, locate drinking water, gather wood for cooking and heating, build an outside toilet, and construct a woodshed. We had to make many preparations for our first mountain winter. It was still summer, and the weather was warm and pleasant. But we knew it was going to get cold, with snow so deep that it might keep us from traveling anywhere, even for necessities.

At first there were people with us, planning to live on our land as neighbors, and to share with us the experiences of learning wilderness life. But they didn't remain here long. The young California couple was the first to become discouraged when they realized their lack of money would keep them from building anything but the most primitive shelter. Back in the city that had seemed like a wonderful idea. But they hadn't reckoned on the endless hordes of mosquitoes, or on the quantities of bears and other creatures that seemed eager to bother humans who lacked sturdy homes. In addition, they had romantic theories about all living things, which kept them from eating meat, among other foods (although they said they didn't mind killing vegetables). It was too late to plant a garden for the year, and they needed plenty of cash to pay for their vegetarian diet. The upcoming hunting season would have been of no use to them. To top it off, they got dysentery, though luckily the rest of us didn't. After that they split up and went back to city life, separately.

We felt a bit guilty over their failure, wondering if we should have been more willing to share our own meager funds. Lack of money kept several other interested friends from joining us in the mountains, as well. It seemed that we were the only ones who had spent time preparing for the move. We had saved up money to acquire our land and get settled, and had also brought tools and materials with which to work that land and make some of our own clothing, furniture, and utensils. It did not seem right that we should be expected to share with those who had not bothered to bring anything they could share with us, except their company.

The young fellow who came with us from the neighboring tribe also had no money, though he said he was used to living without any, and that it didn't bother him. He would hunt for meat, and be satisfied with the addition of a few sacks of carrots and potatoes. As a "Treaty Indian" in Alberta he was allowed to hunt any time of the year on unoccupied "Crown land," as public land is called in Canada. He didn't care that the modern government of British Columbia, where we were, was trying not to honor this part of the promised "aboriginal rights."

His simple philosophy about life was quite in harmony with the way I thought we should try to live together in a camp. However, his attitude about hunting upset me. He seemed to think that wild animals were there for the taking by ambitious native hunters. Perhaps I was too idealistic in hoping that we could find some way of hunting "peacefully" and with little bloodshed. It seemed as though he went around constantly "sniffing" the air for wild scent, his gun nearby and ready to shoot. I didn't realize I was learning some of this from him, even while I consciously thought such behavior was outdated.

Even worse, our friend had to go back to his reserve after a few weeks here, to stand trial on a charge of allowing several elk to waste during an earlier season. He and a friend had shot the elk on a remote part of their tribe's land during late winter, when the snows were melting. They tried to drive in to haul out the heavy carcasses, but they were unable to get near them. The elk were too big and awkward to drag out on foot, especially with the poor weather conditions. Our friend and his companion had intended to pass the meat out among relatives and elders, who would have been glad to get it. Instead, they were forced to leave the elk until they spoiled.

We bought enough lumber so that this friend could build himself a little cabin. He added bits and pieces scrounged from abandoned cabins in our region. He worked eagerly until it was completed, and then he hunted. There were fresh tracks of deer and elk near our homes, yet he was unable to see any of the animals, let alone shoot one. He considered this a bad sign for himself. He said he liked the place very much, otherwise, and we felt good about having someone with us from the same tribe. He was one of the few younger people interested in carrying on Blackfoot traditions with us.

Like a true descendant of great Blackfoot horsemen, our friend was eager to get horses for riding. Back on the reserve he had his own, but we decided it would be too much trouble to bring them over and get them used to mountain living. Often this means several seasons of extra feeding, since prairie horses are used to better grazing conditions than our tree-covered slopes provide. With our lack of money we thought it would be better to get plain, tough, local ponies, who would be used to the woods and mountains.

I was eager for horses, too—some of my ancestors in Europe were fantastic horsemen long before the Blackfeet ever saw the first of these animals. I was anxious to learn life with horses from an Indian viewpoint, since my own experiences had not been too good. In Europe I only saw horses used for working, and their size frightened me. Later my own horses always got away, so that I never learned to have confidence in my relationships with them.

We heard about a rancher up the valley from us who had a nice little Appaloosa stallion that he wanted to sell. Years before, the man had been one of the cowboys who helped round up the last wild horse herds in this area. He claimed the stallion was a descendant of these mustangs, which made it sound like a perfect animal to have in our camp.

We found this old rancher living in a modern, split-level house near a log cabin that had once been his home. He had the horse in a well-built corral nearby. It was a nice-looking animal—short, with a long mane and tail, and with a buckskin-colored body covered with golden spots over a pure white rump. The Appaloosa looked proud and excited, and we both liked him right away. The owner put a bridle on the horse and I jumped up on his bare back. Within an instant I was down again, lying in barnyard manure! My brashness resulted in a quick buck, after which the animal stood and watched me out of the corner of one eye. Childhood fright battled manhood pride, as I got up and decided to give it another try. The stallion bucked me off again, so I tried it a third time. He finally gave up and took me for a pleasant ride.

The owner bragged his fancy horse up quite a bit, in the manner of experienced horse traders. He said the stallion was the ultimate descendant from the wild herds of the valley—the result of breeding for beauty and endurance. He also claimed the Appaloosa was the only survivor from the few mustangs that he and another cowboy had saved from the roundup, which took place sometime in the thirties. The rest were sold to canneries for dog food, while their range was taken over by cattle.

We finally concluded a deal in which I gave the man one hundred dollars in cash (which we sorely needed for getting settled), as well as a modern, 7mm European hunting rifle, with scope, that I got in trade for some old farm equipment when I left the first homestead. The gun was a powerful sporting weapon that I used only once, after which I preferred the feel of my old, lever-action Winchester.

That horse turned out to be the cause of considerable trouble for us. Beverly was against the purchase from the start, when she said that stallions are especially hard to care for. I thought she just didn't want horses around, since her oldest brother was killed on one. I later wished I had followed her advice.

We borrowed a trailer to haul the horse home with. When we tried to get him into it he gave the first indication that following orders was not part of his personality. With a lot of pulling and cursing we finally got on the road and brought him to our simple, wilderness corral. It consisted of poles and barbed wire, hurriedly attached to fence posts and trunks of convenient trees. Using barbed wire anywhere, and driving nails into living trees are remnants of two pioneer methods that I have come to despise, since then.

The stallion was certainly exciting to ride. He was fast, and he seemed to love racing up and down our long, open field at top speed, especially after being corralled much of the day. He should have had a large, fenced pasture, and we should have waited to get him until we had one built. Racing a fast horse has its limited appeal, just like racing a fast auto. Once the initial thrill wore off I decided that a slower form of travel would be safer and more enjoyable. This half-wild horse knew absolutely nothing about being relaxed. It was hard work getting him to go slowly, at all. He bolted at the slightest nudge, and even with a release of tension on the reins.

When our friend came back from his court hearing about the elk, he brought along a truckload of hay from the reserve. We needed lots of it, since the horse was confined to his corral. On the prairie it cost only half as much as in the mountains, because most of it is grown there. Even so, I wondered how we would get another load or two to last us through the winter.

Mail order sales of our small books brought the only income we had for making monthly payments on the land. There were eight or nine volumes in the series, and I was working on more. The subject of Indians and living in Nature was quite popular at that time. Unfortunately, the money never came steadily, and there was seldom enough for printing new books after reprinting old ones. The lack of funds kept us from advertising, also. We relied on word-of-mouth business, along with occasional reviews and other media mentions. These were mostly in the so-called "alternative publications."

Once a week we drove to town to pick up mail, send orders, and do our banking. If there was money left over we bought food and building supplies. The owner of a small lumber mill sold us his rejects very cheaply—sometimes only ten dollars for a truckload of two-by-fours. This lumber had cracks and warps so that it could not be used for construction in towns and cities, but it worked fine for us.

Our postal address was over an hour's drive from home, which helped cut down the temptation of going there often. We originally got a remote post office box to check the flow of uninvited visitors. Hardly a week went by that letters did not arrive, saying things like: "I'm coming to the Canadian wilderness and want your help!"

Some wanted advice on getting into the country, or buying land, while others simply wanted to share our lifestyle, which they supposed was like the ideals described in our books. Very few of the writers gave us the impression that they really understood the serious aspects of wilderness living, or Indian culture. They sounded "fed up with cities and modern society," and often said so. They expected a mere physical relocation would cure all that bothered them.

Living so far from our mailbox did not always keep seekers from finding us, we quickly learned. We tried to accommodate those who showed up, although there was little spare room in our cabins. I spent a lot of time at my desk, writing, while Beverly ran the daily household. Our friend often went hunting. When the weather got cold and gloomy he tried sitting at his desk, too, although he couldn't find any work that interested him for long. Outsiders who came were faced with the same problem—what to do with themselves to get settled. There seemed to be a shortage of training in useful skills!

Our lack of specific tribal goals and activities caused the various visitors to drift on after a time. Some didn't even stay long enough to eat meals, or to spend the night. Yet even these short visits became distracting to our family efforts at harmony. Our friend finally gave up and decided to go back to his reserve. Beverly drove him over there, since she had grown lonesome for her people, too. Suddenly I found myself all alone, surrounded by nothing but wilderness and wondering what had become of my envisioned "new tribe."

This first experience of being here by myself might have caused me to pack up and move away if Beverly had not assured me that she would be back in a few days. As it was, I finally gave up waiting and walked to the highway, from where I hitchhiked to the reserve. By then I not only missed her companionship, but I was also lonesome to see our old people again.

During the time I was home alone there were several distractions. First, a young couple came with dogs, which they treated like children. One dog got carried away by the wilderness and disappeared. Much time and energy was spent trying to locate him. He eventually showed up, dripping slobber and looking as though he'd given the country a good going over. Dogs running loose in the woods almost invariably chase every deer and wild thing that they see, causing much unnecessary terror and confusion. We learned to ask visitors to keep their dogs on leashes, although it took years to learn how to make sure it was done.

An even greater distraction during my lonely stay was caused by our stallion. One morning a bunch of strangers came to see *him,* instead of me, and he went nearly berserk! The strangers were a herd of scrawny horses that belonged to a cranky old hunting guide who still held to the outdated pioneer attitude that Nature is here for man's taking. When the hunting season was over, and his last customers gone, he simply turned his horses loose to fend for themselves all winter. Only if things got too severe did he scout them up and bring a few bales of hay. Otherwise they had to compete with deer and elk for food. These wild animals didn't need the extra company, since they were already being fenced out of much important winter range by farmers and ranchers.

The guide's horses found their way to the hay bales that our friend brought over the mountains. Like flies on a warm meal in the summertime, those horses wouldn't stay away from the hay. We had it stacked outdoors, next to the corral, because there was no other place to store it. Within a couple days most of it was eaten, and the rest was scattered on the ground and spoiled.

Our stallion didn't care at all about the food—what interested him was that a bunch of mares were gathered within mounting distance, but on the other side of a fence. I chased the wandering herd away before I took him out for exercise and water, but I could hardly keep him under control. By the time I put him back the hay was finished, and the herd had moved on. It was led by a big, heavy-footed gelding who was beyond doing anything for his women except to drive them away from the eager young stud.

The departure of the mares proved too much for the stallion's restraint. He ran after them with abandon, taking part of the corral with him on the way out. When he got to the herd the gelding came out to defend it. A battle ensued that shattered my remaining peace. They bit, kicked, and squealed so loudly that I was sure one or both would be badly hurt before they were through. Periodically the whole bunch would take flight, leaving a cloud of dust in their wake, but the fighting continued, even at top speed. Twice I saw the big gelding go down, but he refused to give up. Finally they all disappeared into the forest, and I was relieved just to be rid of the violence. I intended to see the guide and give him some of my opinions, after Beverly returned with the truck. That night I had strange visions. When I stepped outside, before going to bed, it seemed there were many unseen eyes and unheard voices around me. I stood alone for a long time in the silent darkness.

Beverly's parents were surprised when I suddenly showed up out of the dark. When her old grandmother saw me she covered her mouth with one hand and said: *"Key-eye-yah!,"* which is an ancient Blackfoot expression used by women to indicate surprise. Roughly it means: "Well, *my* goodness!"

Beverly had taken the kids to a Halloween party in Standoff, the reserve's only village. Her mother went right to work, preparing a meal for me, and soon I was enjoying boiled meat, raw kidney (with fat), and fresh celery stalks. When Beverly drove up I hid behind a bed, thinking to surprise her. But I forgot that my rubber overshoes were by the back door, and they gave away my presence. She said our old people had jokingly wondered if I was not afraid to stay home alone in a country so full of bears. Wolf Old Man was especially concerned, since the traditions he was teaching us forbade the killing of these animals, or even touching any part of them.

The Old Man was back in the hospital again for the winter. He would have preferred staying home, but said he was afraid to cause trouble for others if he got sick there. He was eager to hear about our new home, and said he would like making the long trip just to see it once. He was pleased when we gave him some red earth paint, and even more so when he learned that we had found it ourselves along a creek in the mountains. Only once had he been to a place where it was gathered, somewhere out on the plains, in the time of his youth. He said he looked for the place again in later years, but it appeared to have been covered by a landslide. Although red-colored earth is not uncommon, the kind used for sacred paint is. The rest will not color skin properly. Wolf Old Man said ours was just the right shade and texture. When word of our find got around, others asked for some, as well. After that we made frequent contributions to various ceremonies in which painting was important.

There were six beds in the hospital room where Wolf Old Man was staying. All were occupied by elderly men, including the two oldest on the reserve—Wolf Old Man and Guy Wolf Child. The third oldest man, who was a brother of Beverly's grandmother, was also in the same room. He was deaf and nearly blind, and existed mostly in a world of his own. Although he was nearly as thin as a skeleton he had an inner strength that kept him going far beyond any particular reason. Since he was a relative, we always stopped to greet him, although it is doubtful that he knew who we were.

People frequently came to Wolf Old Man at the hospital, for his prayers, advice, and other blessings. Sometimes he brought them to a nearby private room for this, if it was not occupied. He carried on his role of leading medicine man in the tribe as though he were at home in his cabin.

Back at the family house Beverly's father told me a curious story relating to the smoking of a pipe. During the previous winter he had brought me to a special event during which—for the first time ever—Catholic Church leaders prayed and smoked together with traditional Bloods. I was asked to bring my smoking pipe so that it could be used for this occasion. Atsitsina and I wore blanket coats and moccasins, while Beverly wore a long dress and her shawl. Other tribal elders included Pat Weasel Head, John Many Chief, and the tribe's head chief, Jim Shot-on-Both-Sides, who wore a buckskin suit and feather headdress. There was also a half-breed man from the Montana Blackfeet, wearing a blanket coat and carrying a beautifully beaded pipe bag that contained his own smoking pipe. The Catholic bishop came to the reserve from Calgary, wearing his robes. At the appropriate time he sat down with the old leaders and medicine men to smoke my pipe.

Since the time of that event my father-in-law had somehow forgotten that it was *my* pipe that had been used. He said a good friend of his recently brought the same half-breed to a well-known medicine man for a healing ceremony that was held by a neighboring tribe. The man again brought his beaded bag and pipe, from which he offered the medicine man a smoke, along with the request that he be cured of a certain physical ailment. The medicine man had already heard of the church event with the bishop, and he knew that this elderly half-breed was there, with his pipe. The medicine man was one of the "born-again" traditional Indians who bitterly disliked "white men" and "white churches." As the filled pipe was handed to him, he suddenly said he was receiving "instruction from the Spirits" that the pipe was tarnished and had "lost its powers" because it had been smoked by white men. The pipe's owner was very embarrassed, and probably felt quite guilty. He was told to take the pipe out into the forest and dispose of it as an offering, which he did. The story quickly made the moccasin-telegraph. However, there were some enlightening discussions after it was learned that *my* pipe was actually the one used, instead of this man's. My father-in-law decided the whole matter had become clouded by more mysticism than was warranted.

When we got ready to end that visit on the reserve, Beverly's parents asked us to return the following weekend for a smoking ceremony that they were sponsoring to help one of Beverly's brothers, who was ailing. Even though they were both lifelong Catholics, they saw no conflict in hosting a "prayer meeting" of tribal elders, and felt confident that the "native religion" would add strength to their son's recovery and goodness to their love for God and Jesus.

Back home, before we could make the return trip, another young "spiritual seeker" showed up on a cold autumn day. He had written to us, saying he was just out of high school, couldn't get along with his parents or friends, and didn't want to look for a job. He said he wanted to try living the way I described in one of my first small books. He claimed it had "saved" him from giving up life altogether. After reading this, I dreaded his arrival, knowing he would have ideals and expectations that I could not fulfill. I sensed he would be disappointed. I had already determined to change the direction of my writing away from encouraging a concept of "get back to the wilderness," and toward more historic commentary about cultural lifestyles. Still, I was sometimes frustrated to find romantic idealism creeping into my work even when I tried to write without it.

The young fellow was a total tenderfoot—he had never even camped with the Boy Scouts. He had never thought about living without running water, electric lights, or bath and flushing toilet. When he realized there was no choice about the matter, he gamely said he would try to enjoy the simplicity. I told him that we were going back across the mountains in a few days, and that he would be left here alone. His face suddenly paled, and he licked his lips.

When we drove away the following weekend, the young fellow smiled weakly and waved. We concluded that if he was still there by the time we got back he would not stay much longer, and we were right. During the few days and nights that he was totally alone, his parents, and their home in the city, took on new appeal for him. He seemed almost to have visibly matured.

We arrived on the reserve two days before the ceremony was to be held, because Beverly wanted to help her mother make the preparations. We were not worried about leaving a stranger at our home. The medicine pipe bundle always came with us, and we didn't own much else that we considered valuable (except for the land, which always takes care of itself).

After visiting Wolf Old Man and Atsitsina, I took a lone drive down to Browning to visit my elderly friends. As usual I brought along albums with tribal photographs. This was my "work" within the tribe, and elders that I knew often encouraged it. Eagerly they added names and information to my notebooks. My visits were like favorite television programs for people who were beyond having any interest in TV. They had seen very few of the photos before, even though all showed relatives, friends, or at least familiar places. I felt bad when someone got emotional over seeing a dear one who was long gone. It embarrassed me to explain that I could not give the photos away without spoiling the work I was trying to do with them. I sometimes spent goodly sums of money having duplicate prints made, for which I accepted no payment other than friendship and information.

There were some elders who would only give information if they were well paid. They were regular informants for museums and other funded agencies. I knew a couple of these "professional elders" well, but I never asked them to help me, because I could not afford their services. In later research work I found some of what they contributed, and was impressed. But when I checked into their lengthy stories in more detail I sometimes learned that they "padded" their stories with extra color and length. They had learned to combine traditional knowledge with clever skills, giving complex and correct-sounding answers to questions that they either misunderstood or didn't have the right knowledge for. Historians are faced with serious responsibilities to verify these things before they are used to make permanent written records of oral cultures.

In Browning there was a strange old woman who asked me several times to write down her story for one of my books. I never learned what name she was born with, but she called herself Princess Lexipar. She claimed she was a "genuine Indian princess," although it has become generally understood that this title was made up by non-Indians to bestow honorary respect on certain native women. Lexipar claimed the title because of her "grandfather," who, she insisted, was the famous Sioux chief Rain-in-the-Face. The story was amazing, though highly questionable, and she was a captivating teller of it.

Princess Lexipar was the wife of John Bird Earrings, who was my best source of information about old Blackfoot photo scenes. He refused to "sell" his knowledge to strangers, whom he lectured on Jesus and the Bible instead. But he took kindly to me from the moment we met, when I was dressed in costume and he led me around the Indian Days dance floor during my first visit. On different visits I brought him blankets, foodstuff, two pipes, and tobacco. He seemed pleased to get them from a friend, and didn't consider them the same as cash payments.

John was eighty-six years old that fall. As a young man, shortly after the turn of the century, he had often served as interpreter to old warriors and their wives, especially when they went traveling to other parts of the country. He went to world's fairs and expositions in San Francisco, Chicago, St. Louis, and other places. Because of that he knew many faces from the past. In addition, his father was one of the tribe's leading medicine men, who received many visitors. John had a fantastic personal history, but his talks were ruled by traditional modesty, which focused attention on everyone but himself. Thus, I learned of many events he had been involved with, but seldom of his own part in them.

When I first met John and Lexipar they were living in a small, dark log cabin along one of Browning's dusty back alleys. By then John had been twice-widowed. He had also given up country life on his reservation ranch and moved into town. He brought me to his house after the dance, as though he were the tribal ambassador welcoming a special guest. He was the first to show me the hospitable character for which his forefathers were noted.

It was John's open welcome of strangers that helped bring him together with Lexipar. She was about twenty years younger than he, and no one was sure where she came from. The two certainly made an unusual couple. He was tall and thin, with high cheekbones and the hawklike nose of his ancestors. She was short and plump, with light skin and blue eyes. She had thick, dark hair that she wore in two long braids. She also wore moccasins, a beaded belt, and a long dress of calico cloth. Except for her distinct facial features she could easily have passed for an old Indian woman.

The log house had a small porch with a dirt floor that seemed very primitive. In the main room the floor was made of well-worn planks. The walls and ceiling had a darkened gloss from years of smoke and cooking. Lexipar stood at a big wood-burning stove preparing a meal. The warm house was almost stuffy. It smelled strongly of food and old clothing. It was as though I had entered a place left over from another era, although this was in the 1960's. It looked like the movie set for a story about pioneer life on the prairies, with a mixed marriage providing a plot.

During that first visit John had no trouble keeping my attention with his continuous flow of interesting conversation, which he punctuated by signs made with his hands. He was a devout Catholic and he made sure everyone knew it. He was also a sidewalk politician, and he had interesting ideas for curing the country's ills. It was an unusual experience to sit with this old Indian man, in his primitive home, hearing him preach loudly in clear English. Although he wore a huge, six-inch crucifix which was suspended by a stout leather strap, there was no mistaking the air of mystery learned in the household of his father, the medicine man.

John gave interesting discourses on his thoughts about Jesus Christ (as the savior), the federal government (as the oppressor), and himself (as the one who would chase away all politicians not working for God and country). He always climaxed his talks by saying he was going to take "two secketarries and two stenagress" and become President of the United States, throwing out the "whole damned crookit bunch" in the process. Whenever he used a swear word for effect he immediately added: "Excuse me, God!"

At the end of these talks he usually chuckled to himself, then looked at me with a grin. His eyes would squint, as if to say: "I suppose you think I'm just a crazy old man!" But he took his crusade quite seriously, and gave his talks anytime, anywhere, and to anyone who would listen. He felt the country should be in the charge of its native people, who would rule by tribal and community governments, "without sennatarrs, congressmen, Presidents, or New World politics." He felt everyone had a right to live in the country, but that European politicians had usurped the native governments illegally. He wrote volumes of declarations and announcements about these ideas, which he kept in a worn, old leather briefcase. He frequently went to the tribal office, government office, or to his church, and asked for photocopies to be made of his writings. These he passed out on the streets and at powwows. He was a man far ahead of his time, politically, even though some people said he was unbalanced. Government workers and modern Indian politicians considered him a nuisance, or worse. He made open accusations about conniving and swindling regarding tribal laws and finances.

John combined his well-learned school education with the ancient Blackfoot custom of fierce personal independence, which used to keep chiefs humble and working for the good of their people. Those who stepped out of line found themselves without followers. He publicly called for the resignation of questionable tribal leaders, for the opening of all meetings to tribal members, as well as for the publication of all economic affairs. He said his people were being herded like sheep on their own reservation. He wanted them to stand up against those who treated them unfairly. He did not restrict these opinions to audiences around Browning, either. He showed me letters indicating direct contacts with state senators and other important persons, along with newspaper clippings telling of his trips and invitations to several presidential inaugurations.

While John talked, Lexipar puttered around her kitchen and acted as if she didn't hear what he said, or else didn't care. Sometimes he finished talking and turned to her, asking: "Isn't that right, Tiny?" The name fit her, especially in his presence, since her head barely reached his shoulders. In response she usually blushed, nodded her head in agreement, and then tried to get away from the center of attention

Eventually John would take a rest, light up a cigarette, and hum an old Indian tune. His thick glasses reflected so much light that his eyes were hidden from all but a head-on view. He looked like a wise old owl, and gave me the impression that there was nothing he feared.

It was then that Lexipar would quietly come over and show me a framed postcard picture of the heroic Rain-in-the-Face. She would hold it as though it was sacred and ask me, in a low tone: "Did I ever tell you about my grandfather? He was a big Sioux chief, and he ate Custer's liver at the Battle of the Little Bighorn!" Time and again she told me one or another variation of the story.

The first time I met her, when she and John still lived in the old log house, her father was with them, also. He lived in a tiny, closet-like room on one side of the house. He was very wrinkled, and he appeared even older than John. He was short and thin, with scruffy white hair and a fiery glint in his eyes. He spoke with a scratchy, loud voice that made me imagine him as an old gold miner, chasing trespassers off his claim. He was seldom seen around town, and had a reputation for detesting people. He seemed like an old, cranky mouse, staying by himself in his dark, cramped den.

He was actually the first one who told me about Rain-in-the-Face. It was when John took a break from his long conversation with me. The old codger called me into his room and said, almost threateningly: "I'm gonna show ye somethin' ye ain't never seen before, and ye ain't likely to see agin!" Then he reached under his bed and brought out an ancient eagle-feather headdress that had obviously been around for many years. He held it up in the air with a look of triumph, though he made sure to keep it back far enough that I wouldn't be tempted to reach for it.

"This here belonged to my dad, Rain-in-the-Face," he said, very matter-of-factly. Then, with a savage gleam on his face, he added: "He wore it when he rubbed out that General Custard and his boys!" When he was satisfied that I was impressed by the headdress, he quickly put it away, telling me: "I never wear it to the dances here—these fellows might try and get it away from me! You know the Sioux and these Blackfoots was enemies. Why, they might even try and scalp me, you never know!" At that he cackled loudly, as though the thought of it excited him.

John's father-in-law died there, in his little room. The next time I saw John he said "Tiny" took it so hard that she left him, cut off her braids in mourning, and headed for the Coast. However, he didn't seem particularly concerned, saying: "Oh, well, I got her easy and now she's gone again—I just stole her from an old friend in the first place, you know." I learned that on her arrival in Browning, some twenty years earlier, Lexipar had married an Indian who was a generation older than John, though a friend of his. She said once that this man did not treat her very well, and John knew it. One day he came for her and said he would take her shopping. He did, and afterward he brought her to the local justice of the peace, who promptly married them, after which John took her to his own home. The other man had never married her legally, so John got away with his daring maneuver.

By the time of my late-autumn visit, just before the smoking

ceremony, Lexipar was back in Browning with John. Her braids had
grown again, and John was growing braids, too, although his were
thin and stubby compared to hers. He had mellowed out a lot, besides. He still raked the government and tribal council over hot
coals, but he did it with a quieter voice, and with more sense of
humor. He frequently sang old Indian songs, and he even told old
Indian stories, which he had earlier avoided.

This time I had a tape recorder so that Lexipar could tell me her
story. Following are some excerpts from the transcript I made of it:

". . . Well, my father said that back when they lived in Brooklyn, New York, him and his father—that's Rain-in-the-Face—had a
war horse that come up from the Battle at the Little Bighorn. He
said that he used to get up on a stool and wash him—scrub him with
a brush. My dad was just a little feller, then. And later on, when his
dad came in the house, he asked my dad: 'Did you wash my horse
good?'

". . . Then Rain-in-the-Face would say to my father: 'Now I've
got to go and get some firewater.' My father said: 'Firewater?
There's plenty of that in the faucet!' And his dad would tell him:
'No, not *that*, I mean *real* firewater,' and he would start licking his
chops. He said: 'I'll be right back.' And that time he was really
dressed up, too—he had on buffalo horns, feathers down the back,
and a dark buckskin suit that was all brown from smoke . . ."

Although the story of Rain-in-the-Face living in Brooklyn with a
war horse and a headdress seemed farfetched, I was interested in the
many little details that Lexipar provided. I asked her which part of
Brooklyn this took place in, to which she answered:

"I'm not sure, I just know it happened soon after Rain-in-the-
Face quit fighting with the white man. My dad told me he ran away
from home once and rode on the subway trains. This was when he
was just five years old! He rode the subways first, then he went up
an elevator and rode those other kinds of trains that go on top of
buildings [elevated trains]. He just put a nickel in and got a ride. He
said when he got off the trains he was by the back of this store and
this man was hauling something around that turned out to be hogs'
heads. So my father asked for some, 'cause he knew that his mother

could cook them. The man said: 'I'll give you some,' and he gave my dad a whole sack full.

"So my dad was walking down this street in New York with a sack of hogs' heads and a cop came up and said: 'Is your name Bill?' 'Yup, that's my name.' 'Well, you're a wanted man—your father is looking for you! Your father's name is Rain-in-the-Face?' 'Yup!' 'All right, then come with me.'

"This cop drove my dad clear across New York and back to Brooklyn. He told him he was under arrest. When they got there the cop said: 'Well, Rain-in-the-Face, here is your boy. How old is he, anyway?' When he found out he said: 'Say, isn't that kind of young to be going around town with hogs' heads?' But my dad just told him that white people don't know what to do with hogs' heads, that's why he brought them. Us Indians know how to cook them good, you know!"

Interestingly, my mother-in-law substantiated that last statement. Her old, full-blooded grandmother had often made head cheese, after learning the art from her German husband. It caught on among her friends and relatives, and for some fifty years making cheese from animal heads was common in some Blackfoot households. Of course, this was not traditional food, since pigs only became known to native people after they settled on reservations. In fact, many Indians dislike hogs and say they are too filthy to be eaten.

Lexipar said she ended up on the Blackfeet Reservation after her father got fed up with wandering from city to city and decided to move "back to the Indians." She didn't make it clear why they didn't go to the Sioux, but she evidently found her peace among a people who accepted her stories as entertaining and harmless.

Beverly's parents had their smoke ceremony the following night, after my visit with John and Lexipar. Blood elders knew John by the name Roached Hair, and spoke with respect of him. One person mentioned that he had been a hardworking rancher and farmer in his younger years. Someone else said he was a ladies' man before that, to which everyone agreed. They considered that an accomplishment.

The ceremony was small—only five of us sang, instead of the usual eight or ten. Someone else was having the same kind of ceremony the next night, and several elders felt it would be too much to attend both. Those who were closest to us supported ours, while friends and relatives of the others chose theirs. White Horse led the ceremony for Beverly's father, who was his nephew and the sponsor. Pat Weasel Head came to support his adopted younger brother, and we brought Wolf Old Man from his residence at the hospital. On the way we stopped at his house so he could pick up the ceremonial things he needed. Only Atsitsina didn't make it, since he was sick.

The men got stuck several times for songs that they could not recall. Each time they were helped by Pat Weasel Head's wife, Paula (or Ponah, as she was commonly called), who had great knowledge of ritual things. She grew up close to her father, who was the keeper of many bundles and a participant in all their rites. She became Beverly's advisor in traditional matters, and told her several times: "If our customs did not require ceremonies to be led by men, I would be able to lead them all." She was once the head of the women's secret society. During our time she served as "grandmother" to the younger members.

Our trip back through the mountains was a quiet one. Beverly and I were absorbed with thoughts about the upcoming winter—the first in such isolation for both of us. I was especially looking forward to staying home for a while, because it seemed that we came back from each trip with new thoughts and distractions. I wanted to concentrate on living in harmony with Nature and practicing traditional customs. Impatiently, I tried to force Beverly to rush along and keep up with my disciplined efforts, even though she frequently asked me to let her follow in her own time. She didn't want to be forced into loving Nature the way that she had been forced to accept the Bible by dominating nuns and priests. We had difficulty agreeing on how much of our daily life should be devoted to the strict old ways.

Although our simple household was not exactly comfortable in the modern sense, we had no physical complaints, only emotional ones. Before moving to the land we had built up mental expectations of each other. Although we had discussed these thoughts, there was no way to make definite plans and decisions until we began *doing*, instead of talking. There were no books describing precedents from which we could learn. It was still a new social alternative for young, educated couples to move *away* from technology and cities, rather than *toward* them. Of course, it was a totally new alternative to make such a move while trying to practice ancient Blackfoot traditions. Modern history has generally seen tribalism and individualism discarded rather than adopted.

Beverly was perhaps better qualified for rustic life than I was, since she grew up without electricity and running water. Her first home was basic, like our cabin, without luxuries. But she and her family lived that way out of necessity, and now I was asking her to do it by choice. She felt ready to try, but there seemed no end to "modern" things I wanted to do without. We had no radio in our vehicle, or in the house. I didn't want newspapers or magazines, and certainly no TV. I felt it was not possible for us to have much direct say about the course of the modern world, anyway, so I saw no need to concern ourselves about its daily activities. These seemed mainly to make people tense, I thought.

Attitudes like mine were sometimes criticized as being antisocial by those more active in world affairs, among them some close friends. But I considered this a personal matter, the choice of which each human being should be entitled to make freely. After all, I was not criticizing those who wanted to live in crowded cities, so why should they bother us if we didn't?

Some of our friends said moving to the land was "escaping reality," and we talked about this. Is it *really* possible to "escape" reality? We cannot see how, as long as one continues to remain alive. True, there are ways of altering one's state of reality, for instance, by eating, exercising, drinking, using drugs, or watching TV. Based on the life-view of our elders, each of us *should* change our realities if that will give us more happiness and satisfaction—as long as it brings no harm to anyone else.

It has also been said that people living by themselves avoid responsibilities to society. But how is it possible to live without making some sort of contribution? Pioneers of the past left established societies and moved off by themselves, yet history frequently mentions their contributions. Some were sourdough prospectors and hardy frontier trappers who never saw other people for seasons at a time.

Our first important goal on the land was to find a dependable source of drinking water. We had no pipes to hook up with, like our friends in town, or even a creek or handy spring. The only open water was the nearby back channel of a river, which we considered too warm and slow-moving to be safe. With lots of money we could have called someone out to drill a well, even though we had no power with which to pump up the water. But hiring someone to drill in an unknown place is like sitting down at a poker table. We might have reached water in a few feet, or in a few hundred. At that time the price was already over five dollars per foot, water or not, and now it costs more than twice that much.

We finally hired a man with a small bulldozer who dug a pit for water near the river channel. He also made several holes for outside toilets. Bringing this machine to our land was the first sign of my weakening discipline, since I originally wanted to do everything by hand. I realized how impractical this was after I spent many hours digging up a foot of rocks and dirt with a shovel. The bulldozer completed the job in half an hour. We stood a large metal culvert into the water pit before the bulldozer shoved the dirt back around it. By lowering a bucket down the culvert on a rope, we got clean water.

Building a home without power tools and electricity can intimidate a fledgling pioneer. Even more so when that pioneer also lacks training in the technical skills needed for construction. We learned to cope with such challenges in ways that would have brought shame to my precision-minded European forefathers. With only a few basic tools we decided to build our home for the purpose of coziness and convenience, rather than for architectural perfection.

It was hard to saw a pile of lumber by hand and still have all the pieces come out exactly as measured. We finally quit using our tape measure so much. We learned to build things one section at a time, measuring each of the pieces mainly with our eyes, and also by holding them next to each other. Sometimes we ended up with whole sections that were a bit too long or too short, but there were always methods for improvising, until the end result was functional. As long as we stuffed all the cracks with insulation and covered up the outside walls, our house stayed pleasant and warm, even if it was a bit crooked here and there.

By the time the first snowflakes fell on our new home, we were settled in—Beverly and I, with sons Wolf and Okan. Our dream of a tribal camp had barely come alive. It was evident that we would be tending the "campground" by ourselves during the upcoming harsh and cold season. Our main concerns became firewood, groceries, and meat.

I waited for a real snowfall before setting out in search of wild meat. It came during the final week of hunting season. I didn't want to hunt while the ground was bare and dry, knowing there was a much greater risk of losing a wounded animal. Cold, frozen ground without snow shows few signs for a tracker to follow. Although Beverly had year-round hunting rights on government lands, guaranteed through aboriginal treaties, I was limited to the regular hunting times.

During my first effort at hunting I saw several deer, but they were so nervous and observant that I never got a clear chance to shoot any of them. I think they sensed being my potential victims. At one place along the trail I heard a loud snort in some thick trees to my right. The sound reminded me of a sweaty worker blowing flies from his forehead. "Pheww," it went, and for a second time, giving me goosebumps and a tight feeling around my heart. There was no other sound, and I could see nothing—except my breath hitting the cold air in clouds of mist. There was a breeze blowing toward me from the sound, so the maker of it could not smell me and was probably as curious about my identity as I was about "its."

Cautiously I raised my rifle to my shoulder, thinking I might get a chance to shoot. I pulled the hammer back gently with my right thumb. I stood still and waited—almost breathlessly—until my arms began to shake, making the rifle tremble. Just then I heard a loud crashing in the forest. The animal had decided to run. It raced between trees and snapped dry branches that cracked loudly. The noise was coming my way, making the swelling in my heart grow larger. My forehead broke out in a cold sweat.

Less than thirty steps in front of me a gully ran down from a ridge and out from the forest. The animal was in that gully when it suddenly made a turn and appeared on my trail, facing me. Our excited eyes met each other at a surprisingly close range. The only thing between us was my rifle—now aimed right at the middle of the creature's head!

In an instant I summed up that I was facing a very large and heavy buck deer. It had a thick neck to support its massive set of many-pointed antlers. Bushy hair bristled on its neck, either from anger or fear. Mist came out of its flaring nostrils. There was no time for second thoughts, so I pulled the trigger and prepared for an explosion that would shatter the deer's life.

But the only sound I heard was a metallic "click!" I had forgotten to pump a shell into the chamber of my rifle when I first set out on the hunt. That "click" set off the buck's nerves and muscles, as he jumped off the ground and practically spun in midair. Before I could take the rifle from my shoulder and correct my mistake, he was back down in the gully, crashing headlong through the terrain. For some time I could hear the racket, until finally his noises were swallowed up in the distance. It was a wilderness lesson for him and me both!

Had there been a chance for second thoughts, perhaps I would not have been so eager to shoot this stallion of a deer, especially during his rutting period. Such an animal represents strength and cunning that should be passed down to offspring of his kind. Besides, younger bucks usually have more tender meat than the big, old ones.

Unfortunately, the encounter gave me an eagerness that experienced hunters call "buck fever." A primitive urge within me suddenly longed for the taste and smell of fresh blood, and I noticed numerous signs of wildlife recently made on the trail. I think this urge for blood is within many animals, as well as in humans. In modern society people try to suppress their instincts, often only with great difficulty. Games of sport are among the acceptable releases.

Soon I saw other deer, and felt that I must get one of them. I felt challenged to succeed in this ancient ritual of hunting. I expected success behind every large rock and clump of trees, where I thought animals might be hiding. It was like a roulette wheel of animal targets, spinning and stopping, and I knew that eventually it would give me a prize.

Snow fell continually while I was walking, turning the hills ever more still and white. It was easy to tell fresh tracks, because they had sharp outlines clear down to the ground. The snow was already ankle-deep, like a feather blanket, and older tracks quickly filled in. The only problem with the tracks was that most of them led into thick clumps of trees that I could hardly penetrate, especially not without making noise. I had to try catching a deer out in the open, like that big buck.

My next chance finally came after I followed a fresh set of tracks uphill for about ten minutes. On top of a small ridge I saw two young bucks running away from me. I guessed that they hadn't seen me, but were frightened by sounds I had made passing through a bunch of dry brush. I was sure they could not have gotten my scent, and they affirmed this by suddenly stopping and looking back at me. I quickly aimed at the nearer one, fired, and watched it fall, but in a moment it was back up and running. Its big white tail no longer waved in the air, which meant it was wounded. When I rushed to the scene of its fall I found much blood in the snow, along with tufts of deer hair and bits of bone. It was a gruesome sight, but the freshness only heightened my excitement.

With more skill as a hunter I would have sat down right there and given the animal a while to find shelter. With all the bleeding it would not have gotten far, anyway. But I had yet to learn how to read these natural signs, so I immediately set out on the blood-splotched trail. My persistence drove the animal to make desperate efforts at getting away. It rushed downhill, leaving signs to show where it had fallen. Finally it reached another thick piece of forest, just as its heavy blood flow seemed to stop. Suddenly its tracks were no longer so conspicuous, as they mingled with those made by other deer in the area.

It has occurred to me that without snow on the ground I would probably have lost this deer, although it would have died shortly, anyway. I can only imagine how many wild animals are wounded and lost by inexperienced hunters every year. Luckily, I finally caught up with this one and put an end to its miseries with a bullet through its head. By that time my excitement as a bloodthirsty hunter had turned to near-remorse for the killing I had done. I felt humbled as I knelt by the deer's side, knowing I had summarily ended its life. I removed my hat and said words that came from deep in my heart.

As winter arrived we still had our Appaloosa stallion running wild with his companions. Now and then I saw signs of them in the nearby hills and forests, although they would not let me get close. Since our friend had returned to his home on the reserve, I was left alone to be responsible for the horse. I was angry with the owner of the other horses because they had eaten my stallion's hay and lured him from the corral. I expected the man to catch our horse for us and replace the hay. Imagine my surprise when I learned that the law was against me!

The bad news was brought by an RCMP constable who had been called out by the horse herd's owner. He was threatening to sue *me* for letting the stud run with his mares! I was outraged, since the stallion was a registered animal and the mares were just common stock. With the right facilities I could have earned money for the stud's services. The outfitter said pregnant horses would be useless for his work during the next hunting season.

The Mountie informed us that range laws in our district allow ordinary stock to roam free, but require breeding stallions and bulls to be kept inside stockades much taller and sturdier than the small one we had built. He gave me one week to catch the horse, after which, he said, he would have to shoot him. No wonder the Appaloosa's previous owner had been so anxious to get rid of him!

Beverly was right, stallion-keeping turned out to be no simple matter.

At about this time there was a temporary "tipi camp" along a mountain creek some distance from us. We knew one member, who said the others were "hippies from the States." They had come to Canada to try out their own form of tribal living. They were opposed to the concept of private property, and we found little in common with them. However, they were searching for more horses and sent word that they'd like the stallion.

We found these folks living in a half-dozen tipis pitched near the bend of a logging road. Continuous noise from rushing creek water tumbling over rocks covered most sounds made by passing trucks and cars. For a couple of seasons the tipi dwellers lived nearly undisturbed by the world around them. Although they had four-wheel-drive trucks and used chainsaws to cut firewood, they talked about taking horses and heading for places that no vehicles could go.

The encampment looked romantic and primitive from the outside, but the tipi interiors we saw were far different from those we had become used to. Each one was heated by an efficient metal stove, with stovepipes that went out through asbestos-lined holes in the tipi coverings. The smoke flaps of the tipis were tightly closed, robbed of their duties by the chimneys. Without the usual open view to the sky the tipis seemed different. They were furnished with large, modern beds and warm carpeting, and at least one had a stereo system, with quality speakers, powered by a spare car battery. Loud rock music sometimes boomed through the camp.

The novelty of such a camp was good material for winter gossip in our valley. Some said it was a haven for draft dodgers who were illegally in Canada. Others claimed the group was wealthy and planned to buy a large, well-known ranch. After some of the members were seen bathing in the creek—naked!—rumor said they were indulging in primitive sexual rites. A neighboring landowner threatened to have them arrested or moved away.

Our stallion soon ended up in this camp after we agreed to accept a silver necklace and an old turquoise bracelet for him in lieu of cash. The heavily bearded fellow who took charge of the horse had been living in one of the "new-age communes" near Taos, New Mexico, where such jewelry was almost as important for "Indian-style living" as horses are up here, in the North. I was glad to get the jewelry, since it needed no hay and would not run away from me. We warned the bearded fellow that life in the camp would surely become more exciting with the stallion, but he said horse-breeding was so important to their plans that they didn't mind putting up with the trouble. He knew no more about caring for a stallion than I had a few months earlier.

Members of that tipi camp eventually drifted apart because they lacked experience and common goals. The owner of the stallion was the first to leave, moving to the shore of some wilderness lake, where it is said the horse ran away and was never found again. We did not do much better with the jewelry, although we at least had the pleasure of giving it away. One piece went to my mother and the other to the wife of an elderly Indian friend. The horse turned out to have been an expensive lesson.

We really felt prepared for winter after I managed to shoot an elk, one of the first to come down into the valley because snows were getting deep up in the mountains. It was a young bull, not nearly so massive as some of the old ones, but I still had a lot of work getting him back to our house. It was the very end of hunting season, and most of the first snowfall had already melted again. I wanted to do all my hunting without motor vehicles, so I stubbornly determined to drag the meat down the hills and through the forest on our toboggan, even though that meant crossing fields of mud and stones.

For several days Beverly cut up the meat until her hands could hardly hold on to a knife anymore. What had been an animal as large as a young pony was now a thin bunch of meat hanging like rags from strings stretched below the ceiling of our cabin. When it was dried it became "Indian jerky," which is easy to store without refrigeration. The bull took up just one large canvas sack, which we stored inside a wooden trunk, where mice couldn't bother it. Beverly used the meat as an addition to soups and stews, or boiled it with potatoes and served it as though it were a piece of steak. Often we took the raw, dried pieces and chewed on them alone. The animal gave us lots of protein, made us feel good and healthy, and yet saved us the high cost of fresh meat as well as the concern about what additives had been put into it.

Among the machines that I detested most were chainsaws, because of their noise and bad smell. I had several old-fashioned handsaws that worked only when I did. I started out to cut all our firewood using only these. I was not willing to admit that I was spending too much time and energy on this endeavor, especially as the cold weather forced us to use more wood in our stoves for all our heating and cooking. The house was so poorly insulated that the stoves worked overtime to make up the difference. To top it off, neither of the two stoves we had was very efficient. They could not be closed tightly against drafts and air leaks; thus a lot of the heat rushed right up the stovepipes and out of the house through the chimneys.

Beverly's parents realized our plight the first time they came over for a visit. They grew up around woodstoves in a land where trees are not very abundant. They thought we were fortunate to have so much wood right by our house, and could not understand my opposition to using chainsaws. As a result, they *gave* me a chainsaw for Christmas, knowing I could not refuse the present, and rightly guessing I would not be crazy enough to deny myself the use of it. They probably did it more out of concern for the warmth and safety of their daughter and grandchildren than for any pity on my self-punishing ways.

To soften the impact of this technological intrusion, they got the smallest chainsaw they could find. I unwrapped it at their house during a big family Christmas gathering, and some of the younger relatives laughed and snickered when they saw it. They knew that we seriously depended on wood for our household needs, and they probably had enough sense to realize that an ordinary-sized chainsaw would enlarge our woodpile much quicker than the tiny thing I was holding. I later traded it for a bigger one.

While we were at the reserve for the holidays, we learned another lesson the hard way. At home we left a good supply of potatoes, carrots, and other vegetables, along with some canned goods. During our absence temperatures plunged way below zero, and our lonely house turned into an icebox. When we got back we found all our fresh supplies frozen solid. There was only a little that we could salvage. We realized the need for some kind of frost-proof cellar, even though several more winters passed before we had the spare funds to build one. Meanwhile, we tried not to leave our house during severe cold spells again. In addition, Beverly's dad taught us to wrap freezables with a thick buffalo hide, like the one we keep on our floor. When blankets are piled on top of this, the warmth prevents freezing in all but the most icy weather.

I was already in the habit of considering winter my "writing season," since there were few dances and ceremonies to lure us away. I built a little addition to our cabin, with a small wood heater of its own, where I went every day for a few hours of privacy while I tried to get my thoughts written down on paper. I was easily distracted by the beauties and mysteries of Nature that were continually evolving outside a big window in front of my desk. I had heard of writers who shut themselves into windowless rooms to avoid distractions, and I soon understood why. Still, I had no desire to give up this free luxury.

I managed to write a dozen pages every day, even with time off for gazing outdoors. I also began reading to our kids each evening, which gave me practice in word usage. One evening the older boy, Wolf, said to me: "Gee, these books are a hassle!" I was surprised and asked him why, so he said: " 'Cause they always get finished!"

Wolf adapted to isolated living very quickly, since he was just a small boy, too young for school. He was used to playing alone, and by the age of four often occupied himself quietly for hours at a time. He even helped entertain his baby brother, Okan, who was still being nursed by his mother. Our household life was simple, and the boys were always in the midst of it. Okan slept by our bed, tightly wrapped in a "moss bag" of buckskin—though Beverly kept him covered with cloth diapers instead of the traditional pads of moss. He spent most of his early months laced into this bag. In the daytime he slept very soundly in a small hammock over our bed. One of us would swing him for a while if he cried. Beverly always took him down from the hammock at night, because her grandmothers said strange Spirits might come to him if he were left there.

While Okan was nursing, Beverly developed a lump in her breast that became sore and tender. Neither of us knew what it was, but the symptoms seemed serious. On our way to the reserve for a late-winter visit we decided to see the doctor who had attended the childbirth. He examined the lump and said it was mastitis. He suggested that Okan be weaned immediately so he wouldn't get the infection and possible die from it.

Beverly was quite upset by this news, especially since the condition had already given her headaches and fevers. The doctor prescribed antibiotics and plenty of rest. But at her mother's house Beverly got quite a different story. Her mother and grandmother said lumps in the breasts of nursing mothers are not unusual, nor are they hard to cure. They told her to apply frequent hot pads of tobacco boiled in tea. They thought the condition would go away in a day or two. Beverly's grandmother said she once had a lump that would not go away in spite of this treatment, so she finally had it lanced. She told about another case in which the lump took so long to go away that the child had to nurse on just one breast, while the other went dry. They said they had never heard of a child dying from this, or even getting sick, "except maybe from prescriptions taken by the mother."

The lump soon went away, all right, but Okan got weaned anyhow. We learned that another child was only five months away. We had been depending on the old story that nursing mothers will not get pregnant, so we had taken no other precautions. Although we had talked of eventually having more children, we wanted to get our new home set up first.

With the first grass of spring came new people to join us, this time a young couple from the East whom we had met earlier. They wanted to live out in Nature and take part in some sort of group effort. Our books inspired them to think about helping us form a "tribe." They were a bit more experienced than others we had known, having already lived on a small farm in Colorado for a couple of years. After they sold this they moved here to try subsistence living. For a start they dug up and fenced a small vegetable garden.

Next to arrive for the "tribal camp" was a young, long-haired, bespectacled fellow from Alabama. He hauled all his worldly belongings up here in an old, funky, pickup truck that didn't appear to have strength for such a long journey. He spoke with a heavy southern drawl that took us a while to understand. He had lived in a tipi at the shore of some isolated Alabama lake, and he was somewhat disappointed that the rest of us preferred to stay in wooden cabins. He became the first one here to live in a tipi, which he reverently called his "law-dge." We hoped that his example would give the rest of us inspiration to try full-time tipi life, as well, although we wondered how the boy from the South would make out during the cold winter.

There were now enough "hands" to work on our intended "campsite," but we had little money for the necessary supplies and materials. Our books still provided the only income. We began building a rustic little barn to house chickens and rabbits. Since none of us knew much about this work, it turned out rather poorly. We would have done well to select a plan from a qualified handbook, instead of building whatever came to our minds on the spot. Since we all had different ideas about what was important, in the end none of us was really satisfied. In addition, our lack of money had forced us to scrimp on material and hardware. Instead of ending up with good doors tailored to frames, for instance, we nailed old boards together and hooked the resulting piece so that it swung on leather hinges in an opening left at the front of the barn. The few windows we had were too small, and fit so poorly that they were drafty. It made little difference when the young couple later took them out to use in their own home.

In the midst of spring work we learned that the first medicine pipe ceremony for that year was to be held soon. It seemed that we were just beginning to develop an effective group effort at home when our energies were needed elsewhere. When we got back we learned that practically all work came to a halt during our absence.

Somehow our leaving was considered a sign for everyone to take a vacation. We felt caught between two very different tribes.

This first ceremony was held inside an old house in Browning. The weather was cold and damp, and the gathering would have been miserable out in a tipi. That's why the ceremonies are always held a bit later among the Bloods, who prefer to hold them outdoors. Still, a large crowd was there, eager to celebrate the return of spring and the coming of summer.

At this time the only leader of medicine pipe ceremonies among the Montana Blackfeet was an old man named Richard Little Dog, who learned the ritual from his father. The man was a quiet, short-haired widower, who sang so softly that it was often hard for others to follow him. He had transferred his own medicine pipe bundle to Bob Scriver, the son of an early reservation trader, who served as Browning's justice of the peace. Although a non-Indian, Scriver had developed faith in ceremonial ways practiced by his lifelong neighbors. As a sensitive artist and sculptor he appreciated the creative symbolism of their ceremonial objects. His interpretations of these and other western traditions served as themes for his artistic work on the reservation.

It turned out that Richard Little Dog had recently been in an auto accident and injured his head so that he was no longer able to lead the complicated ceremonies. After a debate among the bundle keepers they finally decided to hire one of the Blood elders who was present. They did this with some reluctance, since there are variations in the way each division performs the ceremony. They wanted to maintain their old tribal form, distinct from the Bloods.

During the ceremony we learned of the tragic death of Pete Stabs-by-Mistake, who had often treated me kindly and helped identify many of my old Blackfeet photographs. His father had been sort of a tribal "superstar" in the 1920's and 1930's—an extremely handsome and well-dressed man who posed for many visiting tourists and photographers. He appeared in magazines and advertisements throughout the world, especially in connection with Glacier National Park, where he brought his family to live for many summers.

Pete Stabs-by-Mistake was proud to talk about his father, and about others from the time of his youth. He was an old man, living with his wife in a little log house on a strip of open prairie that was not far from the peaks of the Rockies. Here was part of an outlying community called Heart Butte, because of a fascinating hill of the same name that stood between Pete's house and the mountains. During Pete's young days his grandfather—a grizzled old warrior named Mountain Chief—was leader of the Heart Butte people.

We were shocked to learn that friendly old Pete had been murdered by some of his own acquaintances. It seems that he had gone to town one morning and picked up his pension check at the post office, along with some other mail and money. It was thought that he had several hundred dollars with him. He told a number of people of his good luck, and, knowing him, he was probably also generous with the money. That evening some of the area's toughs paid the old couple a visit at their house. The youths had been drinking, and they began to demand that Pete share his money with them. Pete was still tall and husky, although he was around eighty. A scuffle broke out, and before it was over Pete lay on the floor near his badly injured wife. The hoodlums then took the money and, apparently figuring to cover their crime, set fire to the house. Pete's wife managed to drag herself outside, but before anyone could come and see if the old man was still alive, he burned with his house.

There were actually two medicine pipe ceremonies held that weekend in Browning. One was the day after the other, and both were in the same house. Pat Weasel Head and his wife came there with us. We spent the night in one of the town's rickety, windblown motels. The old couple kept us entertained with humor, as well as with anecdotes about earlier visits to the same town. More than fifty years before, Pat had ridden all the way down on his horse on an overnight trip. He said it was a common event in those days, when Blackfoot society still depended on horses. Pat was even then still seen frequently going around the reserve on horseback.

The second medicine pipe ceremony was the longest and most crowded that we ever attended. The bundle belonged to George and Molly Kicking Woman, a very popular and respected couple. For many years George was elected to the tribal council, while his wife was noted for herbal cures and other traditional wisdom. As a modern-day chief George was the only council member to follow the ancient custom that chiefs should also be keepers of medicine pipe bundles. Most of his fellow members hardly understood the Blackfoot language, much less the ancient ceremonial rites.

I counted over one hundred people crowded into two rooms of the small house. Close to that many more came and went around the outside. When it was time to receive the blessings of facial paintings it seemed as if every kid in Browning showed up. The face-painting ritual lasted for a couple of hours, during which the crowd could do little but watch, or visit with each other. The ceremony began in the morning and did not finish until way after dark.

During breaks in the ceremony the other bundle keepers discussed plans for their own openings, and we selected the following weekend. Wolf Old Man happened to be present, and he thought we should go ahead and have the obligation completed. He gave public notice of the fact with a loud announcement to the gathered crowd.

For that ceremony we set up our yellow tipi in a grassy patch near the house where Beverly grew up, on the reserve. Atsitsina came early and helped us get everything arranged. By the time we brought Wolf Old Man from his house, not far away, a crowd was already starting to gather. A wind was also starting to blow quite strongly, but the Old Man said that was the case every time this bundle had been opened. Later the wind rattled our tipi poles and shook the canvas cover so loudly that it seemed to represent all the world around us. All day we were snugly gathered in our firelit circle, performing ancient and inspirational rites.

Paula Weasel Head filled the role of Wolf Old Man's partner, since he had no wife. She knew the ceremony nearly as well as he did. Her husband, Pat, sat at the Old Man's left, ready to assist him. At one point Pat asked Wolf Old Man if the complex work of leading such ceremonials was not becoming too difficult for a man of his age and disabilities. To this Wolf Old Man matter-of-factly said: "I will not be leading these ceremonies anymore." We didn't know how true his statement would become in another season.

Atsitsina led the four drummers and singers because he had a strong voice and knew the tunes well. Next to him sat his nephew, Beverly's father, to whom he was teaching this part of his knowledge. They were using the original drums from the Longtime Medicine Pipe, which had been brought by Many Gray Horses. He also helped with the drumming and singing.

The Longtime Medicine Pipe had been transferred to Many Gray Horses and his wife during the previous Sun Dance encampment, as planned. But the bundle was taken away from them and brought back to the Provincial Museum in Edmonton afterward. The Horns Society had been involved in this affair, and their spokesmen signed papers agreeing that the pipe bundle was only going to the reserve on loan. They were trying to arrange for the return of bundles belonging to their society at the same time. At that time museum officials hoped the Bloods would be satisfied just to borrow these ancient bundles for their annual ceremonies.

When permanent return of the bundles was refused, the Horns went to higher government authorities, who were in charge of the museum's funding. The politicians realized that most of the tribe backed the demands of the Horns so they agreed to help. They were concerned about alienating this large voting force, and they also did not want the situation to be made public.

Negotiations over these important cultural matters went on for some time. Museum officials tried to find ways to keep their prized relics, which they considered so old as to be in danger of disintegrating from use. They suggested that Indian people study the original sacred objects at the museum and then make duplicates of them. Later they said they were willing to give up the old things and keep the duplicates themselves. At one point Indian negotiators demanded return of *all* Blackfoot religious artifacts in the collections of major museums, which would have meant several thousand pieces. There were not even enough interested people to look after so many sacred things properly, nor were there qualified leaders to perform all the transfer ceremonies, should they be needed.

We paid close attention to these affairs, since they were important to the survival of the tribal culture that we were dedicating ourselves to. While doing research in various museums, I had built up strong feelings myself. Most cultural materials seemed to be virtual prisoners, locked away from the people who could best use them. It was exciting that some sacred articles in museums were now being demanded by their most legitimate caretakers.

I became so concerned about these museum matters that they began to appear in my dreams. During one of these dreams Beverly and I were with Many Gray Horses and his wife, and we were coming back from the museum with the Longtime Pipe Bundle. It was a lengthy dream, and I felt puzzled by its meaning. After discussing it, Beverly and I decided to go see the elderly couple. It is a custom to share personal dreams with those who appear in them.

I told my dream in the English language, which this conservative elder never spoke. However, his wife was fluent in both languages, and she helped Beverly to translate it very carefully. He listened without comment, and remained silent for some time after I was finished. Finally he said, in Blackfoot:

"I have been suspicious of you. I am an old man and I have grown not to trust any white man. But I have also watched you at ceremonies, and I cannot find anything wrong. You pray mostly in English, which is a language I do not understand. I am not sure what you pray about. That is why I keep my distance from you. If someone mistreats their religion and prayers, all those around them are likely to suffer."

He paused again, letting his comments settle with us. There was nothing for me to do but accept him as a stoic and honest old Indian. Finally he continued:

"But now I accept your dream! We will do what it has suggested. You are the only one who has come with an offer to help bring back the Longtime Pipe, which belongs here . . ." He went on to say that he heard constant rumors about the bundle, and about the current negotiations with the museum people. He did not like this and said it was not right, since the bundle had been transferred and paid for, and was thus his, period. He wanted no part of political maneuvers, and said the matter should not even be discussed by any other than medicine pipe keepers and leaders.

The time for fulfilling this dream was to be in the spring, when all medicine pipes are supposed to be brought outside to help greet the return of Thunder. This was an instruction given to the original medicine pipe keeper through a mystical relationship between that man's daughter and the Spirit of Thunder. During the ceremony for our own bundle Wolf Old Man called on the Spirit of Thunder and asked for good luck and success on our journey to bring the Longtime Pipe back from the distant city.

I went to the museum alone first, to spend a couple more days completing research of archives and materials that I had been working on for several seasons. My studies seemed valuable when I combind them with the traditional knowledge our elders were sharing through their stories and actions. I had a feeling that my museum work might become difficult to carry on after we reclaimed the pipe bundle, and I was correct.

There was a young ethnologist at this museum who understood some of the cultural problems among Indians caused by certain museum practices. He agreed that especially sacred artifacts should remain among the people to whom they have the most meaning. Several times we discussed the idea of museums on Indian reserves, where these materials would be safe, yet readily accessible to those who might need what they offer.

This young museum official even agreed that the Longtime Pipe should be returned to the Bloods, although his superiors would have considered the notion pure treason if he had told them his views. He thought a lengthy court battle would be required for this to happen, and he understood why Many Gray Horses refused to consider it. I told him that the elderly couple was planning to follow me in order to visit with "their pipe." I did not tell him all that was planned. Traditional customs regarding dreams would not have allowed it.

Beverly brought Many Gray Horses and his wife from their isolated ranch house on the appointed day. One of the couple's daughters—a young woman of Beverly's age—rode along with them as far as the city of Calgary, where she was attending the university. Sitting together in the vehicle, she and her father symbolized the opposite extremes in Blood lifestyles. She lived with a language that her father could not even speak, and studied the details of things that he knew little or nothing about. She later traveled to faraway places in the world, including Africa, where a black tribal chief wanted her to marry his son. The parents were very proud of their daughter, even while mystified by much of what she did.

Beverly said the trip to the museum was a nerve-racking one. For most of the three hundred miles they sat in silence, and she sometimes had a hard time staying awake at the wheel. The road to Edmonton from the reserve is not noted for scenic splendors or interesting diversions. It is heavily traveled, wide, and smooth. Most of the time it rolls across open prairie like an endless gray ribbon. Ranches and occasional prairie towns are its main highlights, if they can be called that. Beverly said the old couple prayed quietly, and often, but they hardly talked. They had never been to the museum, and were not sure what to expect.

We met at the museum entrance, and from there we went to the public display of Blackfoot culture, which was housed in several large glass cases. In the center of one room stood a full-sized tipi, painted yellow. Visitors could go inside and see a Blackfoot medicine pipe bundle opened up on the floor. In a nearby case were parts of the bundle we had come after, although the Longtime Pipe itself had been taken away and rewrapped. This was as promised during our visit with the elders going to Smallboy's camp.

Many Gray Horses immediately said they had done just as bad by taking the pipe away and separating it from the rest of the bundle. The young ethnologist came up to us at about this time and welcomed the old couple with words of respect and signs of humbleness. When we told him the old man's complaint about separating the bundle, he seemed to realize that a time of reckoning had arrived.

A custodian was called to unlock the offensive display case so that its contents could be removed for our proposed ceremony. When museum officials learned that something was going to happen, they wanted to be sure it was kept private, with no publicity.

Patience turned to chagrin as we all stood around and waited for the custodian to figure out the right combination of keys and methods to open the case. Several people tried getting the lock to work. The museum staff must have felt awkward in the presence of the silently staring elders. After more than an hour we finally got the things we needed, and were led to a large storage room where the sacred pipe itself lay in a metal closet. The staff members then left us to pray alone.

I reminded Many Gray Horses that it was up to him which parts of my dream he wished to carry out. So he told me to go and ask the ethnologist to return. To him he explained that it was not good to pray with the ancient bundle inside a large, modern building, and that he wished to take it outside. The ethnologist listened carefully, then said he would speak to his superiors and get their answer. While he was gone, I showed Many Gray Hoses some of the drawers and closets that were crammed full of tribal artifacts. He said he had not seen so many in all his life. He was totally amazed and also very disappointed that his people had given up so much. In this context the Longtime Pipe Bundle seemed almost like a small matter.

After a time the ethnologist returned and said we could bring the bundle out of storage and to an upstairs courtyard that was still within the building. He said his superiors feared public attention if we went all the way outside. A main city throughfare ran right beside the museum. Perhaps they thought publicity would bring to light some of the intrigue behind their collection, which would damage the museum's reputation. Citizens of the province might have reacted angrily to news that one of their tax-supported institutions spent many thousands of dollars relieving a group of fellow citizens of their precious cultural and religious belongings, often through questionable methods.

Many Gray Horses realized that going outdoors with the bundle was an important part of fulfilling the dream, so he refused to settle for anything less. He explained that being in a courtyard would be like walking around the inside of a tipi. The ancient instructions for medicine pipes say they must be taken outdoors to greet the return of Thunder. Another conference was called, after which the ethnologist came back and said the request had been approved.

We were then led through a maze of artificially lit corridors to reach the museum's back door. Along the way we passed a security station, where armed and uniformed guards checked everyone going in and out. There was a wall of television screens that silently monitored valuable museum displays, including the now-empty case for the Longtime Pipe. The guards nodded respectfully when the ethnologist advised them that we were taking an "artifact" outside with permission.

Because it was known that this ethnologist had some doubts about museum policies regarding religious artifacts, I did not want to make him look like an accomplice to our plans. I convinced him not to come with us alone during our outdoor venture. He responded by bringing the head of the museum himself—a scholarly man near retirement age, who was a devout believer in conservative museum policies. To him, the idea of our ceremony with the bundle was quaint, at best. He acted as though he thought it was a nuisance. His primary interest was the safekeeping of his museum's collection, and the bundle was its most valuable artifact. It was like a "Rembrandt," or a set of "Crown jewels."

The four of us were wrapped in blankets and wearing beaded moccasins. The two women wore long, colorful dresses, as well. There was no way we could look inconspicuous on the museum lawn. Many Gray Horses led the way, carrying the bundle's accessories, including a heavy bag of rawhide with long leather fringes. His wife followed with the large, heavy bundle. It was supported on her back by a sturdy leather strap that went around her shoulder. It was the size of a small child, covered by a fringed woolen shawl.

The sky was clear and bright, and birds were singing in nearby trees. It was a wonderful spring day, perfectly suited to our purpose. We walked slowly around the big museum complex, stopping at each of its four corners so that Many Gray Horses could pray. The scene was just as I remembered it from my dream. I was nervous with excitement, knowing what an important event it was in traditional tribal history.

After making the fourth stop for prayers, Many Gray Horses

began to walk again, but his wife called him to stop. Not far ahead of us stood our truck, and it was time for us to announce our intentions. The ethnologist and his boss were right behind us, and not far away stood one of the museum guards. Just then another guard drove slowly past us in an unmarked patrol car, which he parked at the main exit. Suddenly I thought that our plans had been discovered, and wondered if the old folks were ready to make a run for it.

Many Gray Horses turned around to explain briefly his feelings about the bundle. He asked me to thank the museum people for having looked after it so long, and to tell them that he was now going to take it back home with him. He said all this in Blackfoot, but I knew what he meant. As soon as he finished, he turned and motioned his wife to follow him.

I began to interpret the old man's words, but I did not get far before the museum boss turned pale and brushed me out of the way in an effort to catch up with the elders. What was going on had suddenly dawned on him. All he could do was to ask in a broken and frustrated voice, "Is he planning to take the bundle now? Is he going to take it now?"

When he reached our vehicle he called out: "Wait! Mrs. Many Gray Horses, this is a very bad thing that you are doing!" His words came slowly, and he pronounced each one clearly, as though speaking to a young child, or to someone who might have trouble understanding. The woman paused and faced him, standing by the open door with the bundle still on her back. Hopeful because of her attention, the official tried to smile as he continued, in a desperate voice: "We could stop you physically, but that would be a very bad thing, also."

At that point Many Gray Horses stepped forward to face the challenge. He was calm and determined, as opposed to the other man's nervous pleadings. He stood and smiled, then finally said: "*Ahh-hahh!*" By this he meant: "Well, what's all the excitement?" Then he proceeded to tell once again his story about being the traditional owner of the pipe.

When he finished talking Beverly interpreted his words. The official had an ownership story of his own that was based on his institution's having paid a lot of cash to buy the bundle. Many Gray Horses laughed, knowing the official was caught in his own game. Originally he agreed to have the bundle traditionally transferred to his employee, Yellow Fly, in order to disarm tribal criticism of the sale. By tribal custom, that made Yellow Fly the keeper and sole spokesman for it. Now that Yellow Fly had transferred those rights to Many Gray Horses, the same customs decreed that the bundle was his.

The official finally realized his predicament, so he changed his approach and asked who would pay back the three thousand dollars that the museum had paid out for the transfer to Yellow Fly. Many Gray Horses laughed again. He said he did not understand the white way of thinking. He explained:

"It is a common tradition that friends and relatives help each other to make transfer payments. In this case, you people helped your friend, Yellow Fly. Last summer I gave him many good horses and a lot of money during the transfer. He should have given you back your share from that." Yellow Fly, of course, had given the museum nothing. Many Gray Horses said to us, in Blackfoot: "This white man is crazy. If he goes to church and puts money on the donation plate because he wants to help out, I wonder if he asks for it back later?" That was how he interpreted the matter of payments.

He finally brought all this idle chatter to an end by asking the official if he had ever been initiated as keeper of a medicine pipe. When told that he had not, Many Gray Horses said he should not even be discussing the subject. He turned abruptly and got into the vehicle, along with his wife and the bundle. For a moment or two their efforts seemed in doubt, as the woman had managed to get the shawl's fringes caught in the doorway. She was halfway in and could go no farther, calling anxiously for help. Beverly finally unhooked the part that was stuck. Later this momentary delay became the source of much laughter, and an anecdote worth repeating many times in tribal circles.

The ethnologist had spent all this time quietly out of the way, writing things down in a little notebook that he carried. He seemed almost to enjoy the predicament in which the Indians had his normally stubborn boss. Finally he quit smiling long enough to say: "Let me ask this, to help clear the matter up: Are you planning to bring the bundle back up here when you are finished?" While Beverly translated the question to Many Gray Horses, I wondered what he would answer. Our departure would certainly have been made much easier, at that point, if he had simply said yes, but it would not have been the truth. He wisely replied: "Many people in the tribe have vowed to be blessed with the bundle when it is opened, so it will take time to get everything prepared. When we are done with what has been planned, I will phone to your place and let you know."

By the time I got in and started the motor, I noticed that the unmarked car was gone. As we slowly drove away, I looked into the rearview mirror and nearly laughed at the sight of our ethnologist friend's dejected-looking boss. He looked like one whose business had just been repossessed by a bank.

When we rolled into traffic Many Gray Horses looked back with a sigh of relief. Then, in contrast to his usually reserved character, he began to talk and joke as though he were an excited young man. He talked about how we would soon be back home with the bundle, although I still expected we might be stopped by police and arrested before we could get out of town. Many Gray Horses said he was not worried about going to jail, as long as the bundle was with him. Under no condition would he let anyone take it away, he assured us.

He talked and entertained us throughout the drive home. Four times we stopped along the road and prayed. The couple had brought tobacco and wild berries to use as offerings, and with these they asked that the Longtime Pipe never leave its home among the Bloods again. Word of our successful venture spread quickly on the reserve after we got back. The elders whom we met were glad it happened and was done.

The story did not take long to reach neighboring reserves, either. The next time we saw the young friend who had stayed with us, he said people on his reserve claimed I had personally taken the bundle and that the RCMP was looking for me. He thought it was a crazy story, and he was very surprised when I told him what actually happened. Some talked about going to the same museum and taking back other family heirlooms that had been lost to them, though none did so. We also heard rumors about me that were circulating in the museum world. I had no one to check these with, but in the following years I found myself unwelcome at several conservative institutions.

Many Gray Horses and his family sponsored the long-awaited opening ceremony for the Longtime Pipe not long after we brought it back. Many people came to take part or to have their faces painted for blessing. Some just wanted to see and be near this ancient relic that was held sacred by their forefathers for countless ages. We brought Wolf Old Man, and it turned out to be the last medicine pipe ceremony for him. He was still staying in the hospital, although winter was long over. He had me stop at his house so that he could paint his face and bring his ceremonial blanket.

At one point during the day the Old Man sang an honoring song for us. In addition, he loudly spoke words of praise about what we had done. Many Gray Horses gave a long talk to the crowd, explaining how everything happened. At the end he said very kind and friendly things about Beverly and me, and advised the crowd to treat us both "like relatives." Seeing Wolf Old Man's proud and happy face—shining with the red earth paint—was a real treat, although the best reward for our efforts was in knowing that our descendants would still be able to call upon the spiritual powers of the sacred tribal relic we had brought back.

Beverly learned to know life and death from a more personal perspective among her people than I did, since I hardly had a family. My own father and old Smiling Bear were the only close persons who had died, but I was not near them at the time. Wolf Old Man was the first person to pass away in the midst of a growing relationship with me. In spite of his advanced age I had not prepared myself for it, and did not expect it would affect me so deeply. I always thought we should feel lucky to have known him at all.

The first indication of his impending death came with a garbled message from friends in the valley, who had gotten it from the RCMP after the Old Man's relatives contacted them. We only heard that we were wanted by the Old Man for some reason or other. When we drove down the highway to the nearest pay phone, we guessed what might be wrong. But by then his condition had settled, and he was said to be resting and stable. Since Beverly was also ready for a hospital encounter any day, to give birth, we decided to go back home and await further developments, rather than disturbing the unborn baby with a long drive.

The next time we went out to phone we heard that the Old Man's condition had not improved, and that the hospital doctors still expected him to go at any time. Since the baby was making no signs of coming, we decided to take a chance on the drive, in order to see Wolf Old Man one more time. We loaded up our bundle, bedding, and spare clothes, waved good-bye to the young couple who said they would look after our place, and headed across the mountains again. We did not know if we were going over to lose an old man or to gain a young baby, or both. As it turned out, it was neither.

The Old Man looked terrible when I first saw him at the Indian hospital. He was on a lone bed in the private room, and he looked unconscious. His skin was pale and drawn, and there were tubes hooked to him. His daughter and an elderly granddaughter were keeping him company. Members of the family had been taking turns staying by him day and night, as is the Indian custom. I volunteered to take the next night.

When Beverly leaned down and spoke to him, he made a feeble response. When she told him who she was, and that I was with her, he roused himself up and said: "Oh, my son—my children—I nearly made a big mistake the other day!" He meant he almost gave up and died. When she told him that young Wolf was there, too, he smiled and called out again: "Oh, my son!" For a while it was hard to control our emotions, as we all stared at this powerful man and watched helplessly while he made his final efforts at living.

That night passed slowly, as I sat on a hardbacked chair and listened to the Old Man's labored breathing. A couple of his grandsons sat with me at first, and told me stories of their experiences with him. They were both elderly men themselves. One was present a number of times when the Old Man used his mystical powers, herbal brews, and ancient rituals to cure various people of their ailments. These men agreed that Wolf Old Man was the last one with such knowledge of traditional Blackfoot medicines. Since he had passed very little of this on to anyone else, it saddened us to know that soon it would be gone with him.

The other grandson told me about the time Wolf Old Man surprised his friends and relatives by coming home from a trading post with a brand-new Victrola and a box full of the early-type, cylindrical records. He liked all kinds of music, but his favorites were Indian religious songs that the trader had produced himself. Learning this made me reconsider my own ban on radios and music, much to Beverly's delight. It also made me wonder what other strict disciplines I was trying to learn from the Old Man that he had not followed himself while my age. I had to remind myself that he had not always been an old man!

As I watched him all night, I found myself wishing we could have another good visit. I thought of many things I wished I had asked him. I wondered what he would say if he knew I had learned to sing several of his medicine pipe songs. In the final hours of the night I decided to sing them for him, even if he did not hear me. We were alone, and the hospital was completely quiet. His door was closed, so I sang with a low voice, and close to his ear. Much to my surprise, when I finished he lightly clapped his hands together—as he often did to express surprise and exclamation. He had apparently been conscious for quite some time, and he recognized me perfectly. He wanted to know where Beverly was, and he asked for a drink of water. Later he sang some songs of his own which must have been his personal power songs, because I did not recognize them.

By the time the nurses and orderly came to check on him and clean up his room the next morning, Wolf Old Man was feeling pretty cheerful. He had evidently decided that the time was not yet right for his passing, although he was in a weak condition. The orderly was a grumpy old white man from the neighboring community. Wolf Old Man called him with a cheerful voice: "Box-ee-coa-sin," or "sticky berry soup," which is the Blackfoot of "Big deal!'' The man grumbled that hospital patients would recover more readily if relatives did not sit around and drain their energies with so much visiting. He did not care for the custom that says sick persons should be cheered and encouraged at all costs, and at least given company in their final hours.

We came home from this trip just in time to get Beverly to our local hospital, where she gave birth to another son. He was given the name Iniskim, in honor of Wolf Old Man's relationship with the sacred stones of the same name. Atsitsina later gave the boy his own name, as he had wanted to do for some time.

The growing family inspired me to work on our rustic cabin so that we would not be too crowded the next winter. Like a child's building-block set, our house was so simple that it was easy for an amateur like myself to make changes and build additions. With the help of visiting friends I quickly set up a ''back room'' that measured about eight by twelve feet. After covering the floor with a used rug we built a platform that ran the length of one wall and was wide enough to sleep on. For the boys it gave a split-level floor for playing and at night it was warm for them to sleep on.

We had another method for insuring that the kids would be warm in their new room. We built the floor of the addition so that it was several inches higher than the one in our main room. We joined the two rooms with a doorway that I sawed out of where there had been just a small window. Since it was higher than the room in which we had the heater, this new room was much warmer than an earlier addition, which we had foolishly built with a floor lower than the one in our main room.

We continued to have visitors throughout our second year here, but there was little talk about living as a permanent group, or tribe. Having three sons in the household, with a fourth on the reserve, made me realize that we had unconsciously created our own tribe. It was an exciting thought that made me look at many things from a new perspective. For Beverly, her childhood predicament had been reincarnated, as she was again surrounded by men and boys. What seemed to be missing was a daughter.

We phoned regularly to the Indian hospital to check on Wolf

Old Man's condition, which went up and down. One day we were stacking firewood when the dreaded news was brought to us. The Old Man had passed away, and his funeral was to be held the next day. There was little time to concentrate on the feeling of shock, as we had to hurry and make our way across the mountains again.

Our hearts felt way down and heavy as we stood by Wolf Old Man for the last time and said farewell to him. His big smile and hearty laughter were gone, and there was not even the labored breathing. His cold corpse lying in the casket seemed unreal. Our emotions longed for the warmth that he had so willingly shared, as did the emotions of many others who considered him a "tribal grandfather."

A funeral service was held for him in the small wooden Anglican church to which he was said to belong. Most Bloods are affiliated either with the Anglicans or the Roman Catholics, because those two faiths were the first to send government-approved missionaries. During his sermon the Anglican priest said Wolf Old Man had lived a successful life by combining the best of the Anglican teachings with his own native ways. He said the Old Man was in the first group of Blood students to attend the Anglican missionary school, although he didn't mention how glad he was to leave it, after only a couple of years. He also claimed that Wolf Old Man had "taught" Sunday school at the church for sixty years, and helped translate the Bible from English into Blackfoot. If all that was true—and it may well have been—the Old Man never said anything about it to us. When we knew him he only went to church if he was specifically invited—as he did to most other religious functions.

Somehow Bible songs and prayers, along with a lengthy sermon, did not seem like a suitable last statement for the old medicine man. I felt relieved when it was time to go outside and drive to the graveyard. The line of cars with burning headlights was long and the crowd large, as we gathered around a deep hole dug into the prairie. A cold wind was blowing, reminding us that soon another winter would cover the land. It would be the first one in almost a hundred years that Wolf Old Man would miss.

When the Old Man's casket was ready to be lowered into the

grave, someone brought his well-used metal suitcase that contained his sacred things for doctoring and leading ceremonies. It was placed on top of the casket, along with the drum he used to accompany his singing, and also his two wooden canes. It looked as though he was packed to go on a sacred journey. The wind blew nearly loud enough to cover our sounds of sadness, as it dried the tears from our eyes.

Although we were gloomy for some time afterward, we tried to follow Wolf Old Man's advice not to mourn, since he was only going to join his many friends and relatives who already dwelled in the "Spirit Land." His passing made us more determined to continue the faith he had taught us. We felt grateful for having known him and seen him using that faith in his daily life. We wondered if our children and grandchildren would someday be inspired by us in a similar way.

EPILOGUE

IN THE YEARS SINCE Wolf Old Man's passing, in 1974, there has been a revival in Blackfoot traditions that would surprise and please him. Many old Indians of his generation thought they were witnessing the final chapter of their own culture and history. Instead, Beverly and I are no longer the only young people sitting regularly with elders, as we were, at many ceremonies and gatherings. Several important medicine bundles are now in the keeping of young families, and there have even been transfers of sacred rights to sponsor the all-important Okan, or Blackfoot Sun Dance ceremony. There is now much hope for a cultural future in the tribe.

Atsitsina got to see more of these changes than Wolf Old Man, but regrettably his heart failed him in the spring of 1976, while he was at home during a late snowstorm. There were many paths left for us to explore together, but now we can only be grateful for those that we had already covered. As though bestowing a farewell blessing, he gave his name, Atsitsina, to our youngest son, during his final visit to our mountain home.

Although Beverly had been used to being in a household full of men since the time of her birth, she wanted very much to have a daughter. She got her wish with our last child, who is now four years old. Her grandfather, Edward Little Bear, gave her the inherited name, ''Nato-Achkuinemaki'' or Sacred Pipe Woman, though she is better known to everyone by her first name, Star.

Wolf Old Man missed one ceremony that surely would have thrilled him, when we transferred the medicine pipe bundle that he

287

helped us get—and that he once owned—to his elderly grandson, Harry Shade, and his wife, Agnes. The event finally answered most rumors about my involvement in traditional ceremonies. But our home seemed empty without the bundle's presence over the head of our bed, where it had hung for four summers and winters. We missed the obligations of making frequent incense and sponsoring various rituals. Then an elderly relative of ours lost both his wife and daughter, so he decided we should take over the medicine pipe bundle that had been in his family for nearly thirty years.

As elderly relatives and friends slowly passed away, we found ourselves compelled to stay at home and try making our family self-sufficient. With four kids around the house, I found little time to dwell on my earlier desires to be part of a "new tribe." I realized that Beverly and I had made a "tribe" of our own!

By this time our participation in cultural activities was accepted by all the traditional elders. But then we were faced with a new challenge, this time from a group of young Indians who said they wanted to learn their own traditions, and resented my already knowing them. During a public campaign to destroy our reputation, they said I was using Beverly to get close to old Indians and learn their ways so that I could write books and get rich from them. They had the mistaken belief that medicine ceremonies involve a lot of "voodoo," and they publicly claimed that I was using this "sorcery." Our elders and friends laughed, knowing that such activity is foreign to our beliefs. But they also gave us reassurance and backing that strengthened our faith.

With the counseling and guidance of Blood elders like Pat and Paula Weasel Head we found strength to overcome this new disappointment. I was jolted into taking another look at myself and my work. I didn't like everything that I saw, and determined to make changes for the better. For a start, I got my whole family more involved in the work of writing books and recording history. One close friend and supporter within the tribe said: "Why don't you guys write a book about yourselves, so we will all know what you are trying to do amongst us?" From that comment came the idea for this volume. . . .